MCSE Test Success:
Exchange Server 5.5

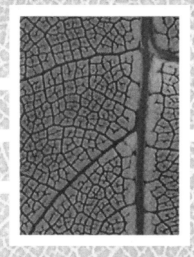

MCSE Test Success™:
Exchange Server 5.5

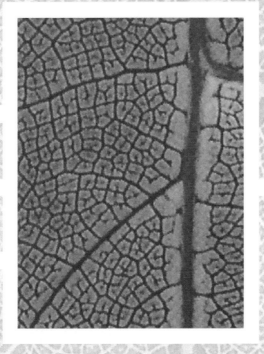

Maria Aurelia Tapia-Ruddy

NETWORK PRESS®

SYBEX

San Francisco • Paris • Düsseldorf • Soest

Associate Publisher: Guy Hart-Davis
Contracts and Licensing Manager: Kristine Plachy
Acquisitions & Developmental Editor: Bonnie Bills
Editor: Pat Coleman
Project Editor: Brenda Frink
Technical Editor: Jim Cooper
Book Designers: Patrick Dintino and Catalin Dulfu
Desktop Publisher: Maureen Forys, Happenstance Type-O-Rama
Production Coordinators: Eryn Osterhaus and Blythe Woolston
Indexer: Lynnzee Elze
Cover Designer: Archer Design
Cover Photographer: FPG International

Library of Congress Card Number: 98-85472
ISBN: 0-7821-2250-7

Manufactured in the United States of America

10 9 8 7 6 5 4 3 2 1

November 1, 1997

Dear SYBEX Customer:

Microsoft is pleased to inform you that SYBEX is a participant in the Microsoft® Independent Courseware Vendor (ICV) program. Microsoft ICVs design, develop, and market self-paced courseware, books, and other products that support Microsoft software and the Microsoft Certified Professional (MCP) program.

To be accepted into the Microsoft ICV program, an ICV must meet set criteria. In addition, Microsoft reviews and approves each ICV training product before permission is granted to use the Microsoft Certified Professional Approved Study Guide logo on that product. This logo assures the consumer that the product has passed the following Microsoft standards:

- The course contains accurate product information.
- The course includes labs and activities during which the student can apply knowledge and skills learned from the course.
- The course teaches skills that help prepare the student to take corresponding MCP exams.

Microsoft ICVs continually develop and release new MCP Approved Study Guides. To prepare for a particular Microsoft certification exam, a student may choose one or more single, self-paced training courses or a series of training courses.

You will be pleased with the quality and effectiveness of the MCP Approved Study Guides available from SYBEX.

Sincerely,

Holly Heath
ICV Account Manager
Microsoft Training & Certification

MICROSOFT INDEPENDENT COURSEWARE VENDOR PROGRAM

To my Father, Raymond Fuentes Tapia

Dad, you taught me that I could do anything I wanted to in this world. This one is for you, of course with a two-burrito minimum.

And to all the children in my life—Daniel, Christopher, Kathy, Shannon, Marc, and the newest two, Victoria and Christopher Alexander. You all gave me faith and the reason to excel. It's all for you.

Acknowledgments

I would like to acknowledge the fine team at Sybex: Bonnie Bills for giving me this wonderful opportunity, Pat Coleman who had the patience of Job, and Brenda Frink, who worked with me until I got it right.

I also thank my children for putting up with me during the writing of this book and my friends who made us dinner on Sunday while I worked all weekend. Without you all, I would have been lost.

Thanks to Mom and Bunnie; you know why.

Contents at a Glance

Table of Contents

Introduction

One of the greatest challenges facing corporate America today is finding people who are qualified to manage corporate computer networks. Many companies have Microsoft networks, which run Windows 95, Windows NT, and Microsoft BackOffice products (such as Microsoft SQL Server and Systems Management Server).

Microsoft developed its Microsoft certification program to certify those people who have the skills to work with Microsoft products and networks. The most highly coveted certification is MCSE, or Microsoft Certified Systems Engineer.

Why become an MCSE? The main benefits are that you will have much greater earning potential and that an MCSE carries high industry recognition. Certification can be your key to a new job or a higher salary—or both.

So what's stopping you? If it's because you don't know what to expect from the tests or you are worried that you might not pass, this book is for you.

Your Key to Passing Exam 70-081

This book provides you with the key to passing Exam 70-081, Implementing and Supporting Exchange Server 5.5. Inside, you'll find *all* the information relevant to this exam, including hundreds of practice questions, all designed to make sure that when you take the real exam, you are ready for even the picky questions on less frequently used options.

Understand the Exam Objectives

To help you prepare for certification exams, Microsoft provides a list of exam objectives for each test. This book is structured according to the objectives for Exam 70-081, which measures your ability to design, administer, and troubleshoot Exchange Server 5.5.

At-a-glance review sections and more than 400 review questions bolster your knowledge of the information relevant to each objective and the exam itself. You learn exactly what you need to know without wasting time on background material or detailed explanations.

This book prepares you for the exam in the shortest amount of time possible—although to be ready for the real world, you need to study the subject in greater depth and get a good deal of hands-on practice.

Get Ready for the Real Thing

More than 200 sample test questions prepare you for the test-taking experience. These are multiple-choice questions that resemble actual exam questions—some are even more difficult than what you'll find on the exam. If you can pass the Sample Tests at the end of each unit and the Final Exam at the end of the book, you'll know you're ready.

Is This Book for You?

This book is intended for those who already have some experience with Exchange Server. It is especially well suited for:

- Students using courseware or taking a course to prepare for the exam, and who need to supplement their study material with test-based practice questions.

- Network engineers who have worked with the product, but want to make sure there are no gaps in their knowledge.

- Anyone who has studied for the exams—by using self-study guides, by participating in computer-based training classes, or by getting on-the-job experience—and wants to make sure that they're adequately prepared.

Understanding Microsoft Certification

Microsoft offers several levels of certification for anyone who has or is pursuing a career as a network professional working with Microsoft products:

- Microsoft Certified Professional (MCP)
- Microsoft Certified Systems Engineer (MCSE)

- Microsoft Certified Professional + Internet
- Microsoft Certified Systems Engineer + Internet
- Microsoft Certified Trainer (MCT)

The one you choose depends on your area of expertise and your career goals.

Microsoft Certified Professional (MCP)

This certification is for individuals with expertise in one specific area. MCP certification is often a stepping stone to MCSE certification and allows you some benefits of Microsoft certification after just one exam.

By passing one core exam (meaning an operating system exam), you become an MCP.

Microsoft Certified Systems Engineer (MCSE)

For network professionals, the MCSE certification requires commitment. You need to complete all the steps required for certification. Passing the exams shows that you meet the high standards that Microsoft has set for MCSEs.

The following list applies to the NT 4 track. Microsoft still supports a track for 3.51, but 4.0 certification is more desirable because it is the current operating system.

To become an MCSE, you must pass a series of six exams:

1. Networking Essentials (waived for Novell CNEs)

2. Implementing and Supporting Microsoft Windows NT Workstation 4.0 (or Windows 95)

3. Implementing and Supporting Microsoft Windows NT Server 4.0

4. Implementing and Supporting Microsoft Windows NT Server 4.0 in the Enterprise

5. Elective

6. Elective

Some of the electives include:

- Internetworking with Microsoft TCP/IP on Microsoft Windows NT 4.0

- Implementing and Supporting Microsoft Internet Information Server 4.0

- Implementing and Supporting Microsoft Exchange Server 5.5

- Implementing and Supporting Microsoft SNA Server 4.0

- Implementing and Supporting Microsoft Systems Management Server 1.2

- Implementing a Database Design on Microsoft SQL Server 6.5

- System Administration for Microsoft SQL Server 6.5

Microsoft Certified Trainer (MCT)

As an MCT, you can deliver Microsoft-certified courseware through official Microsoft channels.

The MCT certification is more costly, because, in addition to passing the exams, it requires that you sit through the official Microsoft courses. You also need to submit an application that must be approved by Microsoft. The number of exams you are required to pass depends on the number of courses you want to teach.

For the most up-to-date certification information, visit Microsoft's Web site at www.microsoft.com/train_cert.

Preparing for the MCSE Exams

To prepare for the MCSE certification exams, you should try to work with the product as much as possible. In addition, there are a variety of resources from which you can learn about the products and exams:

- You can take instructor-led courses.

- Online training is an alternative to instructor-led courses. This is a useful option for people who cannot find any courses in their area or who do not have the time to attend classes.

- If you prefer to use a book to help you prepare for the MCSE tests, you can choose from a wide variety of publications. These range from complete study guides (such as the Network Press *MCSE Study Guide* series, which covers the core MCSE exams and key electives) through test-preparedness books similar to this one.

After you have completed your courses, training, or study guides, you'll find the *MCSE Test Success* books an excellent resource for making sure that you are prepared for the test. You will discover if you've got it covered or if you still need to fill in some holes.

For more MCSE information, point your browser to the Sybex Web site, where you'll find information about the MCP program, job links, and descriptions of other quality titles in the Network Press line of MCSE-related books. Go to http://www.sybex.com and click on the MCSE logo.

Scheduling and Taking an Exam

Once you think you are ready to take an exam, call Prometric Testing Centers at (800) 755-EXAM (755-3926). They'll tell you where to find the closest testing center. Before you call, get out your credit card because each exam costs $100. (If you've used this book to prepare yourself thoroughly, chances are you'll only have to shell out that $100 once!)

You can schedule the exam for a time that is convenient for you. The exams are downloaded from Prometric to the testing center, and you show up at your scheduled time and take the exam on a computer.

Once you complete the exam, you will know right away whether you have passed. At the end of the exam, you will receive a score report. It will list the six areas that you were tested on and how you performed. If you pass the exam, you don't need to do anything else—Prometric uploads the test results to Microsoft. If you don't pass, it's another $100 to schedule the exam again. But at least you will know from the score report where you did poorly, so you can study that particular information more carefully.

Test-Taking Hints

If you know what to expect, your chances of passing the exam will be much greater. The following are some tips that can help you achieve success.

Get There Early and Be prepared

This is your last chance to review. Bring your Test Success book and review any areas you feel unsure of. If you need a quick drink of water or a visit to the restroom, take the time before the exam. Once your exam starts, it will not be paused for these needs.

When you arrive for your exam, you will be asked to present two forms of ID. You will also be asked to sign a piece of paper verifying that you understand the testing rules (for example, the rule that says that you will not cheat on the exam).

Before you start the exam, you will have an opportunity to take a practice exam. It is not related to Exchange Server and is simply offered so that you will have a feel for the exam-taking process.

What You Can and Can't Take In with You

These are closed-book exams. The only thing that you can take in is scratch paper provided by the testing center. Use this paper as much as possible to diagram the questions. Many times diagramming questions will help make the answer clear. You will have to give this paper back to the test administrator at the end of the exam.

Many testing centers are very strict about what you can take into the testing room. Some centers will not even allow you to bring in items such as a zipped-up purse. If you feel tempted to take in any outside material, be aware that many testing centers use monitoring devices such as video and audio equipment (so don't swear, even if you are alone in the room!).

Prometric Testing Centers take the test-taking process and the test validation very seriously.

Test Approach

As you take the test, if you know the answer to a question, fill it in and move on. If you're not sure of the answer, mark your best guess, and then "mark" the question.

At the end of the exam, you can review the questions. Depending on the amount of time remaining, you can then view all of the questions again, or you can view only the questions that you were unsure of. I always like to double-check all my answers, just in case I misread any of the questions on the first pass. (Sometimes half the battle is in trying to figure out exactly what the question is asking you.) Also, sometimes I find that a related question provides a clue for a question that I was unsure of.

Be sure to answer all questions. Unanswered questions are scored as incorrect and will count against you. Also, make sure that you keep an eye on the remaining time so that you can pace yourself accordingly.

If you do not pass the exam, note everything that you can remember while the exam is still fresh on your mind. This will help you prepare for your next try. Although the next exam will not be exactly the same, the questions will be similar, and you don't want to make the same mistakes.

After You Become Certified

Once you become an MCSE, Microsoft kicks in some goodies, including:

- A one-year subscription to Microsoft Technet, a valuable CD collection that contains Microsoft support information.

- A one-year subscription to the Microsoft Beta Evaluation program, which is a great way to get your hands on new software. Be the first kid on the block to play with new and upcoming software.

- Access to a secured area of the Microsoft Web site that provides technical support and product information. This benefit is also available for MCP certification.

- Permission to use the Microsoft Certified Professional logos (each certification has its own logo), which look great on letterhead and business cards.

- An MCP certificate (you will get a certificate for each level of certification you reach), suitable for framing or sending copies to Mom.

- A one-year subscription to *Microsoft Certified Professional Magazine*, which provides information on professional and career development.

How to Use This Book

This book is designed to help you prepare for the MCSE exam. It reviews each objective and relevant test-taking information and offers you a chance to test your knowledge through study questions and sample tests.

The first five units in this book correspond to the Microsoft objectives groupings: Planning, Configuring, Maintaining, Monitoring, and Troubleshooting. The sixth unit is a final review, which contains test questions pertaining to all the previous units.

For each unit:

1. Review the exam objectives list at the beginning of the unit. (You may want to check the Microsoft Train_Cert Web site to make sure the objectives haven't changed any.)

2. Read through or scan the reference material that follows the objectives list. Broken down according to the objectives, this section helps you brush up on the information you need to know for the exam.

3. Review your knowledge in the Study Questions section. These are straightforward questions designed to test your knowledge of the specific topic. Answers to Study Questions are listed in the Appendix at the back of the book.

4. Once you feel sure of your knowledge of the area, take the Sample Test. The Sample Test's content and style matches the real exam. Set yourself a time limit based on the number of questions: A general rule of thumb is that you should be able to answer 20 questions in 30 minutes. When you've finished, check your answers with the Appendix in the back of the book. If you answer at least 85 percent of the questions correctly within the time limit (the first time you take the Sample Test), you're in good shape. To really prepare, you should note the questions you miss and be able to score 95 to 100 percent correctly on subsequent tries.

5. After you successfully complete Units 1–5, you're ready for the Final Exam in Unit 6. Allow yourself 90 minutes to complete the test of 56 questions. If you answer 85 percent of the questions correctly on the first try, you're well prepared. If not, go back and review your knowledge of the areas you struggled with, and take the test again.

6. Right before you take the test, scan the reference material at the beginning of each unit to refresh your memory.

At this point, you are well on your way to becoming certified! Good luck!

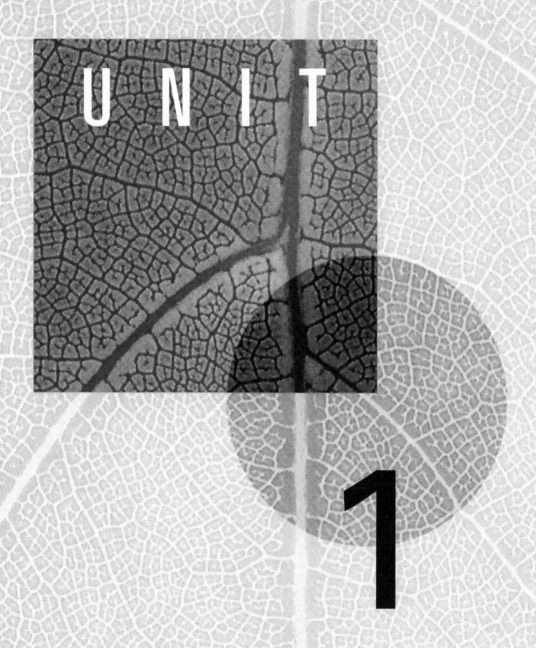

UNIT

1

Planning

Test Objectives: Planning

- **Choose an implementation strategy for Microsoft Exchange Server. Elements include:**

  - Server locations

  - Address space

- **Develop the configuration of an Exchange Server computer.**

- **Identify strategies for migration from previous versions of Exchange Server to Exchange Server 5.5.**

- **Develop a long-term coexistence strategy. Protocols include:**

  - IMAP (Internet Messaging and Addressing Protocol)

  - LDAP (Lightweight Directory Access Protocol)

- **Develop an infrastructure for Exchange Server.**

  - Identify public folders, including server-side scripting.

  - Identify private information store databases.

  - Plan Internet connectivity and access.

- **Choose installation and integration strategies for Exchange Server client applications. Elements include:**

  - Network installation

  - Client computer installation

  - Scripted client application installation

  - Forms interoperability

  - Schedule+ interoperability

  - Calendar interoperability

- **Develop long-term administration strategies.**

  - Plan a backup strategy.

  - Plan a disaster recovery strategy.

  - Plan information store maintenance.

  - Plan remote administration.

- **Plan information retrieval strategies.**

- **Develop security strategies.**

- **Develop server-side scripting strategies.**

Exam objectives are subject to change at any time without prior notice and at Microsoft's sole discretion. Please visit Microsoft's Training & Certification Web site (www.microsoft.com/Train_Cert) for the most current exam objectives listing.

The most time-consuming task when implementing or migrating to Exchange Server is planning, which requires that you make important decisions about configuration:

- First and foremost, you must plan around the Microsoft organization. You need to define sites, decide which servers will participate, and think about how you build your sites. Will you organize sites according to geographical location or by function? You'll also need to determine address space resolution based on the connectivity you need.

- If you are upgrading from previous versions of Exchange, you must determine the method you will be using. Is your current Exchange configuration sufficient, or will you be adding more sites, servers, or connectors?

- The Internet Mail Service supports new protocols. In your configuration, which protocols will you support? For example, Network News Transfer Protocol (NNTP) provides access to Internet newsfeeds—you can import newsfeeds into public folders and export public folders into newsfeeds. What other protocols will you support and how will you configure them?

- You must make critical decisions regarding placement of public folders: Do you want to centralize your public folders onto a dedicated public folder server or store public folders on all servers within a site?

- What will be the naming conventions for users, and which servers will hold mailboxes? Are you planning unlimited growth, or will you manage growth by placing storage limits on mailboxes? Will users be able to send e-mail to all users in the world, only within your company, or only within specific sites?

- How will you handle installation? Which servers will participate in a site, and which servers will be bridgehead servers? Which servers will connect to the Internet?

- Which clients will your site support? How will you implement the installation of these clients? You'll also need to make decisions regarding the network installations of these clients: Which servers will hold the source files, and will the installation contain scripts to execute when connections are made?

- Domains provide a single management domain for security purposes. Will your sites participate in domain validation? If not, what are your plans for validating users when they connect to Exchange resources?

- Will you be using server-side scripting to implement applications? Which users will be given permissions to create scripts?

In this unit, we will cover the implementation strategy for your Exchange Server 5.5 deployment.

Choosing an Implementation Strategy for Microsoft Exchange Server

One of the first decisions you must make when implementing Exchange Server is how to structure your organization. Because Exchange is organized hierarchically (see Figure 1.1), you can distribute data across several servers, across a LAN (local area network), or across a WAN (wide area network). The Exchange hierarchy is composed of the following:

Organization—The top-level container. The organization usually describes your company or corporation and contains your public folders and references all users of your company.

Site—A collection of Exchange servers distributing information within a high-bandwidth environment, usually a LAN. The connection between servers in a site must support synchronous *Remote Procedure Calls* (RPCs) and must be permanent.

Locations—A subgroup of servers linked by high-bandwidth networks. Locations are clusters built into sites and are used primarily by public folders. Locations are contained within a site.

Servers—A single and separate functional component of a site or a location. The server contains its own information store and connectors.

In addition to these components, the Exchange hierarchy contains two types of objects:

- A *container* contains other objects. The organization holds sites; therefore, the Organization object is a container.

- A *leaf object* contains no other objects. It contains properties and characteristics, but does not refer to other objects within its properties.

FIGURE 1.1

A view of an Exchange organization

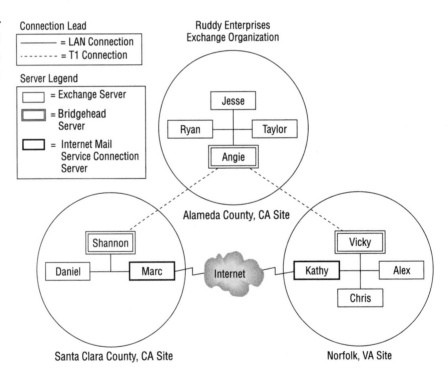

Server Locations

When planning server locations, think about network bandwidth and messaging traffic. High-speed and high-bandwidth network connections typically connect Exchange *intrasite servers* (within a site). These high-speed links allow automatic replication of Directory database data within a site. If high-speed lines connect all your servers, you can separate your sites by geographical or functional boundaries to make smaller sites of a more manageable size.

In addition to the proximity and speed required for intrasite servers, all servers should operate in the same domain context. It is possible for users to reside in different domains, but to utilize this feature you must build and maintain trust relationships.

Your site-to-site connections are typically slower links, since message traffic between sites consumes less bandwidth than the message traffic between servers within a site. The communication between sites is known as *intersite communication* and is performed by intersite servers. To connect sites, you must configure a site connector to replicate Directory database information between sites, since Directory database information is not replicated automatically between sites. For messages to be transferred between sites, you must configure a site-messaging connector in addition to the directory site connector.

For more detailed information on the network types used for intrasite and intersite communication, see Table 1.1.

T A B L E 1.1 Network connection types and site configuration	Connection Type	Site Configuration
	Ethernet, FDDI, Token Ring, ATM, and T1	Intrasite connection: You can configure servers within one site. Fast connections allow for continuous replication of data and fast messaging transfer. You can use locations to subgroup clusters of servers within a site. Locations are typically connected by the higher-bandwidth connections.
	Frame Relay, Fractional T1, 56K, ISDN, and X.25 Leased Line	Intersite connection: Configure servers as separate sites. Slow connections are used to schedule the replication of data between sites and to schedule message transfer between sites.

Address Space

Address space is a set of address components that third-party gateways and connectors use to identify the messages for which they are responsible. The address space contains information that is used to create routes for messages sent outside a site.

When planning address space, you must determine the type of addresses your Exchange Server site will handle. For example, if your site supports Internet mail, you must configure the Internet Mail Service, which automatically adds the address space of SMTP. If you are sending mail to an X.400 mail recipient, you must configure an X.400 connector, which adds the address space of X.400.

Exchange Server 5.5 gives more control over message routing than earlier versions of Exchange. You can now add scope restrictions to the Address Space property page, and you can configure address space in much finer detail. Table 1.2 gives examples of address space entries.

T A B L E 1.2: Sample address space entries

Address Space Entries	Example	Description
SMTP	*.*	Internet Address Entries—Entries are usually in the format username@organization.com.
X.400	C=US;a=;p=RudEnt;o=SC	X.400 Address Entries—Used for X.400 compliant mail systems.
MS	Uses default X.400 addresses	Microsoft Exchange native entries.
Microsoft Mail	RUDDYENT/SCPO	Consists of Microsoft Mail network name and postoffice name.

You can use address space to control where messages are sent. If the Internet Mail Service address space has been modified to contain *.com instead of *.*, the only types of addresses that will be accepted are those ending in .com.

Developing the Exchange Server Configuration

Before installing Exchange Server 5.5, you must ensure that the prerequisite software is installed to support Exchange components on servers and that the hardware platform can support multiple Exchange end-users. Table 1.3 lists the software requirements to support Exchange Server 5.5 features. Table 1.4 compares the minimum and recommended hardware and software requirements to run Exchange Server 5.5.

T A B L E 1.3: Software prerequisites

Software Required	Exchange Feature
Windows NT Server 4 or later with Service Pack 3	Basic Exchange Server
TCP/IP for Windows NT	Needed for Internet Mail Service
Microsoft Internet Information Server (IIS) Version 4 or Version 3 with Active Server Pages	Needed for Exchange Web Access and Outlook Web Access
Microsoft Cluster Server Software	Used if planning to install Exchange on a pair of clustered servers
Windows NT Services for Macintosh	Microsoft Mail connector used to exchange mail with MS Mail for AppleTalk networks

T A B L E 1.4: Hardware requirements

Minimum	Recommended
Intel Pentium 90 MHz (or faster) or Digital Alpha 4/275	Intel Pentium 166 MHz or faster or Digital Alpha 5/500
24MB RAM	At least 32MB RAM (48MB for RISC-based systems)
250MB free space—after NT Server has been installed and minimum page file allocated (50MB)	Minimum 250MB free space across multiple disk drives
	Sufficient disk space for public folder information and users' mailboxes
	Multiple disk drives to balance I/O
	At least one striped drive set
	Sufficient disk space for NT Server page file (100MB plus mount of physical RAM)

Creating the Site Service Account

Before you install Exchange on your server, you must create a *Site Service account*, which is used to exchange data between servers within a site. You use the same service account for all Microsoft Exchange servers within a site. Never use the Administrator account as the Site Service account; this account should be used for support of Exchange services only.

You assign the following characteristics to the Site Service account from the User Manager for Domains application:

- User cannot change password.

- Password never expires.

- Clear the User Must Change Password at Next Login checkbox.

- Clear the Account Disabled checkbox.

During installation, setup grants the current account administrator permissions on the Exchange Server computer. This allows the current user to grant access to the Exchange hierarchy to other users.

WARNING Create the Site Service account before you install Exchange, and specify the Site Service account during installation. If you do not, the account you are using to install (usually the Administrator account) will become the Site Service account.

Determining Naming Conventions

Before you install Exchange on your server, you need to determine the naming conventions that will identify servers, sites, and organizations. Each object in the hierarchy contains two name properties:

- Display

- Directory

Although you can change the display name on certain Exchange objects, you cannot change the directory name without reinstalling Exchange Server. Make these names descriptive:

- Server names should indicate location and functionality.

- Site names should indicate functionality or geographical location.

- User names should be consistent across the organization.

Upgrading to Exchange Server 5.5

Two paths are available when upgrading to Exchange Server 5.5: upgrading from Exchange Server 4 and upgrading from Exchange Server 5.

Upgrading from Exchange Server 4

How you upgrade to Exchange Server 5.5 depends on whether your site is a single-server site or a multiserver site. If it's a single-server site, you can upgrade directly to Exchange Server 5.5 without any intermediate steps.

 Back up all Exchange databases before attempting any upgrade.

To migrate a multiserver site to Exchange Server 5.5, first be sure that each server is running Exchange Service Pack 3. If some are not, first install Service Pack 3, and then upgrade all servers to Exchange Server 5.5.

If you cannot upgrade all servers to Service Pack 3 before upgrading to Exchange Server 5.5, you should perform the following upgrade steps:

1. Identify your Directory Replication Bridgehead servers.

 To view the list of bridgehead servers, select the Directory Replication connector in the site you are working with and choose File ➤ Properties. Select the General tab to view the list.

2. Upgrade all bridgehead servers to Exchange Server 5.5.

3. Allow at least one directory replication cycle to run.

4. Stop, start, and restart all Exchange 4 servers in the site.

5. Upgrade all servers within your site to Exchange 5.5, in any order.

 You must upgrade your Directory Replication Bridgehead servers first. If you do not, directory replication stops, and you will be not able to restart directory replication until all servers are upgraded to Exchange Server 5.5.

Upgrading from Exchange Server 5

Upgrading to Exchange 5.5 from Exchange 5 is fairly easy and straight-forward. The Exchange 5.5 Upgrade contains two new options.

Standard Database Upgrade—Upgrades your databases within the current locations. If a failure occurs during the upgrade, you must restore your databases from your backup and run setup again.

Fault-Tolerant Upgrade—Copies the databases to a temporary location before you actually begin the upgrade. If a failure occurs, only the temporary databases are affected. You can restart the procedure to continue. Once the databases are upgraded, this procedure copies the upgraded directories back to their original locations.

If you are upgrading from Exchange 4, the fault-tolerant upgrade is not available. To use the fault-tolerant option, first upgrade to Exchange 5 and then upgrade to Exchange 5.5.

Developing Long-Term Coexistence Strategies

Microsoft Exchange Server 5.5 can function and provide client support with a multitude of other e-mail clients and networks. Connectors provide access to each of these clients, and Microsoft provides connectors for many third-party mail systems, in addition to those connectors provided by third party vendors. Connectors provided by outside vendors are called *gateway*s.

Coexisting with E-Mail Clients

Exchange Server 5.5 can coexist with a variety of e-mail clients, including:

- cc:Mail
- Microsoft Mail

- Protocol support for Internet mail clients:

    - ETRN

    - Secure Multipurpose Internet Mail Extension (S/MIME)

    - Secure Sockets Layer

    - Simple Authentication and Security Layer (SASL)

    - HyperText Transfer Protocol (HTTP) for Web browsers, including Outlook and Exchange access

    - Internet Message Access Protocol Version 4rev1 (IMAP4rev1)

    - Post Office Protocol Version 3 (POP3)

Coexisting with Network Operating Systems

In addition, Exchange Server on Windows NT 4 can coexist with various network operating systems, including:

- Novell's NetWare (protocol support built-in with Window NT NWLink)

- Banyan VINES (with protocol support for ncacn_vns_spp)

In the next section, we'll look at which client mail systems or protocols are supported.

Developing the Exchange Server Infrastructure

Exchange is made up of five core and optional components. The core components are required (with the exception of the Internet Mail Service). In earlier versions of Exchange Server, the size of the Exchange database was limited, but in Exchange Server 5.5, the only limit is what your hardware resources can handle.

The five core components are:

- Information store

    - Public information store contains public folders and any applications that are to be shared across multiple users.

    - Private information store contains private mailboxes.

- Directory service defines objects.

- System Attendant is responsible for maintenance and logging.

- Message Transfer Agent (MTA) transfers messages from one Exchange server to another.

- Internet Mail Service (IMS) provides connection remotely though the Internet or an intranet to other Exchange sites or servers.

Although the Internet Mail Service is considered a core component, it is the only core component that is optional. All other components are gateways or connectors to foreign mail systems.

Planning the Exchange Information Store

Public folders contain information that a group of users share. Public folder contents are stored as messages in a *public information store.* Your user's public folder information is stored in a folder hierarchy, which is made available to all users. Using this hierarchy, users can connect to the public folder without knowing the path or the server name of the public folder that is storing the data.

Public information stores are created on every machine by default. You can create a dedicated public information store server that stores all public folders in a location or in a site. Follow these steps:

1. From the Administrator program, open the site container.

2. Select the private information store object, and choose File ➤ Properties to open the Private Information Store property page.

3. In the Public Folder Server text box, enter the name of the public folder server.

There can be more than one dedicated public folder server within a site. You can configure each server to point to any dedicated public folder server within a location or within the site.

Table 1.5 presents a list of public information store configuration options that you need to plan.

T A B L E 1.5:   Public folder implementation features

Implementation Feature	Configuration Options	Advantage	Disadvantage
Top-level folder creation	The default is to allow all users to create top-level folders. Turning off this option doesn't allow users to create public folders.	Users can easily create folders to store data. Users can also configure who has permissions to view or access data within the folder without administrator intervention.	Users may create public folders at will and for the wrong purpose. Turning off this feature will force the administrator to manage the public folder information store and create folders for users.
Specifying a container for public folders	The default storage location is the recipients container of the site where the public folder will be stored. You can specify which recipients container holds public folders for organizational purposes.	Users can see which public folders are available to receive mail messages from the default recipient container.	If public folders are not displayed within the default container, inexperienced users will have trouble navigating through the hierarchy to find them.
Message tracking	The default is not to enable message tracking.	Less overhead required to support public folders.	Unable to track access or permissions on public folder if tracking is not enabled.
Storage warnings	This feature is not enabled, by default.	Less overhead required to track message storage limits.	No enforcement of limits on public folders, allowing unlimited growth.

Planning Private Information Store Implementation

Private information stores typically contain information that is specific to one user. For example, mailboxes are found in a private information store. Here are some configuration settings to consider in your implementation:

- Balance the load of user mailboxes across several servers. Doing so distributes network traffic evenly across more than one server.

- Add users who typically work together on one server. This lessens network traffic by limiting the number of messages to be sent off site.

- Plan mailbox storage limits and age limits. These limits help control disk space usage.

- Determine who will create and maintain distribution lists.

- Determine whether users can recover deleted documents or folders. If so, establish the time frame within which a user can effectively retrieve a deleted document before it's gone for good.

The planning information you generated for the public folders can also be used to create your private information store.

Directory Services

A directory service provides the following:

- A database of addresses, mailboxes, public folders, distribution lists, and descriptive information about servers, sites, and services

- Replication of this information to all servers within a site

- Write access to *POP3* (Internet Post Office Protocol Version 3) mail using *LDAP* (Lightweight Directory Access Protocol)

Directory Service Virtual Organizations

Another aspect of planning is determining which sites in your organization will share directory information. Exchange 5.5 now supports *virtual organizations* for providers hosting more than one organization on their servers. Users can see only the organization to which they are assigned. If you will be hosting several organizations on one server or within a single site, it's a good idea to plan the hierarchy for each organization within the Exchange databases. Each virtual organization should have a unique naming convention for users, mailboxes, servers, and sites. You can also assign administrators to specific organizations to further separate the organizations.

Directory Replication Requirements

As I mentioned, directory replication within a site is configured to occur automatically. Therefore, network connections between sites must be stable and fast enough to support Remote Procedure Calls (RPCs). For directory replication to occur across sites, you must configure a Directory Replication connector that is scheduled to run at regular intervals.

Differential Address Book Downloads

Exchange Server 5.5 also supports differential address book download. Users can download from the global address list only those changes that have occurred since the previous download, thus minimizing server connect time for downloads. You must decide which address book components users can download.

System Attendant

This component is responsible for several maintenance functions that keep Exchange server running efficiently. Here are some of the tasks it performs:

- Reclaiming space by deleting old directory objects (Tombstones).

- Creating and maintaining site Routing tables.

- Maintaining the server Message Tracking log. This is necessary if you plan to track messages between sites.

- Generating all required electronic mail addresses for new recipients when created through the Exchange Administrator or the User Manager for Domains.

- Running monitoring tools on services running on servers within a site.

- Maintaining messaging connections and logging errors if connections fail.

- Enabling and disabling signatures and encryption on mailboxes.

When planning for the implementation of the System Attendant, consider the following parameters:

- Tombstone (deleted objects) lifetime
- E-mail address generation

 In the Exchange startup sequence, the System Attendant must be the first service started. The Exchange System Attendant is a dependency for other core components.

Message Transfer Agent (MTA)

The component responsible for the transfer of messages is the *Message Transfer Agent* (MTA). The Exchange MTA conforms to the *Consultative Committee International for Telegraph and Telephone* (CCITT) electronic mail standards for 1984 and 1988. The MTA performs the following tasks:

- Posts, fetches, and routes messages to other Exchange servers' MTAs, foreign X.400 MTAs, or to Microsoft Mail connectors
- Converts messages from *Microsoft Database Exchange Format* (MDBEF) to native X.400
- Expands distribution lists on a specific server or a group of servers

Your planning and configuration considerations for the MTA are:

- Passwords for local MTA agents
- Routing instructions for specific routing entries

Internet Mail Service

The Internet Mail Service (IMS) provides users with the ability to connect to the Internet and send mail to other systems that use *Simple Mail Transfer Protocol* (SMTP). The IMS also provides access to an *Internet service provider* (ISP) for direct connectivity to the Internet. In addition, you can use the IMS to connect to another Exchange site through the Internet.

Advantages

- You can limit the amount of data transferred.

- You can restrict communication to one-way, if necessary: Messages can be delivered but not received, or messages can be received but not sent.

- Communication can be bi-directional, supporting both incoming and outgoing messages.

Disadvantages

- The IMS runs continuously and cannot be scheduled.

- All messages must be converted from MDEMF format to SMTP format and vice-versa as they travel through the IMS.

- Traffic on bridgehead servers used by the IMS to connect several sites or to connect to an ISP is high volume.

Configuration Considerations

Before you install the IMS, you must plan the implementation, including making decisions about the issues listed below. You can modify some options after installation, but it's always a good idea to have a handle on these issues before you start.

Configurations—Which servers will connect directly to the Internet through your ISP? Will a firewall be part of the configuration? Or will messages be forwarded to a host that will connect to the Internet?

Installation requirements—You must install TCP/IP network services for Windows NT to be able to use the IMS on a specific server.

Number of connectors—Will you have minimal network traffic through the IMS, or will you be controlling traffic by configuring the servers to:

- Only accept messages (incoming only)

- Only send messages (outgoing only)

- Receive and send messages (incoming and outgoing)

- Forward all mail to relay hosts for final delivery (using mail hubs)

- Send mail to final destinations using *Domain Name Services* (DNS)

Access to SMTP systems—Which servers or users will be able to send messages to the Internet?

Message content options—Will MIME be supported or UUENCODE?

Optional Exchange Components

You can add the following components as needed:

Microsoft Mail Connector converts and exchanges messages with Microsoft Mail 3.*x* postoffices and Exchange.

Directory Synchronization exchanges directory object information with Microsoft Mail 3.*x* postoffices. Microsoft Mail exchanges its global address list with Exchange.

Connector for Lotus cc:Mail exchanges Lotus cc:Mail messages and directory entries between Exchange and cc:Mail postoffices.

Schedule+ Free/Busy Connector exchanges Calendar free and busy information with Schedule+ 7 and Schedule+ 1.

Key Management Server uses encryption and signatures for advanced security.

Developing Long-Term Administration Strategies

Exchange Server 5.5 provides a graphical user interface known as the Administrator program (Admin.exe) to manage the Exchange organization. Commonly referred to as the Exchange Admin program, this utility can be run by any user who has appropriate permissions.

You can install this program on more than one Exchange server and also on a Windows NT workstation. Although you can install the core components and connectors only on a Windows NT server, you can install the Exchange Administrator program on an administrator's NT 4 workstation where the majority of management will be done. If the Exchange Administrator program is installed on an NT workstation, Exchange administrators can connect and manage all servers within the site.

By default, the Administrator account that installed Exchange is given administrator privileges to manage Exchange, in addition to the Site Services account. As an Exchange administrator, you can do the following from the Exchange Administrator program:

- Grant permissions to other NT accounts to manage:

  - Servers

  - Mailboxes

  - Distribution lists

- Connect to multiple servers in a site, with each server contained within its own window.

- Configure the following objects:

  - Organization

  - Sites

  - Site Configuration container

  - Servers and connectors

  - Scheduled maintenance for the five core components and connectors

By default, the Exchange Administrator program displays only permissions for container objects. To view permissions for all objects, choose Tools ➤ Options and select the Permissions tab. Then check the *Show permissions for all objects* checkbox.

Before you configure and build your Exchange hierarchy, it's a good idea to assign roles and permissions to those users who will be supporting Exchange. The following seven predefined roles have been assigned permissions to perform specific tasks. For more information on the specific tasks, see the Exchange Server 5.5 "Getting Started Guide" in the Microsoft documentation set.

- Admin

- Permissions Admin

- Service Account Admin

- Viewing-Only Admin

- User

- Send As

- Search

Each of the above roles has a specific set of permissions, which can be any combination of the following:

- Add Child

- Modify User Attributes

- Modify Admin Attributes

- Delete

- Logon

- Modify Permission

- Replication

- Mailbox Owner

- Send As

- Search

Exchange objects inherit permissions from their designated containers. Some containers exist within the context of other containers. The containers are:

Organization object—Other containers do not inherit permissions placed on this object.

Site object—Permissions on the site allow a user to modify the site object and all the recipients within the site. Permissions here do not get propagated to the Site Configuration container.

Site Configuration object—Permissions on the site container allow a user to manage the entire Site Configuration object, including servers.

In addition to these predefined roles and permissions, the administrator can create custom roles with specific permissions to fit the needs of the organization.

Backup and Disaster Recovery Strategies

Backing up the Exchange Server files, including the Directory database, is an important part of your disaster recovery plan. In case of software or hardware failure, you can quickly re-create the data with minimal loss of data and down time.

Hardware Configuration

You'll want to plan for tape drives and other storage media during the hardware acquisition phase. Will a single tape drive serve your site, or will you need several tape drives to support your backup strategy? Observe the activity on the Exchange site to determine which server will suffer the least from the overhead of creating backups and the normal processing associated with Exchange Server.

Logging

Because Exchange Server is a transaction-log–based application, you may want to consider *circular logging* if disk space is a critical resource. Circular logging is the ability to store transactions in a single log file until they have been written to the Exchange database. When more space is needed to write new transactions, Exchange overwrites the transactions in the log file that have been committed to the Exchange Directory database.

Advantage   Circular logging saves critical disk space.

Disadvantage   You cannot use incremental or differential backups. Also, you can only restore to the last full backup if there is a data loss. Only use circular logging as a last resort. In addition, Microsoft discourages circular logging.

Backup Schedule

Directory   Back up the Directory database on each server at least once each week. To minimize down time of servers, plan one or two backups of Directory databases each night.

Information Stores   Back up the information stores nightly, depending on each server's activity.

Information Store Maintenance Planning

As I mentioned, you can specify various options and settings to manage information stores. Administrators can also designate specific servers as dedicated private information store servers and designate others as dedicated public folder servers.

Public folders consist of two components:

Hierarchy—Folder information that displays the directory information of the public folders of the site. The hierarchy contains pointers to the specific server information store that contains the data. This information is replicated automatically as part of directory replication.

Data—Contents of public folders. This data is not replicated within the site.

You can duplicate the public folder contents across sites by creating public folder replicas. *Replicas* are instances of public folder contents, or exact duplicates of the folder contents. Since there are no master replicas in your Exchange hierarchy, all copies are considered peer replicas.

Advantages

- Public folder contents are accessible from multiple sites. Replicas are excellent tools to share stable organization-wide data.

- Network traffic can be contained within one site whenever users connect to public folder data.

Disadvantages

- You must schedule public folder replication. For dynamic public folder contents, you must schedule the public folder replication more frequently than stable contents.

- For public folders that will be modified, content conflicts can occur on replicas that exist on different sites.

Remote Administration Planning

Windows NT 4 provides users with dial-up access, known as *Remote Access Services* (or RAS). As an Exchange Server administrator, you can connect to remote sites using RAS and manage the sites from your Exchange Administrator program. You probably don't want to connect sites over a slow phone line, but for remote management purposes it works just fine.

The rest of remote administration follows the same concepts covered in the previous section on administration.

Planning Mailbox Document Recovery

Microsoft Exchange Server 5.5 provides a feature that lets users retrieve documents that have been deleted and removed from the Deleted Items folder.

As part of planning, you must choose a time range in which users can retrieve deleted documents. After the time limit expires, users will no longer be able to reclaim the document; the document is deleted permanently.

You can place retrieval limits on:

- Users' mailboxes

- Server information stores

Advantage   Allows users to retrieve documents without having to restore the entire information store.

Disadvantage   The administrator must dedicate more space for document retrieval stores. Instead of a message being deleted immediately, the document is retained for weeks or even months.

Developing Security Strategies

Planning security also involves planning NT domain relationships across your organization. Microsoft recommends placing your site within one NT domain. If you do, you will not have to build trust relationships between domains in your site or specify a username and password every time you want to connect to another server in your site.

If this is not a possibility for you, consider using the Override property page for every object that needs to communicate across your site or between sites.

In addition, you will review advanced security. Advanced security allows users to digitally sign and to seal messages using encryption algorithms. Using advanced security does entail more planning, usually involving decisions about which encryption algorithm you will use and which of your users will participate in advanced security. Let's review these two topics

Windows NT Domain Models for Exchange Organizations

Exchange uses the features of Windows NT to provide security and security auditing. Windows NT 4 provides a flexible security model based on the Windows NT domain model.

A *domain model* consists of domains and trust relationships. The type of domain model you use in your Exchange organization depends on the number of users in your organization and your existing domain or workgroup configuration.

For a detailed explanation of Windows NT domain models, see the Network Press title *MCSE: NT Server 4 in the Enterprise Study Guide, 2nd Edition*.

Single Domain Model

In the single domain model, shown in Figure 1.2, all accounts are created within a single domain. (A PDC is a primary domain controller, and a BDC is a backup domain controller. The office SRV is a member server.) Because there is only one domain, Windows NT trust relationships are not needed. This is the simplest domain model to manage. Single domain models are used for a site that has fewer than 40,000 users.

FIGURE 1.2

The single domain model

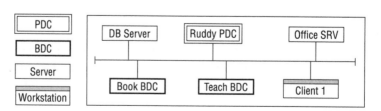

Single Master Domain Model

In the single master domain model, shown in Figure 1.3, one domain provides a security context for all user accounts, and multiple resource domains provide resources. A trust relationship is established so that the resource domains trust the users on the user domains. Single master domain models are used for a site that has fewer than 40,000 users.

FIGURE 1.3

The single master
domain model

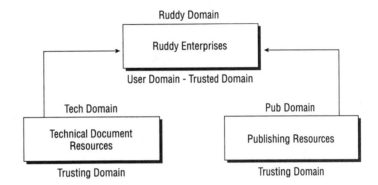

Multiple Master Domain Model

In the multiple master domain model, shown in Figure 1.4, two or more domains provide user accounts, and several trusting domains provide resources. Multiple master domain models are used for sites that have 40,000 to 100,000 Windows NT users.

FIGURE 1.4

The multiple master
domain model

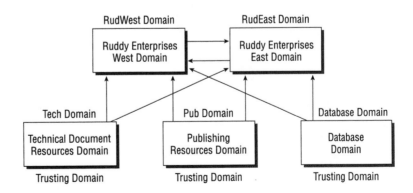

Implementing Key Management Server

Exchange Server 5.5 provides data encryption and digital signatures. If your site requires any of these services, you must install the Key Management Server component of Exchange Server 5.5.

Administrators must authorize each Exchange user to use security features by creating key pairs (encryption keys). To authorize users, access the Mailbox Properties Security tab and enable security for the user.

Developing Server-Scripting Strategies

Exchange Server 5.5 includes the Microsoft Exchange Scripting Agent, which allows users to write applications driven by Exchange events using Microsoft VBScript or Microsoft JScript.

The Scripting Agent is event driven and will automatically execute the script whenever specific events, such as posting a message, creating a message, receiving a message, and posting to a public folder, occur.

Administrators must determine which users can develop scripts and authorize them to create, edit, and save scripts. Because scripts can corrupt server information stores, assign authorization to develop scripts only to those users who must do so.

Users of Outlook 8.03 (or later) can create scripts within the Outlook interface if authorized. By default, Notepad opens and allows users to edit event scripts.

Choosing an Implementation Strategy for Microsoft Exchange Server

1. Exchange Server 5.5 supports intersite communication using network _____
_____ .

2. The top-level container in Exchange is known as the _____ .

3. To send a message to a foreign mail system, there must be an _____
_____ entry.

4. What must you install before you can install the Internet Mail Service?

_____

5. True or False. Administrators can connect servers within a site over a 56K line that does not
support RPCs.

6. True or False. Exchange Server will not support NT clusters.

7. True or False. Exchange sites must be organized by functional boundaries.

8. True or False. All Exchange servers must operate in the same domain context.

9. Address space is associated with _____ .

STUDY QUESTIONS

Developing the Exchange Server Configuration

10. The Windows NT account used for Exchange maintenance and services is known as the

_____ _____ account.

11. Exchange Server runs on Windows NT 4 and NT Service Pack _____.

12. True or False. You can install Exchange on the following operating system configurations: Windows NT 4 Domain Controller, Windows NT 4 Backup Domain Controller, and Windows NT 4 Member Server.

13. A collection of public folder servers linked by a high-bandwidth network is known as a

_____.

14. True or False. The supported network hardware types for servers communicating in a site are FDDI, Ethernet, and ATM.

15. To connect Microsoft Mail for Macintosh, you must have what installed on your Windows NT Server?

_____

16. The minimum recommended hardware processor requirement is a _____

_____.

17. True or False. A Site Service account is used for logon validation.

Upgrading to Exchange Server 5.5

18. When upgrading from Exchange Server 4 to 5.5, you must upgrade all _____ _____ first.

19. True or False. You can upgrade from Exchange Server 3 directly.

20. True or False. The types of upgrade installations are fault-tolerant and standard.

21. Before upgrading, you should _____ the Exchange databases.

22. True or False. Before upgrading, you should copy the NT directory to all the Exchange servers.

Developing Long-Term Coexistence Strategies

23. The _____ Mail Service provides SMTP connectivity.

24. True or False. The following protocols support access to the Exchange Directory database from an Internet mail client: TCP/IP, LDAP, POP3, and NNTP.

25. True or False. To allow Microsoft Mail clients to send messages to Exchange users, you must install the Microsoft Mail connector.

26. True or False. Exchange Server supports the following Internet access protocols: S/MIME, IMAPv4, POP3, and LDAP.

Developing the Exchange Server Infrastructure

27. The Exchange Directory database consists of what two types of objects?

_____

28. List the five core components in Exchange.

_____

_____

_____

_____

_____

29. The core component responsible for expanding distribution lists is the _____

_____.

30. The core component that stores definitions and properties of all Exchange Server objects is known as the _____.

31. _____ _____can be placed on public folders and mailboxes to control growth.

32. True or False. The Exchange Directory database is replicated automatically within a site.

33. Connectors provided by third-party vendors are known as _____.

34.   The Exchange _____ _____ is responsible for maintenance and logging.

35.   The _____ _____ _____ is responsible
for defining Exchange objects.

36.   The _____ _____ _____ is responsible
for forwarding messages from one Exchange server to another.

37.   The _____ _____ _____ provides access
to other Exchange sites or to the Internet.

38.   The information store contains what two components?

_____

_____

39.   The System Attendant generates _____ _____ for all
users who are added to the system.

40.   True or False. Exchange provides a Web browser.

41.   True or False. Exchange passes public folder contents to newsfeeds.

42.   True or False. Exchange users can access their mail through a Web browser.

43.   True or False. You can rename Exchange directory objects at will.

44. True or False. Folders are containers of shared data.

45. True or False. The private information store contains shared data.

46. True or False. Users who work together should be added to the same Exchange server.

47. True or False. Exchange clients use a full address book download to access the global access list offline.

48. True or False. The System Attendant is an optional component for Exchange Server 5.5.

49. True or False. The Internet Mail Service can only be directed one way. There is no bi-directional communication with the Internet.

50. True or False. One of the disadvantages of the Internet Mail Service is that each message must be converted from SMTP format to MDBEF format.

51. True or False. Exchange supports only two connectors per site.

52. The Directory database is replicated within a site _____
minutes after the last change

53. The number of messages that Exchange users can store in their mailbox is controlled by

_____ _____ _____ _____

_____.

54. True or False. Exchange Server 5.5 uses the following supported protocols: TCP/IP, NWLink, and NetBEUI.

Developing Long-Term Administration Strategies

55. List the seven default roles in Exchange permissions.

_____

_____

_____

_____

_____

_____

_____

56. True or False. A user without system rights can administer Exchange.

57. True or False. A container is an object that can contain other objects.

58. True or False. A leaf object contains only properties.

59. True or False. Message Tracking is not enabled by default.

60. User mailboxes are created through _____ and

_____.

61. True or False. You can install the Exchange Administrator program on the following platforms: NT Server 4, NT Server 3.1, and Windows 95.

62. True or False. Exchange objects inherit their permissions from their designated container.

63. Public folders contain two components: the _____
and the _____.

Backup and Disaster Recovery Strategies

64. True or False. You can save disk space by enabling circular logging to write over the parts of the transaction file that have been committed to the database.

65. When planning your hardware configuration, include hardware purchases of
_____ _____ devices to support your backup strategy.

66. Directory databases should be backed up at least _____
a week.

Planning Mailbox Document Recovery

67. True or False. Deleted Exchange messages can be retrieved whenever users want because there is no time limit on message retrieval.

68. Retrieval limits can be placed on user _____ and
_____.

Developing Security Strategies

69. Encryption and digital signatures are supported by the Microsoft _____ _____ Server.

70. True or False. Exchange supports the following domain models: single domain, single master domain, and multiple master.

Developing Server-Scripting Strategies

71. True or False. Server scripting is available only on PDCs.

72. True or False. Server scripting uses VBScript, JScript, and Notepad as development environments.

SAMPLE TEST

1-1   When communicating between sites, what connector type must be installed and configured to connect between sites?

    A. Bridgehead

    B. Site connectors

    C. System Attendant

    D. Microsoft Mail connector

1-2   What component of Exchange Server 5.5 is responsible for transferring messages?

    A. Directory Replication connector

    B. Site connector

    C. Message Transfer Agent

    D. Logging Replication Agent

1-3   On what platforms can the Administrator program be installed if the Exchange administrator wants to connect to and manage all servers within a site?

    A. NT Workstation 4

    B. NT Server 4

    C. NT Server 4 Primary Domain Controller

    D. NT Server 3.51

1-4   When upgrading from Exchange Server 5 to Exchange Server 5.5, what two options are available?

    A. Standard upgrade

    B. Migration upgrade

    C. Fault-tolerant upgrade

    D. New install without core components

SAMPLE TEST

1-5   Which tool is used to assign characteristics to the Site Service account?

    A. Exchange Administrator program

    B. Windows NT User Manager for Domains

    C. Windows NT Server Manager

    D. All the above

1-6   Each object in the hierarchy contains two name properties. Which of the following choices reflect those two properties?

    A. Display name

    B. Directory name

    C. Connector name

    D. Private information store name

1-7   Name two e-mail environments that can co-exist with Exchange Server 5.5.

    A. cc:Mail and Microsoft Mail

    B. Higgins Desktop and cc:Mail

    C. ALL-IN-ONE and cc:Mail

    D. cc:Mail and WhiteHouse Mail

1-8   What task must you perform to use the fault-tolerant upgrade option in the Exchange Server 5.5 Upgrade procedure from a current Exchange 4 server?

    A. Upgrade to version 5 and then use fault-tolerant-upgrade to 5.5

    B. Run setup

    C. Upgrade to 5.5 directly without backing up any files

    D. Upgrade to 4.2 and Service Pack 2

1-9 Which of the following is a recommended backup strategy?

    A. Incremental backup of directory and information stores nightly.

    B. Full backup of directory each week and nightly on information stores.

    C. Incremental backup on information stores nightly, weekly for the directory.

    D. Backups are not needed because Window NT provides a fault-tolerant environment.

1-10 Which two components make up public folders?

    A. Hierarchy

    B. Data

    C. Directory object properties

    D. Directory object characteristics

1-11 Which entry is used to control where messages can be sent or forwarded?

    A. Storage Limits

    B. Connector Storage Warnings

    C. Address Space Warnings

    D. Address Space

1-12 After installing Exchange Server 5.5, Harold's NT Administrator account is also the Exchange Site Services account. What has happened?

    A. Harold created the Site Service account with the same user ID as his NT account.

    B. Harold failed to create the Site Service account prior to installation.

    C. Harold installed Exchange Server on a primary domain controller that was not synchronized with the domain.

    D. Harold failed to install Exchange Server 5.5, but instead installed Exchange Server 5.

1-13   Elaine's company has changed its corporate identity and now wants to change the name of the organization that appears in Exchange Server. What must she do to change the name of the organization?

    A. Elaine can change only the display name of the organization. The directory name of the organization can be changed only if she reinstalls Exchange Server 5.5.

    B. Elaine can change the display and directory names as long as she changes the names on the bridgehead servers first, then any server within that site.

    C. Elaine cannot change any name properties in Exchange Server 5.5.

    D. Elaine can change only the directory name, not the display name.

1-14   Which items are Exchange Server 5.5 core components?

    A. Information store

    B. Internet Mail Service

    C. Message Transfer Agent

    D. System Attendant

    E. Directory services

1-15   When upgrading from Exchange Server 4 to 5.5 in a multiple-server site environment without Exchange Service Pack 3, what must you upgrade first?

    A. Connectors

    B. The directory service

    C. System Attendant

    D. Bridgehead servers

1-16   The Internet Mail Service provides connectivity to what objects?

    A. SMTP Mail Relay Hosts.

    B. Internet service providers.

    C. Internet mail only.

    D. This service does not connect with the Internet.

1-17   How many users can be managed on a single domain model running Exchange Server 5.5?

    A. 15,000

    B. 35,000

    C. 1,000

    D. 40,000

1-18   Anna Maria has an Intel Pentium 66 MHz with 32MB of memory and a 1.2 GIG hard drive with approximately 600MB of free space. Should she install Exchange Server 5.5?

    A. No, minimum requirement is 90 MHz.

    B. Yes, as long as she does not install any additional connectors or gateways.

    C. Yes.

    D. No, Exchange Server can only be installed on a Digital Alpha.

1-19   What characteristics should not be assigned to the Site Service account from NT User Manager for Domains?

    A. Password expiration date of 90 days

    B. User cannot change password

    C. User must not change password at next login

    D. Account must be enabled

SAMPLE TEST

1-20   Which services are provided by directory services?

> **A.** A database of addresses, mailboxes, public folders, distribution lists, and information about servers, sites, and services
>
> **B.** Replication of information to all services within a site
>
> **C.** Write access from POP3 Internet mail clients using IMAGv4 and POP3 clients
>
> **D.** Site connector services to Internet Mail Services

1-21   When upgrading from Exchange Server 4 to Exchange Server 5.5, what two factors determine the upgrade method?

> **A.** Single-server site or multiserver site
>
> **B.** Multiple server and connectors
>
> **C.** Single-servers and directory services
>
> **D.** Multiple server and domain relationships

1-22   Which of the following is not a consideration when planning the implementation of the Internet Mail Service?

> **A.** Configuration settings
>
> **B.** Exchange Server 5.5 installation requirements
>
> **C.** Number of domain name servers in the Internet
>
> **D.** Access to SMTP systems

1-23 When upgrading from Exchange Server 4 to Exchange Server 5.5, how do you prepare your current Exchange databases?

    A. Archive all messages more than 120 days old.

    B. Shut down the PDC in the domain.

    C. Back up all the Exchange databases.

    D. Plan all Internet connections.

1-24 What software must you install before installing Exchange Server 5.5 with the following features: Internet Mail Service, Exchange Web Access, and Installation on Clustered Servers?

    A. Windows NT 4 with Service Pack 3, TCP/IP protocol, Internet Information Server with Active Server Pages

    B. Windows NT 4 with Service Pack 3, TCP/IP protocol, Internet Information Server with Active Server Pages, and Microsoft Cluster Server

    C. Windows NT 4, TCP/IP protocol, Internet Information Server with Active Server Pages, and Microsoft Cluster Server

    D. Windows NT 4 with Service Pack 3, NWLink protocol, Internet Information Server with Active Server Pages, and Microsoft Cluster Server

UNIT

2

Installation and Configuration

Test Objectives: Installation and Configuration

- **Install an Exchange Server computer.**

- **Configure Exchange Server for message recipients.**
  - Configure mailboxes.
  - Configure custom recipients.
  - Configure public folders.
  - Configure distribution lists.
  - Configure site addressing.
  - Configure container-level search controls.
  - Configure Address Book views.

- **Configure connectivity to a mail system other than Exchange Server. Connector types include:**
  - X.400 Connector
  - Microsoft Exchange Connector for Lotus cc:Mail
  - Microsoft Mail Connector

- **Configure synchronization of directory information between Exchange Server and other mail systems. Types of directory synchronization include:**
  - Manual
  - Automatic

- **Configure directory replication.**

- **Import directory, message, and scheduling data from existing mail systems.**

- **Install and configure Exchange Server client computers.**

- **Configure address lists and accounts by using the Administrator program.**

- **Configure the message transfer agent within a site.**

- **Configure the message transfer agent among sites.**

- **Configure Internet protocols and services. Protocols and services include:**
  - POP3 and IMAP4
  - Active Server and HTTP
  - NNTP
  - LDAP

- **Configure message tracking.**

- **Configure server locations.**

- **Configure security.**

Exam objectives are subject to change at any time without prior notice and at Microsoft's sole discretion. Please visit Microsoft's Training & Certification Web site (www.microsoft.com/Train_Cert) for the most current exam objectives listing.

Installing and configuring Exchange Server is fairly simple if you've done your planning. To configure correctly, you need to know how to do the following:

- Install an Exchange computer
- Configure Exchange Server message recipients
- Configure connectors to other mail systems
- Synchronize the Exchange Directory database and other mail systems' global address lists and directory information
- Configure directory replication
- Import directory, messaging, and scheduling data from existing mail systems
- Install and configure Exchange clients
- Configure the MTA (message transfer agent) within a site
- Configure the MTA for intrasite messaging
- Configure Internet protocols and services
- Configure message tracking
- Configure server locations
- Configure security

In this chapter, I'll cover each of these in detail. Let's start with installing and configuring Exchange Server 5.5.

Installing Exchange Server

In Unit 1, we looked at planning issues having to do with sites, servers, and components. Now we are ready to take the next step—installing Exchange Server. To install Exchange Server 5.5, your server must be running Windows NT 4 with Service Pack 3, you must be logged on as a Domain Administrator, and you must ensure that the Site Service account has been created.

Before you begin, verify that:

- PDC (Windows NT 4.0 Primary Domain Controller) or BDC (Windows NT 4.0 Backup Domain Controller) is running.

- All mail applications are stopped. Choose Start ➤ Settings ➤ Control Panel ➤ Services to stop any mail service.

- Your server has been backed up.

In addition, if you are installing Exchange on a cluster, verify that you have created a cluster group and that you have the required configuration on your server. For more information on NT clusters, see the Microsoft NT 4.0 Cluster documentation.

The Exchange Server 5.5 CD contains autoplay code that displays a Web page, which will guide you in running setup.exe. Choose Setup to install Exchange Server 5.5.

To begin, insert your distribution CD and run setup.exe. Table 2.1 lists the installation types and describes their features.

TABLE 2.1	Type	Feature
Exchange Server 5.5 installation types	Typical	The Microsoft Exchange core components and the Exchange Administrator program are installed. No connectors are installed.
	Complete/Custom	You are free to choose which options and connectors you want to install. All components are available to install. You use this option to install the Exchange Administrator on NT Workstation 4.
	Minimum	Only the core components are installed. The Exchange Administrator and connectors are not installed.

During setup, you must specify whether this server will be the first server in the organization or the site or whether this server will join an existing site.

Configuring the First Server in a Site

To configure a server as the first server in the site, during setup from the Organization and Site dialog box, choose Create a New Site and type the name of the organization and site.

Adding a Server to the Site

To add a server to an existing site, verify that an Exchange server in the site is available. If no site server is available, the installation will stop, and setup will prompt you for the site name again. In the Organization and Site dialog box, choose Join an Existing Site. Enter the name of an Exchange server in the site you are joining.

Selecting the Site Service Account

During setup, you will be prompted to select the Site Service account. Choose the account that was created for Exchange Server in the previous steps. Enter the service account name in the form domain\account.

Never use the Administrator account as the service account. Always use a specific account because setup will grant specific rights to this account that may conflict with the Administrator account. It's always a good idea to have a dedicated service account for applications to communicate across servers.

Running Performance Optimizer

The last task in installing Exchange Server is running the Performance Optimizer. The Performance Optimizer prompts you for the number of concurrent users, memory, and hard disks available. With this information, the Performance Optimizer analyzes the optimal hard-disk configuration for your server. You can then choose to move the data files to the suggested locations.

If you choose not to run the Performance Optimizer, you can always run it later by choosing Start ➤ Programs ➤ Exchange ➤ Performance Optimizer.

Running Performance Optimizer is critical to the performance of Exchange Server. Be sure you run it immediately after installing Exchange. Also, run the Performance Optimizer whenever hardware resources change or when you move Exchange Server directory components to another disk.

Granting Permission on the Site and Configuration Containers

Before you can allow other users to manage Exchange, you must grant them access to the site and configuration containers in the Exchange Administrator. The following objects require permissions:

- Site Container—Accounts and groups with site permission can manage recipient objects and create new mailboxes.

- Configuration Container—Users and groups with configuration permissions can administer Exchange Server by managing core components and connectors.

To add permissions, follow these steps:

1. From the Administrator program, select the object whose permissions you want to change.

2. Choose File ➤ Properties to open the Configuration propery page:

3. Select the Permissions tab.

Configuring Exchange Server

Exchange Server passes messages and public folder contents through objects, which are known as *recipients*. In this section, we will create and configure Exchange Server recipients.

Creating Mailboxes

A mailbox is a storage queue associated with a user and contains messages and other items from users' computers. Users can use their Exchange clients to send messages to and from their organization or external organizations using their mailboxes.

You can create mailboxes from two utilities:

Exchange Administrator—Administrators can select the appropriate recipient object and then choose File ➤ New Mailbox.

User Manager for Domains—As part of setup, Exchange installs the Exchange add-in User Manager for Domains. Administrators can then create mailboxes for new Windows NT users.

If you are using User Manager for Domains, set Exchange options to establish the default action whenever you are administering existing NT user accounts. You have the following options:

- Always create an Exchange mailbox when creating Windows NT accounts
- Always delete the Exchange mailbox when deleting Windows NT accounts
- Always prompt for Microsoft Exchange Server
- Default Microsoft Exchange Server
- Default Microsoft Exchange Recipients container

Administrators can also create mailboxes for users migrating from Net-Ware, LAN Manager, or existing Windows NT networks. The tool for creating user mailboxes and NT accounts for NetWare users is Directory Import.

Extracting User Account Lists from Windows NT

To extract a list of NT user accounts and create mailboxes, choose Tools ➤ Extract Windows NT Account List. Once you create this list, you can edit it to remove the accounts that will not need a mailbox and then import the account list to create mailboxes using the Directory Import tool.

Extracting User Account Lists from NetWare

To extract a list of NetWare user accounts and create Windows NT accounts and mailboxes, choose Tools ➣ Extract NetWare Account List. This extraction tool prepares NetWare 2.*x*, 3.*x*, or 4.*x* accounts running in bindery emulation mode. You must have supervisor rights on the NetWare server. After you create this list, follow the steps for importing the account list later in this section.

Using the Directory Import Tool

The Directory Import tool uses a user account list to create large groups of user mailboxes. You can set the recipient container that these mailboxes will be assigned to, as well as the template that will be used to assign default properties. You can choose to create NT accounts if the list is from NetWare or another foreign mail system not being used in a Windows NT user environment.

To import the list, choose Tools ➣ Directory Import.

Configuring Mailbox Properties

Figure 2.1 shows the mailbox General property page, and Table 2.2 lists the tabs for this page and describes what each contains.

FIGURE 2.1

The Mailbox object
General property page

	Tab	What It Stores
T A B L E 2.2 The tabs in the Mailbox property pages	General	Basic information such as the user name, full name, phone number, and location. You can also use this tab to select and store the primary Windows NT user account associated with the mailbox.
	Organization	Information about the mailbox owner's manager and any direct reports.
	Phone/Notes	Detailed telephone numbers and notes for the mailbox.
	Permissions	Used to assign access to this mailbox for a user or a group of users to manage.
	Security	Used to manage advanced security.
	Custom Attributes	Definable field attributes, such as a badge number or an employee identification number. There are ten custom attribute fields.
	Limits	Storage limits on a user's mailbox. Administrators can define warning limits as well as prohibitive limits. In addition, administrators can specify a time range for recovering deleted documents per mailbox.
	Advanced	Trust levels, display names, Address Book views, and Internet Locator Service parameters. To move a mailbox from one server to another, you can use the Home Server field to select another server within the site.
	Distribution Lists	The distribution lists of which this user will become a member.
	E-mail Addresses	Custom recipients' e-mail addresses. You can also use this tab to create a new address for a custom recipient.
	Delivery Restrictions	Instructions for rejecting or accepting messages from any sender.
	Delivery Options	Delivery options for a recipient or for a recipient who has permission to send messages on behalf of another recipient.
	Protocols	Protocols for individual mailboxes.

Creating Custom Recipients

A custom recipient is a directory entry that points to a foreign mail user. Using the Exchange Administrator, you can create custom recipients for commonly addressed mail recipients who do not have an Exchange Server account. The custom recipient is listed in the Address Book, but this listing is only a redirection instruction to forward mail to the foreign mail system.

To create a custom recipient, follow these steps:

1. In Administrator, choose File ➤ New Custom Recipient.

If you are not currently working with a recipients container, Exchange will prompt you to switch to a recipients container.

2. Select the type of custom e-mail address and click OK to open the Custom Recipient Mailbox property pages.

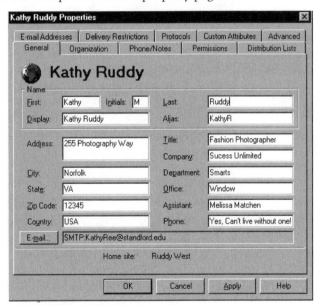

Table 2.3 list the tabs for these property pages and describes what each does.

TABLE 2.3 Tabs in the Custom Recipient Mailbox property pages	Tab	What It Stores
	General	Basic information such as the user name, full name, phone number, and location.
	Organization	Information about a mailbox owner's manager and any direct reports.
	Phone/Notes	Detailed telephone numbers and notes for the mailbox.
	Permissions	Used to define users or groups of users who have access to this object.
	Distribution Lists	Setting this property allows you to specify the distribution lists of which this user will become a member.
	E-mail Addresses	Custom recipients' e-mail addresses. You can also use this tab to create a new address for the custom recipient.
	Delivery Restrictions	Instructions for rejecting or accepting messages from any sender.
	Protocols	Choose the protocols that the user will be using. The protocols that appear in this field come from the server. The server protocol property list is used to create a user's default protocol list. You can edit this list to add or remove the default protocols.
	Custom Attributes	Definable field attributes, such as a badge number or an employee identification number. There are ten custom attribute fields.
	Advanced	Display names, trust levels, ILS information, container name, customer recipient options, and message size limits.

Configuring Public Folders

As I discussed in Unit 1, all users can create top-level public folders by default. You can change your configuration container property to remove this setting and only allow Exchange administrators to create public folders. This will help you control the number of public folders created in your site, but will also place the responsibility for creating public folders on the administrators.

Replicating a Public Folder

As you may recall, a public folder is made up of two components:

- Hierarchy
- Content

The hierarchy is replicated as part of the Directory database information that is replicated automatically within a site. The content is maintained locally on the server that initially created the public folder.

To distribute the load of public folder connections, you can create replicas of public folders on more than one server. A *replica* is a copy of the content of the public folder that is stored on one or more site servers. All replicas are equal copies of the content; therefore, there is no master replica to maintain.

A replica is pushed to a public folder server by use of Public Folder properties. An instance is pulled into a public information store and maintained by the Information Store properties. In the next unit, I'll discuss how to configure and maintain instances by public information store.

The Public Folder Replicas property page lists the servers where the selected public folder is replicated. To add a server to the replicas list, follow these steps:

1. Start the Administrator program.

2. Double-click the Organization object to open it.

3. Double-click the Public Folders container to open it.

4. Select the public folder you want to replicate.

5. Choose File ➤ Properties to open the Public Folder property page:

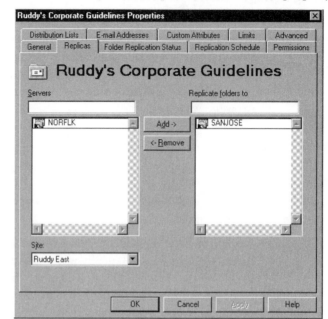

6. Select the Replicas tab.

7. In the Servers control, select the server to which you want to push the replica.

Checking Folder Replication Status

You can use the Folder Replication Status tab on the Public Folder property page to check the status of the public folder replicas. On this tab you can view the status of all servers who host a replica of the public folder.

Setting Up Replication Schedules

You can automate the replication of public folders to all servers hosting a replica by setting up replication schedules. You can set replication schedules for a specific public folder or for all public folders on a server.

The schedule for a specific public folder will override the replication schedule set for the public information store on a server.

Figure 2.2 shows the Replication Schedule tab of the Public Folder property page for a specific public folder. Table 2.4 explains the options in this tab.

FIGURE 2.2

The Replication
Schedule tab of
the Public Folder
property page

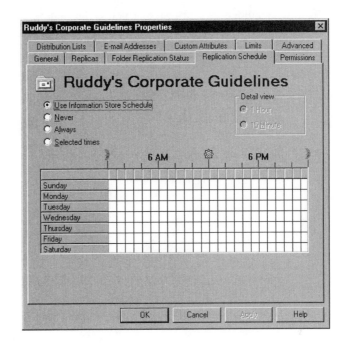

FIGURE 2.2

The Replication
Schedule tab of
the Public Folder
property page

TABLE 2.4	Option	Value
Public folder replication schedule options	Frequency	Use Information Store Schedule—Defaults to the settings in the Public Information Store properties on this server.
		Never—Disables replications.
		Always—Runs replication every 15 minutes.
		Selected Times—Runs replication according to the times selected in the schedule grid.
	Time Detail	1 Hour—Displays the schedule grid in 1-hour increments.
		15 Minute—Displays the schedule grid in 15-minute increments.

Once the folders are created and configured for replication, you can set the remaining public folder properties in the Public Folder property pages that open as a result of setting the schedule. Figure 2.3 displays the Public Folder property pages, open at the General tab. Table 2.5 lists the tabs in this property page and describes what each stores.

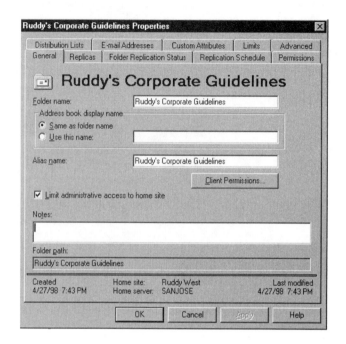

Tab	What It Stores
General*	The name properties of the public folder as well as client access permissions.
Replicas	Copies of the original public folder.
Folder Replication Status	Status of replicas.
Replication Schedule	Replication schedule grid.

T A B L E 2.5 *(cont.)*	Tab	What It Stores
The tabs in the public folder property pages	Permissions	Permissions for those users who have access to the folder.
	Distribution Lists	The distribution lists to which this public folder belongs.
	E-mail Addresses	The e-mail addresses generated for this folder.
	Custom Attributes	Attributes for Administrator-defined fields.
	Limits	Storage limits on public folder contents. Also used to set recover limits on deleted items.
	Advanced	Trust levels, home server, replication importance level, and container name.

*The display name for the folder can be different from the actual directory name for the folder. In addition, you can create several alias names for those clients that do not support long file names.

Creating Distribution Lists

You use Exchange Server distribution lists to address a large group of recipients by associating the list with a user-friendly name. You can create distribution lists from the Exchange Administrator if you have permissions on the recipient's container.

It's a good idea to assign permissions to a super user who will be responsible for maintaining distributions lists in your site.

To create distribution lists, open the Exchange Administrator and select a recipient's container. Choose File ➣ New Distribution Lists to open the Distribution List property pages, as shown in Figure 2.4. Table 2.6 lists the tabs in these property pages and describes what each does.

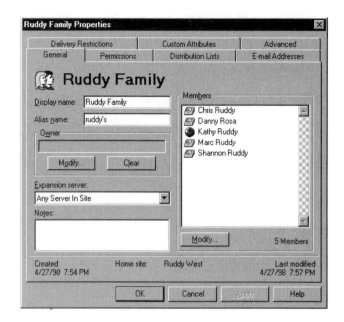

FIGURE 2.4

The Distribution List property pages

TABLE 2.6

The tabs in the Distribution List property pages

Tab	Used To
General	Define display and alias names, assign ownership, specify the server responsible for expanding the current distribution list, and define membership lists.
Permissions	Grant permissions to users or to groups.
Distribution Lists	Assign distribution lists to which the current distribution lists belongs. You can, thus, nest distribution lists within distribution lists.
E-mail Addresses	Modify the addresses generated by the System Attendant.
Delivery Restrictions	Accept or reject messages from a specific user or groups of users by address.

	Tab	Used To
T A B L E 2.6 *(cont.)* The tabs in the Distribution List property pages	Custom Attributes	Customize fields for Administrator-defined fields.
	Advanced	Set message size limits that determine the maximum size of a message that can be sent from this distribution list. Also, administrators can set the display name if it is different from the distribution list directory name. There are also distribution list options that control whether this list is hidden from Address Book or whether the membership is hidden from the distribution list.

WARNING Even though the distribution list can be hidden from Address Book, a user can still use the distribution list if he or she knows the name of the list. All the user has to do is type the name of the list in the TO: box of a message.

Configuring Site Addressing

The Exchange Server 5.5 Site Addressing properties control how e-mail addresses are generated and how messages are routed. This information affects not only the current site but sites outside your organization.

To customize an address, follow these steps:

1. Start the Exchange Administrator.

2. Double-click the Site Configuration object for the site whose address you are customizing to open the object.

3. Select the Site Addressing object.

4. Choose File ➢ Properties to open the Site Addressing property pages.

5. Select the Site Addressing tab to display the Site Addressing list box. Choose Edit to modify an address, and choose Remove to delete an address.

Table 2.7 lists the tabs in these property pages and describes what each does.

	Tab	Description
T A B L E 2.7 The tabs in the Site Addressing property pages	General	Used to change the display name and assign the routing calculation server for your site. The routing calculation server calculates any routing change for a site and recalculates routing whenever a server, a connector, or a site object is added or modified.
		Select the *Share address space with other X.400 systems* option when transitioning from a non-Exchange Server system to an Exchange Server implementation. Whenever a message is sent to a recipient and the recipient is not found, the message will be forwarded to the non–Exchange Server system for delivery.
	Permissions	Used to define users or groups of users who have access to this object.

	Tab	Description
TABLE 2.7 *(cont.)* The tabs in the Site Addressing property pages	Site Addressing	Used to create and modify addresses that will be created for recipients and Exchange Server objects.
	Routing Calculation Schedule	**Frequency:** Never—Disables replications. Always—Runs replication every 15 minutes. Selected Times—Runs the Routing Recalculation job according to the times selected on the schedule grid control. **Time Detail:** 1 Hour—Displays the schedule grid in 1-hour increments. 15 Minute—Displays the schedule grid in 15-minute increments.
	Routing	Used to view the routing information calculated for the selected site. To manually recalculate routing for a site, click the Recalculate Routing button.

Creating Addresses

The Exchange Server automatically creates three types of addresses during installation:

- MS Mail
- SMTP
- X.400

These addresses are based on the organization and site names assigned. Sometimes these addresses contain invalid characters, so you should edit these names as soon as possible to remove any invalid characters in the Address field. Do this before you create recipients and before any addresses are automatically generated for any Exchange Server containers and objects. In addition to these three addresses, Exchange will also create addresses for any connectors you add.

You may want to remove addresses that will not be used. For example, if you do not plan to connect to any SMTP addresses, you can remove the address from the Site Addressing tab.

Establishing the Routing Calculation Schedule

Whenever there is a change in your Exchange server or site (such as adding a connector), Exchange attempts to update the Routing table with information that reflects that change. This can be accomplished in three ways:

- By automatically updating the system whenever a change is made that will affect how a message is routed.

- By scheduling routing calculation and updates. Although this is the most efficient method, there will be a time when an invalid address is used until the next update recalculation is done and sent to all servers in a site.

- By manually forcing calculation and updates. Use this option when your Exchange Server organization is stable and changes are infrequent.

To select the appropriate option, use the Routing Calculation Schedule tab in the Site Addressing object in the Exchange Site Configuration container.

Building Address Book Views

During the installation of Exchange Server 5.5, an Address Book is created. This Address Book is built from three recipient objects:

- Global address list
- Custom address list
- Offline Address Book

To control the information contained in Address Book, you build views. A *view* is a collection of addresses created by grouping recipients according to a predefined common attribute or from a group of predefined attributes. After you select the attributes, containers are built based on the criteria selected. Recipients are then added to the appropriate address view container. As more recipients are added and more view containers are needed, they are built automatically based on the value of the attribute.

For example, employees of Ruddy Enterprises are placed into a building address view container that is grouped by building number. When a user is added that is assigned an office location of Bldg. 101, the user is added to the existing container for the building. If a new building number is added, a container for that building view is built, and recipients are added to that container as the building attribute is created or modified.

To build a new Address view, follow these steps:

1. Start the Exchange Administrator.

2. Choose File ➤ New Other ➤ Address Book View to open the Address Book property pages:

3. Assign a name to the view, and choose the Group By tab to select the attribute on which to build your views.

The Address Book property pages have the following tabs:

General stores the display and directory names and notes.

Group By is used to create the view. Follow these steps:

1. Select an attribute from the Group Items By box.

2. Click Apply. If you need additional attributes to group recipients, use the Then By boxes.

Permissions is used to define users to groups of users who have access to this object. You can use this tab to assign search permissions to groups of individuals. You'll find more information on this in the next section on container-level search controls.

Advanced is used to determine whether recipient objects should appear in one or more parent containers. Also, as recipients are added and modified, Address Book containers may become empty. You can delete empty containers within an Address Book view using this tab.

You can use the Advanced tab to specify whether an Address Book view container will appear in a parent container. For example, if you have an Address Book view for building numbers within a site, you must choose whether the corresponding containers will be views in the parent container Sites in California.

Setting Address Book View Container-Level Search Permissions

You can determine who has access to specific Address Book view containers by assigning search permissions to users. You can leverage Windows NT 4 groups by assigning the search permission to a specific group of users created from the User Manager for Domains administrator utility. Building users into specific groups allows you to assign permissions to those groups instead of to each individual.

If you assign users to groups when you create their Windows NT 4 accounts, they then have access to those views that have been given search permissions for specific Address Book containers. This is much simpler than editing the Permission property page for every container and adding the user to the permission list.

To assign the search permission on a specific view, open the Exchange Administrator and select the appropriate view. Choose File ➤ Properties to open the property pages, and then follow these steps:

1. Select the Permissions tab.

2. Under the Windows NT Accounts with Permissions box, click Add.

3. Select the user or group and the Address Book view container to which you want to assign search permission.

4. Click Add, and then click OK.

5. In the Roles box, select Search.

Creating and Maintaining Exchange Server Connectors

Exchange Server 5.5 provides three connectors for communicating with many mail and information systems:

- X.400 Connector

- Microsoft Exchange Connector for Lotus cc:Mail

- Microsoft Mail Connector

We'll look at each of them in this section.

Using the X.400 Connector

Exchange Server 5.5 provides connection to CCITT (Consultative Committee of International Telegraph and Telephone) X.400 standards. This connector is different from the default Exchange Site connectors in that it can be scheduled. Also, with this connector you can connect to other X.400 compliant systems, or you can use an existing X.400 network to backbone two or more of your Exchange sites together. Figure 2.5 shows how you can use the X.400 Connector to connect two sites across your local network and across an X.400 backbone.

FIGURE 2.5

X.400 network connections

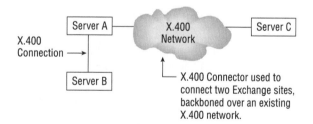

Setting Up MTA Transport Stacks

Before setting up an X.400 Connector in your site, you must set up an MTA transport stack. MTA transport stacks allow an X.400 Connector that uses OSI

(Open Systems Interconnect) standards to use a specific non–OSI-compliant network. The available transport stacks are:

- TCP/IP
- TP0/X.25
- TP4/CLNP

To create the TCP/IP (or any other) MTA transport stack, follow these steps:

1. Start the Exchange Administrator.

2. Select the Site Configuration object for the site in which you are creating the MTA transport stack.

3. Double-click the Site Configuration object to open the container.

4. Choose File ➢ New Other ➢ MTA Transport Stack to open a dialog box that lists the types of transport stacks you can create. Table 2.8 lists and describes the tabs in this dialog box.

5. Choose the appropriate type.

 You use the TCP/IP MTA transport stack to run OSI software on a TCP/IP network.

	Tab	Description
TABLE 2.8 TCP/IP transport stack properties	General	Used to define a new transport display name and OSI address information such as the Transport Service Access Point (TSAP) selector, Session Service Access Point (SSAP) selector, and Presentation Service Access Point (PSAP) selector.
	Permissions	Used to define users or groups of users who have access to this object.
	Connectors	Used to define which X.400 Connectors are using this transport stack.

You use the TP0/X.25 connector to provide X.25 network-compliant communication capabilities to OSI applications, such as the X.400 Connector. Table 2.9 lists the TP0/X.25 Transport Protocol Stack properties shown in Figure 2.6.

FIGURE 2.6

The TCP Transport property page

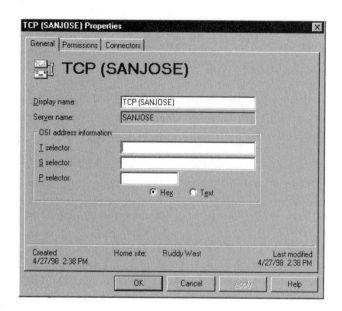

TABLE 2.9

TP0/X.25 transport protocol stack properties

Tab	Description
General	Used to name this transport stack. You can also assign telephone data, facilities data, X.121 address information, and OSI address information.
Permissions	Used to define users or groups of users who have access to this object.
Connectors	Used to define which X.400 Connectors are using this transport stack.

You use TP4/CLNP to provide an OSI interface on a LAN. Table 2.10 lists the TP4/CLNP transport protocol stack properties.

	Tab	Description
T A B L E 2.10 TP4/CLNP transport protocol stack properties	General	Used to define the name of this transport stack and OSI address information.
	Connectors	Used to define which X.400 Connectors are using this transport stack.

Configuring an X.400 Connector

After you create your MTA transport stacks, you are ready to create the X.400 Connector. Follow these steps:

1. Start the Exchange Administrator.

2. Select the Site Configuration object that will host the X.400 Connector

3. Double-click the Site Configuration object to open the container.

4. Choose File ➤ New Other ➤ X.400 Connector to open the X.400 Custom Connector property pages:

5. When you are prompted for which MTA transport stack to use, select the transport stack for the network type used for this connector.

Table 2.11 lists the tabs in these property pages and their uses. At a minimum, you must select options in the General, Stack, Connected Sites, Address Space, and Advanced tabs.

TABLE 2.11	Tab	Description
X.400 Custom Connector tabs	General	Used to define the display and directory name, the remote MTA name and password, the MTA transport stack, message text word-wrap option, and whether remote clients support MAPI.
	Permissions	Used to define users or groups of users who have access to this object.
	Schedule	**Frequency:** Remote Initiated—Sends message queued to the MTA whenever the remote MTA initiates the connection. In the Advanced tab, you must choose the Two-Way Alternate option. Never—Disables the X.400 Connector. Always—Connects whenever messages need to be transferred. This is the X.400 Connector's default option. Selected Times—Runs the X.400 Connector according to the times selected in the schedule grid. **Time Detail:** 1 Hour—Displays the schedule grid in 1-hour increments. 15 Minute—Displays the schedule grid in 15-minute increments.
	Stack	Used to assign the address of the server or foreign connection. Also used to define the outgoing and incoming OSI address information.
	Override	Used to set attributes for a specific connector to a foreign mail system. For example, if a foreign mail system has a different remote MTA name and/or password, use this tab to set those specific attribute values. In addition to the above attributes, you can modify RTS values, association parameters, connection retry values, and transfer timeouts.

	Tab	Description
TABLE 2.11 (cont.) X.400 Custom Connector tabs	Connected Sites	Used to specify which remote systems will connect with this connector.
	Address Space	Used to define the type and format of addresses used to identify messages to another site or to a foreign mail system.
	Delivery Restrictions	Used to accept or reject messages from a specific user or groups of users by address.
	Advanced	Used for setting MTA conformance mode, X.400 connection options, X.400 body part settings, GDI (Global Domain Identifier) settings, X.400 link options, and message sizes.

Using Microsoft Exchange Connector for Lotus cc:Mail

Exchange Server 5.5 includes the Lotus cc:Mail Connector as part of its support for foreign mail systems. This connector provides your Exchange Server organization with the ability to transfer messages and directory information between Exchange and a cc:Mail postoffice. There are some restrictions though:

- You can have only one cc:Mail Connector per cc:Mail postoffice.
- You can have only one cc:Mail Connector per server.

The cc:Mail Connector requires the following software on the cc:Mail side:

- Lotus cc:Mail Post Office Database version 6
- cc:Mail Import version 5.15
- Export version 5.12.

or

- Lotus cc:Mail Post Office Database version 8
- cc:Mail Import/Export version 6.

Run the Exchange Server 5.5 Performance Optimizer with the Connector/ Directory Import option selected. This will optimize the system specifically for Connector and Directory Import performance.

To configure a cc:Mail Connector, from the Exchange Administrator, select your site's Configuration object and open the Connector's property pages:

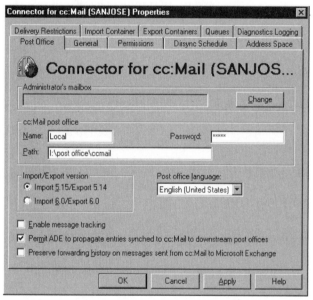

You use the Post Office tab to configure the cc:Mail postoffice with which this connector will communicate. It has the following options:

Administrator's Mailbox—Assigns a user as the cc:Mail administrator.

cc:Mail Post Office—Assigns the network path, the name, and the password to the cc:Mail postoffice.

If you are specifying a connection to a NetWare server, you must be running Windows NT Gateway Services for NetWare. In addition the path must be in UNC format: \\Server\sharename.

Import/Export Version—Specifies the cc:Mail Import/Export version.

Post Office Language—Specifies the local language.

Enable Message Tracking—Specifies whether you choose to track messages to and from this connector.

Permit ADE to Propagate Entries Synched to cc:Mail to Downstream Post Offices—Determines whether directory synchronization data is forwarded to downstream cc:Mail postoffices.

Preserve Forwarding History on Messages Sent from cc:Mail to Microsoft Exchange—Specifies whether the forwarding history is retrained.

Table 2.12 lists and describes the other tabs in these property pages.

	Tab	Description
T A B L E 2.12 The tabs in the cc:Mail property pages	General	Used to assign message size limits for use with this connector.
	Permissions	Used to define users or groups of users who have access to this object.
	Dirsync Schedule	**Frequency:** Never—Disables the cc:Mail connector. Always—Connects whenever messages need to be transferred. Selected Times—Runs the cc:Mail Connector according to the times selected in the schedule grid. **Time Detail:** 1 Hour—Displays the schedule grid in 1-hour increments. 15 Minute—Displays the schedule grid in 15-minute increments.
	Address Space	Used to configure message routing for the connector. With this tab, you can configure address space information to restrict the addresses that can be reached from this connector.
	Delivery Restrictions	Used to enter those local or remote addresses that will not be allowed to send mail through this connector.

	Tab	Description
TABLE 2.12 *(cont.)* The tabs in the cc:Mail property pages	Import Container	Used to specify the recipient container in which imported cc:Mail addresses will be stored.
	Export Containers	Used to specify which recipients will be exported to the cc:Mail Post Office address list.
	Queues	Used to view the information store queues for outgoing and incoming messages. MTS-OUT displays cc:Mail-bound messages, and MTS-IN displays Exchange-bound messages.
	Diagnostics Logging	Used to customize logging information written to the NT Event log. With this option, you can specify the level of logging that will be enabled.

Using Microsoft Mail Connector

Exchange Server 5.5 supports the co-existence of Microsoft Mail by the inclusion of the Microsoft Mail Connector. The connector allows Exchange to import and export messages between Exchange Server 5.5 and Microsoft Mail. Figure 2.7 shows how Exchange objects and Microsoft Mail components interact.

FIGURE 2.7

Exchange and Microsoft Mail interaction

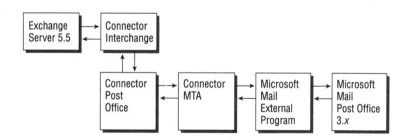

The connector consists of three major objects:

Connector Post Office, which emulates a Microsoft Mail Post Office.

Connector Interchange, which converts outgoing messages to a Microsoft Mail format and converts incoming messages to the Exchange native format.

Connector MTA, which communicates with Microsoft Mail external programs to forward messages to their destination.

To configure the Microsoft Mail Connector, follow these steps:

1. Start the Exchange Administrator program.

2. Double-click the configuration container for the site to open it.

3. Double-click the Connections object.

4. The Microsoft Mail Connector is listed as one of the available connectors. Select the connector to display the MS Mail property pages.

Table 2.13 lists and describes the tabs in these property pages.

T A B L E 2.13 The tabs in the Microsoft Mail Connector property pages	Tab	Description
	General	Used to view the computer name and set message size limits on messages passing through this connector.
	Address Space	Used to configure message routing for the connector. With this tab, you can configure address space information to restrict the addresses that can be reached from this connector.
	Diagnostic Logging	Used to customize logging information written to the NT Event log. With this tab, you can specify the level of logging that will be enabled.
	Interchange	Used to identify an administrator and a primary language and to specify whether to maximize MS Mail 3.*x* compatibility and to enable message tracking. In addition, you can configure a Microsoft Mail AppleTalk MTA for Macintosh users.
	Local Post Office	Used to specify the Microsoft Mail Network, Post Office, and password compatible attributes. Never modify any of the names used in this section without regenerating the MS address type for the connector postoffice. Restart all Microsoft Mail gateways and external programs to continue.

	Tab	Description
TABLE 2.13 *(cont.)* The tabs in the Microsoft Mail Connector property pages	Connections	Used to view, modify, and create connections to external Microsoft Mail Post Offices.
	Connector MTAs	Used to define LAN parameters for each occurrence of an MTA service. For instance, a specific MTA might talk only to a specific group of postoffices and use a unique account and password. You can use this tab to configure the specific attributes for that connection.

Synchronizing Directory Information

As I mentioned earlier, Exchange Server 5.5 provides a way to share recipient information with foreign mail systems so that users can see the addresses of users on Microsoft Mail or cc:Mail and vice versa. The method is known as *directory synchronization (Dirsync)*.

The object that Exchange Server uses to synchronize directory information is the Directory Synchronization Agent, or the Dirsync Agent. This agent imports and exports recipient information to and from Microsoft Mail, Lotus cc:Mail, and other external information systems. In this section, we will look at the two types of directory synchronization:

- Automatic
- Manual

Synchronizing Directories Automatically

The Dirsync Agent is configured to execute in two modes:

- If the agent is configured to compile the master list and forward it, it is known as a *Dirsync Server*.
- If the agent is configured to forward its address list to another server, it is known as a *Dirsync Requestor*.

Configuring a Dirsync Server

Figure 2.8 shows how the synchronization process works.

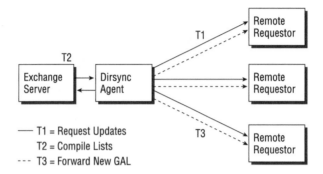

To configure a Dirsync Server, follow these steps:

1. Start the Exchange Administrator program.

2. Select the configuration object for the site you're working on, and double-click to open the site container.

3. Select the connections container, and double-click the Dirsync Server object to open the Dirsync Server property pages.

Table 2.14 lists the tabs in the Dirsync Server property pages and describes what each does.

Tab	Description
General	Used to define the name of the connector and the Dirsync administrator's mailbox. Used to set the copy on outgoing messages and to set the Forward Incoming Dirsync Messages property.
Schedule	Used to define the schedule for the Dirsync Server. The default is to send one message update each day at midnight.

Configuring the Remote Dirsync Requestor

You must define each requestor of directory information in Exchange as a requestor. Follow these steps:

1. Start the Exchange Administrator.

2. Choose File ➤ New Other ➤ Remote Dirsync Requestor.

3. Select a postoffice from the list of MS Mail postoffices.

Use the tabs described in Table 2.15 to assign the appropriate attributes.

	Tabs	Description
T A B L E 2.15 The tabs in the Remote Dirsync Requestor property pages	General	Used to define a display name for the remote requestor mailbox, password, requestor address type, and the requestor language and to specify whether you want to export this information on the next cycle.
	Permissions	Used to define users or groups of users who have access to this object.
	Import Container	Used to define the container in which to place the imported address lists and to identify the trust level of the addresses imported.
	Export Container	Used to specify which Exchange recipient containers will be exported to the external postoffices.

Configuring a Dirsync Requestor

The second way to exchange directory information is to configure Exchange as a requestor of addresses from an MS Mail Dirsync Server. As Figure 2.9 shows, an MS Mail postoffice is responsible for compiling the global address list and forwarding it to all requestors.

To set up an Exchange Dirsync Requestor, follow these steps:

1. Start the Exchange Administrator program.

2. Select the Site Configuration object for your site, and double-click to open the container.

3. Choose File ➤ New Other ➤ Dirsync Requestor to open the Dirsync Requestor property pages.

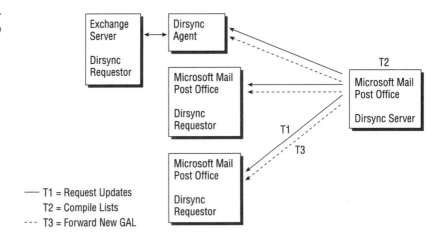

FIGURE 2.9

An overview of the Dirsync Requestor

Use the tabs described in Table 2.16 to assign the appropriate attributes.

You must have only one Dirsync Requestor in your organization per a single directory synchronization server. If you have multiple Dirsync Servers that you want to import, only one requestor per organization should connect to each Dirsync Server. If you have more than one requestor per server, you can inadvertently corrupt your directory information between sites.

TABLE 2.16	**Tab**	**Description**
The tabs in the Dirsync Requestor property pages	General	Used to define a display name for the remote requestor mailbox, password, requestor address type, and the requestor language and to specify whether you want to export this information on the next cycle.
	Import Container	Used to define the container in which to place the imported address lists and to identify the trust level of the addresses imported.
	Export Container	Used to specify which Exchange recipient containers will be exported to the external postoffices.

	Tab	Description
T A B L E 2.16 *(cont.)* The tabs in the Dirsync Requestor property pages	Settings	Used to define a Dirsync password and to choose which of the following settings you want to turn on: Send Updates, Receive Updates, Send Local Template Information, Receive Local Template Information, Import on Next Cycle, Export on Next Cycle.
	Schedule	Used to define the schedule for the Dirsync Server. The default is to send one message update each day at midnight.

Synchronizing the Directory Manually

The Dirsync process executes at the beginning of every hour. If want to start this process sooner or if you have added some requestors or identified a new server, you can start this process manually.

To start a directory synchronization process manually, you must first stop the directory synchronization service. You can do so from the command prompt and from Control Panel.

To stop the process from the command prompt, follow these steps:

1. Start a Command Prompt session.

2. At the command prompt, type **net pause msexchangedx**.

3. Quit the session and return to NT.

To stop the process from Control Panel, follow these steps:

1. From Control Panel, start the Services applet.

2. Select Microsoft Exchange Directory Synchronization.

3. Select Pause.

Ignore the message "Could not pause the Microsoft Exchange Directory Synchronization Service on \\Server. Error 2140." You started the process successfully by issuing the Pause command. To verify, in Windows NT Event Viewer, check that you have enabled Diagnostic Logging for the Directory Synchronization object.

To restart the Dirsync processes, at the command prompt, type:

Net Start MsExchangedx

or in Control Panel, select the Services applet. From the applet, select the Directory Synchronization service and click Start.

Replicating the Exchange Directory

In Unit 1, I mentioned that directory databases are replicated automatically within a site. In fact, whenever a change is made to the directory, Exchange waits five minutes and then starts a replication process within a site. The server then notifies all servers within the site, one at a time. Each server responds by sending a request for the updates. After the server responds, all directories will have the latest information. Figure 2.10 shows this peer-to-peer relationship between servers within a site.

F I G U R E 2.10

Replicating directories within a site

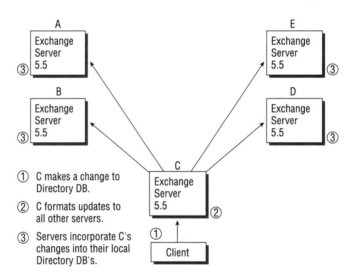

To share directory database information across sites, you must configure a Directory Replication connector, which sends and receives Directory database updates between two connected sites.

Figure 2.11 gives you an overview of the Directory Replication connector in a site-to-site configuration. As part of configuration, you need to identify a server in your site that will connect to a remote server in the target site. These servers are known as *bridgehead* servers, since these servers filter all updates across sites. Local directory replication within a site continues automatically.

FIGURE 2.11

An overview of directory replication between sites

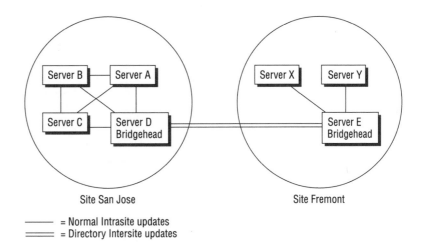

If both servers are on the same LAN, you can configure both connectors from the same source sites. If the remote site is not currently connected, you must configure each server separately.

To configure the source bridgehead server, follow these steps:

1. Start the Exchange Administrator program.

2. Select the Site Configuration object for the site you are modifying, and double-click to open the site container.

3. Choose File ➤ New Other ➤ Directory Replication Connector to open the Directory Replication Connector property pages.

Table 2.17 lists the tabs in these property pages and describes what they do.

T A B L E 2.17	Tab	Description
The tabs in the Directory Replication Connector property pages	General	Used to set up the display and directory names, the target site name, the name of the local bridgehead server, and the name of the remote bridgehead server.
	Permissions	Used to define users or groups of users who have access to this object.
	Schedule	**Frequency:** Never—Disables replication. Always—Runs replication every 15 minutes. Selected Times—Runs the Directory Replication connector according to the times selected in the schedule grid. **Time Detail:** 1 Hour—Displays the schedule grid in 1-hour increments. 15 Minute—Displays the schedule grid in 15-minute increments.
	Sites	Used to define inbound sites (sites from which this server receives updates) and outbound sites (sites to which this server will send updates).

Importing Data from Foreign Mail Systems

During the Exchange Server 5.5 installation, three tools are added to help in migrating groups of users from foreign mail systems to Exchange:

- Source Extractors
- Migration Wizard
- Directory Import and Export (discussed in the earlier section "Creating Mailboxes")

In addition, administrators can write their own source extraction programs using the Exchange Server 5.5 Software Developers Kit.

Using Source Extractors

You use Source Extractors to pull address information, distribution lists, mailboxes, messages, folders, and schedule information across from the following mail systems:

- Microsoft Mail for PC Networks 3.*x*
- Microsoft Mail for AppleTalk Networks 3.*x*
- Lotus cc:Mail (database version 6)
- DEC ALL-IN-ONE, version 2.3 or later
- IBM Profs and Office Vision
- Verimation MEMO MVS 3.2.1
- Novell GroupWise
- Collabra Share

Using the Exchange Server Migration Wizard

The Exchange Server 5.5 Migration Wizard is an easy-to-use administrative tool that helps an administrator migrate a large group of users from one mail system to another. Figure 2.12 shows the Welcome screen of this Wizard.

Currently, the Migration Wizard imports data from the following mail systems:

- Source Extraction Lists

- Microsoft Mail Post Offices

- Lotus cc:Mail Post Office (database version 6)

- Novell GroupWise Post Office

- Collabra Share forums

The Migration Wizard displays several options that you need to configure:

- Selection of Mailboxes to Import

- Mailbox Creation Parameters

  - Recipient Containers

  - Mailbox Template

  - Initial Password Generation

- Folders and Messages to Import

- Shared Folders to Import

- Personal Address Books to Import

- Calendar Files to Import

Installing and Configuring Exchange Clients

Clients are applications that communicate with an Exchange server as the owner of a mailbox. Exchange Server 5.5 includes the following clients:

- Microsoft Exchange Client
  - MS-DOS
  - Windows 3.1
  - Apple Macintosh
  - Windows 95
  - Windows NT
- Microsoft Schedule+ 7.5
- Microsoft Outlook (for Windows 95 and Windows NT)
- Outlook Web Access HTTP Pages (requires IIS and ASP)

Table 2.18 lists the client software installation requirements.

T A B L E 2.18 Exchange client installation requirements

Client	Operating System	Memory	Minimum Disk Space
MS-DOS Exchange	MS-DOS	1MB	2MB
Windows 3.x Exchange	Windows 3.x	8MB	12MB
Windows 95 Exchange (not the Inbox)	Windows 95	8MB	12MB
Windows NT Exchange (not the Inbox)	Windows NT 3.51 Windows NT 4	16MB Intel 20MB RISC	12MB Intel 15MB RISC
Macintosh Exchange	Macintosh	8MB	14MB
Outlook	Windows 95 or Windows NT 4	8MB Windows 95 16MB Windows NT	26MB

Installing Exchange and Outlook Clients

There are two types of installations for Exchange clients:

Local—The client program files are loaded on the user's local computer.

Shared—The client files are placed on a network share, and clients connect to this share to load the Exchange client. This is usually slower than a local installation, but allows for central control of the interface.

Configuring Common Parameters for Exchange Clients

Each Exchange client uses a set of attributes and values to establish a connection with the Exchange server. This collection of configuration data is known as a Messaging Profile, which provides information on the following services:

- Information Services
  - Exchange Server, which is used to define the name of the Exchange server to connect to and the mailbox to open.
  - Personal Folders, which are used for additional storage instead of or in addition to a user mailbox. Personal folders are created and maintained on a user's local computer.
  - Personal Address Book, which is a local file that stores user-defined addresses and/or frequently used addresses.
- Information Storage
  - Information on where to store incoming mail. This can be the user's mailbox or a personal folder.
  - Offline Folder (OST) management
- Message Handling
  - Configuration parameters for receipt of mail
  - Options to configure for reading mail
  - Configuration parameters for reply and forwarding of mail
  - Options to configure for creating mail and checking addresses

Using the Message Transfer Agent

A core component of Exchange Server 5.5 is the message transfer agent (MTA), which forwards messages from the information store from one server to another. There are two types of MTA communication:

- Within a site
- Between sites

The MTA is created during installation and given the same name as the server on which you are installing.

The following sections cover using the MTA to deliver messages within a site (intrasite), between sites (intersite), and to foreign mail systems (using connectors).

Delivering Messages

The MTA delivers messages to another server's information store or forwards messages to a connector. The process of delivering messages to a mailbox on the same server does not involve the MTA.

Delivering Local Messages

Figure 2.13 shows how the MTA delivers a message to another mailbox. Here are the steps:

1. The client sends the message to the server's information store.

2. The public information store receives the message and checks the address. If the address is local to this server, the public information store places the message in the recipient's mailbox.

3. The recipient's client receives notification of a new message.

4. The recipient opens and reads the message.

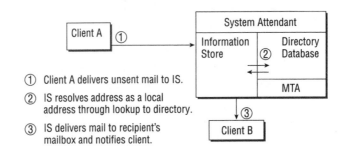

FIGURE 2.13

Delivering a message
to a mailbox on the
same server

① Client A delivers unsent mail to IS.

② IS resolves address as a local
address through lookup to directory.

③ IS delivers mail to recipient's
mailbox and notifies client.

Delivering Messages to Another Server's Mailbox

Sending a message to a public information store on another server involves a slightly different process. Figure 2.14 shows how this works. Here are the steps:

1. The MTA refers to the Directory Service to determine the message's home server and contacts the home server's MTA.

2. The MTA transfers the message to the target MTA.

3. The MTA notifies the information store that a message has been received.

4. The information store resolves the address, determines that it's local, and notifies the client that there is new mail.

Delivering a Message to a Connector

The three main connectors (X.400 Connector, Microsoft Exchange Connector for Lotus cc: Mail, and Microsoft Mail Connector) work basically the same way: The connector submits incoming messages and picks up outgoing messages. Figure 2.15 illustrates this process. Here are the steps:

1. The client sends the message to the server's information store.

2. The public information store resolves the address by referencing the Directory Service.

3. Since the message is destined for a connector, the message is stored in a queue on the server's information store.

4. The connector connects to the information store and scans for any outgoing messages. If it finds a message, the connector converts the message into the outgoing format and delivers it to the connector. If

the connector finds messages to deliver to Exchange, it converts them to the Exchange Server 5.5 format and delivers them to the information store.

FIGURE 2.14

Delivering a message to another server within a site

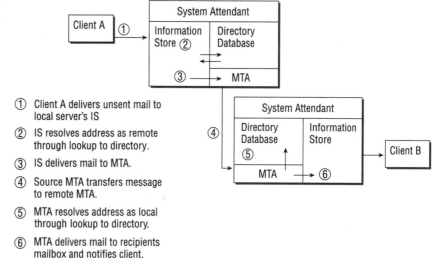

① Client A delivers unsent mail to local server's IS

② IS resolves address as remote through lookup to directory.

③ IS delivers mail to MTA.

④ Source MTA transfers message to remote MTA.

⑤ MTA resolves address as local through lookup to directory.

⑥ MTA delivers mail to recipients mailbox and notifies client.

FIGURE 2.15

Delivering a message to a connector

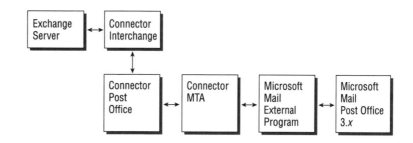

Configuring the MTA for Intrasite Communication

Because the MTA for a server is created at installation, let's take a look at its configuration properties. To configure the MTA, you use the Message Transfer Agent property pages, as shown in Figure 2.16. Table 2.19 lists and describes the tabs in these property pages.

FIGURE 2.16

The MTA property
pages

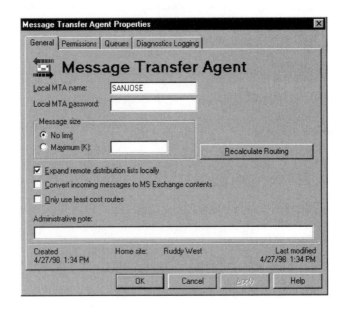

TABLE 2.19

The tabs in the MTA
property pages

Tabs	Description
General	Used to define a local name and a password, to set expansion for remote distribution lists, to recalculate routing, to convert incoming messages to MTA format, and to set the size limits of messages.
Permissions	Used to define users or groups of users who have access to this object.
Queues	Used to display the queues of messages waiting to be delivered by the MTA.
Diagnostics Logging	Used to control how logging will be configured for the MTA.

Transferring Messages between Sites

You can use several connector types to transfer messages between sites. The connector you choose depends on the communication links between sites. Here are the options:

Site Connector is typically used for LAN-connected sites if the connections are stable and high-bandwidth communication is present. You cannot schedule this connector.

Dynamic RAS Connector is typically used to connect two sites of an asynchronous connection using NT Remote Access Service (RAS). No other LAN connection can be present. You can schedule this connector to run at specific times.

Internet Mail Service is a core component that can connect two sites over a private TCP/IP network or an Internet backbone. You can schedule this service. (See Unit 1 for details about this connector.)

X.400 Connector is typically used to connect Exchange Server to an X.400 site and to backbone an Exchange connector over an existing X.400 Connector. This connector is discussed earlier in this unit.

Configuring the Site Connector

The Exchange Server 5.5 Site Connector connects two sites using synchronous remote procedure calls (RPCs). Before you create this connector, you need the following:

- The name of at least one server in the target site
- A LAN protocol that can use RPC
- Administrator permissions on both the local and the target sites
- A list of possible target servers in the remote site

To configure the Site connector, follow these steps:

1. Start the Exchange Administrator program.

2. Select the Site Configuration object for the site you are adding the connector to, and double-click to open the container.

3. Choose File ≻ New Other ≻ Site Connector to open the Site Connector property pages.

Table 2.20 lists and describes the tabs in these property pages.

T A B L E 2.20	Tab	Description
The tabs in the Site Connector property pages	General	Used to assign the Site Connector a name to display as the object name, to configure the Site Connector's usage cost (Exchange Server 5.5 uses least cost routing), to assign the messaging bridgehead server of the remote site, and to store any administrative notes.
	Permissions	Used to define users or groups of users who have access to this object.
	Target Servers	Used to define servers in the remote site that will receive messages. All servers in the remote site are placed in the list by default. To use specific servers in a remote site, you can associate costs with each server. The Exchange MTA will always use the least costly server when communicating across the site.

	Tab	Description
T A B L E 2.20 *(cont.)* The tabs in the Site Connector property pages	Address Space	Used to specify which addresses will travel across this connector.
	Override	Used to define user logon information on the remote site. Use this tab if the remote site is in a separate domain and there is no trust relationship between domains.

Installing and Configuring the Dynamic RAS Connector

You can also use a dial-up connection to transfer messages between sites. The connection must support IPX/SPX or TCP/IP. The Dynamic RAS Connector provides asynchronous connections using RPCs and Windows NT's Dial-Up Networking feature. Before configuring a connection, you need the following:

- Windows NT RAS software installed and configured on the Exchange servers

- A service account with Send As and Mailbox owner permissions for the servers or Configuration containers in the remote site

- The name to use for the MTA transport stack

- The name of the remote server

- A phone book entry for the remote server, including server name and phone number

- A name to assign the Dynamic RAS Connector

- An RAS MTA transport stack configured with the server name using the transport stack

To set up a Dynamic RAS Connector, follow these steps:

1. Start the Exchange Administrator program.

2. Select the Site Configuration object for the site you are modifying, and double-click to open the site container.

3. Select the connections object for the local site.

4. Choose File ➢ New Other ➢ Dynamic RAS Connector to open the Dynamic RAS Connector property pages.

Table 2.21 lists and describes the tabs in these property pages.

TABLE 2.21 The tabs in the Dynamic RAS Connector property pages	Tab	Description
	General	Used to set the display name, the remote server, the MTA transport stack, the phone book entry, and the message size.
	Permissions	Used to define users or groups of users who have access to this object.
	Schedule	**Frequency:** Remote Initiated—Runs only when another MTA initiates the connection. Never—Disables the connector. Always—Sends requests to the target server when a message is in the outgoing queue. Selected Times—Runs the connector according to the times selected in the schedule grid. **Time Detail:** 1 Hour—Displays the schedule grid in 1-hour increments. 15 Minute—Displays the schedule grid in 15-minute increments.
	RAS Override	Used to specify remote logon parameters when connecting to another site. You can also configure a callback and overriding phone number.
	MTA Override	Used to change default server MTA attributes. Change these values only when you need to match a remote Exchange computer.
	Connected Sites	Used to specify servers that will participate in directory replication when connecting to an existing Exchange Server organization.
	Address Space	Used to specify which addresses will travel across this connector.
	Delivery Restrictions	Used to accept or reject messages from a specific user or groups of users by address.

Understanding Internet Protocols and Properties

Exchange Server 5.5 includes new Internet protocols to support a variety of e-mail clients. The protocols depend on the installation of TCP/IP services for Windows NT 4. The support protocols are listed below (an asterisk indicates that a protocol is new in Exchange Server 5.5):

- Simple Mail Transfer Protocol (SMTP)

- Post Office Protocol 3 (POP3)

- Internet Message Access Protocol 4 rev 1 (IMAP4) *

- Lightweight Directory Access Protocol (LDAP)

- HyperText Transfer Protocol (HTTP) and Microsoft Outlook Web Access *

- Internet News Service/Network News Transfer Protocol (NNTP)

Setting the Internet Protocol Scope

The Internet protocols listed above are managed at the site, at the server, or at the mailbox level. The following rules apply to all protocols except HTTP:

1. If a site has Internet protocols configured, the properties for the protocols will be used as defaults for all servers in the site. HTTP is configured at the site level only.

2. If a server has protocols enabled, user mailboxes and recipients are enabled by default. Protocols can be disabled mailbox by mailbox.

3. If a server has protocols disabled, mailboxes and recipients are also disabled and cannot be enabled.

To configure site and server protocol properties, follow these steps:

1. Start the Exchange Administrator program

2. Select either the Site Configuration object or the Server object for the site or server you are modifying. Double-click the object to open the container.

3. Choose File ➤ Properties to open the Protocols property pages:

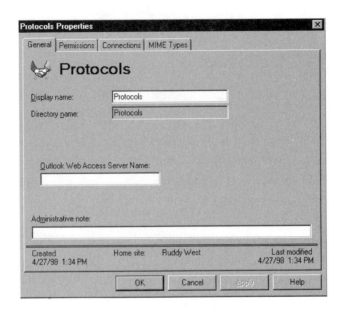

Table 2.22 lists and describes the tabs in these property pages.

TABLE 2.22	Tab	Description
The tabs in the Protocols property pages	General	Used to define the display name and to store administrative notes associated with the protocols container.
	Permissions	Used to define users or groups of users who have access to this object.
	Connections	Used to accept or reject access to mail for POP3, IMAP4, NNTP, and LDAP clients. This option uses rules that define IP addresses and subnet masks to reject or connect.
	MIME Types	Used to assigned file extensions for inbound and outbound attachments.

Using Post Office Protocol 3

Internet mail clients use the Post Office Protocol version 3 (POP3) to retrieve Inbox mail messages from a user's Exchange account on an Exchange server.

This allows users who are temporarily away from their sites to connect and retrieve messages from POP3-compatible clients that are configured to use TCP/IP.

To enable the protocol on a server, follow these steps:

1. Start the Exchange Administrator program.

2. Select the Site Configuration object that contains the server you want to modify. Double-click the object to open the container.

3. Select the Server, and double-click the server object to open the container.

4. Select the Protocols container.

5. Choose File ➤ Properties to open the POP3 Protocol property pages.

Table 2.23 lists and describes the tabs in these property pages.

The POP3 protocol follows the same default hierarchy as the other Internet protocols. See the earlier section "Internet Protocol Scope" for the scope for the site, server, and mailbox.

	Tab	Description
T A B L E 2.23 The tabs in the POP3 Protocol property pages	General	Used to define the display name and to store administrative notes.
	Permissions	Used to define users or groups of users who have access to this object.
	Authentication	Used to specify the methods of authentication from Basic (clear text) to Windows NT Challenge/Response.
	Message Format	Used to define a message format to convert to when a POP3 client retrieves a message. See Table 2.24 for a list of the options in this property page.
	Idle Time-out	Used to define how long POP3 clients can remain idle before the Exchange server closes the connection.

TABLE 2.24	Option	What It Does
The options in the Message Format property page	MIME	Allows you to specify whether the message body is plain text or HTML.
	UUENCODE	Allows you to choose to support Binhex for Macintosh.
	Character Set	Allows you to choose which ASCII set to use.
	Rich Text Format	Allows you to choose whether to use Microsoft Exchange rich text format.

Configuring POP3 Clients

Before you can allow POP3 clients to connect to your Exchange Server, each client must specify the following information:

POP3 account name—This is the alias for the mailbox that supports POP3. The value for this attribute depends on the following:

- If the Windows NT domain and user name are specified as the alias name, both the domain and the user name must precede the alias name. For example, if the alias name is different from the NT account information, you use the following account name: `Windows_NT_domain\user_account\mailbox_alias` name.

- If only the alias name is used as the POP3 account, the Windows NT user account information is the same as the alias name. For example, if only the alias is specified, all NT domains are searched for a user name equivalent to the alias.

- If only the Windows NT domain and user accounts are specified, the mailbox alias is the same as the user account name. The only domain searched is the one specified.

POP3 e-mail address—Use the SMTP e-mail address that Internet users would use to send this mailbox a message.

POP3 server name—This is the name of the Exchange server that hosts the mailbox access through a POP3 client.

SMTP server name—Use this if the Exchange server is running the Internet Mail Server for the POP3 client and allows the client to connect and send mail.

Each client is, therefore, different; the POP3 client configuration must be specified by the third-party vendor's product documentation.

Using IMAP4

The newest protocol to join the Exchange Server 5.5 protocol ranks is IMAP4. This protocol is much more robust than POP3. Although IMAP4 allows the same access to a user Inbox as POP3 does, it also allows access to the entire mailbox and public folders from an IMAP4 client.

 The IMAP4 protocol follows the same default hierarchy as the other Internet protocols. See the section "Internet Protocol Scope" for the scope for the site, server, and mailbox.

To configure the IMAP4 protocol, follow these steps:

1. Start the Exchange Administrator program.

2. Select the Site Configuration object that contains the server you want to modify. Double-click the object to open the container.

3. Select the Server, and double-click the server object to open the container.

4. Select the Protocols Container.

5. Choose File ➤ Properties to open the IMAP4 Protocol property pages.

These property pages contain the following tabs and options:

General—Used to assign the display name. This tab contains the following options:

    Enable Protocol—Click this option to turn the protocol off or on.

    Public Folder Listing—Click this option to turn it off when IMAP4 clients are experiencing poor performance. This does not allow a client to perform a wildcard list command.

Fast Message Retrieval—Click this option to turn off exact message size and to turn on approximate message size reporting. This increases performance for clients that can use approximate message sizes.

Permissions—Used to define users to groups of users who have access to this object.

Authentication—Used to choose one or more of the following authentication types:

- Basic (Clear Text)
- Basic (Clear Text) using SSL
- Windows NT Challenge/Response
- Windows NT Challenge/Response using SSL
- MCIS Membership System

Anonymous—Used to determine if anonymous access is allowed for public folders.

Message Format—Used to enable MIME encoding checkboxes:

- Provide message body as plain text
- Provide message body as HTML
- Character set

Idle Time-Out—Used to define how long IMAP4 clients can remain idle before the Exchange server closes the connection.

Configuring an IMAP4 Client

Before you can allow IMAP4 clients to connect to your Exchange server, each client must specify the following information:

IMAP4 account name—This is the alias for the mailbox that supports IMAP4. The value for this attribute depends on the following:

- If the Windows NT domain and user name are specified as the alias name, both the domain and user name must precede the alias name. For example, if the alias name is different from the NT account information, you use the following account name: `Windows_NT_domain\user_account\mailbox_alias` name.

- If only the alias name is used as the IMAP4 account, the Windows NT user account information is the same as the alias name. For example, if only the alias is specified, all NT domains are searched for a user name equivalent to the alias.

- If only the Windows NT domain and user accounts are specified, the mailbox alias is the same as the user account name. The only domain searched is the one specified.

IMAP4 e-mail address—Use the SMTP e-mail address that Internet users would use to send this mailbox a message.

IMAP4 server name—This is the name of the Exchange server that hosts the mailbox access through an IMAP4 client.

SMTP server name—Use this if the Exchange server is running the Internet Mail Server for the IMAP4 client and allows the client to connect and send mail.

Each client is, therefore, different; the IMAP4 client configuration must be specified by the third-party vendor's product documentation.

If you want to map and use the entire Exchange mailbox, use an IMAP4 client. If you want to pop-in to retrieve your unread mail, use a POP3 client.

Using Outlook Web Access

As discussed in Unit 1, HTTP support is added during the installation of Exchange Server 5.5 if the Web component of Internet Information Server is installed. With the Outlook Web Access component, users can access their Exchange mailbox from a supported Web browser on a Unix, Macintosh, or Windows computer.

You configure the properties for Outlook Web Access from the Site Configuration object. Follow these steps:

1. Start the Exchange Administrator program.

2. Select the Site Configuration object that you want to modify. Double-click the object to open the container.

3. Select the Site Protocols container.

4. Choose File ➤ Properties to open the HTTP (Web) Site Settings property pages.

These property pages have the following tabs and options:

General—Used to define the display name and to enable the protocol. You can configure anonymous access with the following options:

- Allow anonymous users to access the anonymous public folders
- Allow anonymous users to browse the global address list

Permissions—Used to define users or groups of users who have access to this object.

Folder Shortcuts—Used to create links to published public folders. These shortcuts are used to build a list of the public folders to which anonymous users have access.

Advanced—Used to configure the number of Address Book entries returned on a search initiated from the Web browser.

Using Network News Transfer Protocol

The Network News Transfer Protocol (NNTP) allows Outlook users to join online discussion groups (newsgroups) across the Internet. Newsgroups appear to Outlook users as public folders, and the Exchange administrator can also choose which public folders to publish as newsgroup entries.

Before configuring the NNTP protocol, determine what role your server will play in updating newsgroup contents. The updates to newsgroups are known as *newsfeeds*. Your server can be a recipient of a newsfeed or serve newsfeeds to other servers if you will be publishing your public folders. You then need to configure the newsfeeds as either unidirectional or bidirectional.

Exchange Server 5.5 provides a Newsfeeds Configuration Wizard to guide you through configuring the NNTP protocol. Once the Wizard finishes, you can view or change the properties of the newsfeeds. To configure an existing newsfeed, follow these steps:

1. Start the Exchange Administrator program.

2. Select the Site Configuration object that contains the server you want to modify. Double-click the object to open the container.

3. Select the Server, and double-click the server object to open the container.

4. Choose File ➤ New Other ➤ Newsfeed.

Table 2.25 lists and describes the tabs in the Newsfeed property pages.

TABLE 2.25 The tabs in the Newsfeed property pages	Tabs	Description
	General	Used to define the display name, to enable the newsfeed, and to assign an administrator mailbox for newsgroup maintenance.
	Messages	Used to set message size limits for both incoming and outgoing newsfeeds.
	Hosts	Used to create host lists that your newsfeed provider supplies. For a bidirectional newsfeed, the inbound and outbound hosts can be the same.

T A B L E 2.25 (cont.) The tabs in the Newsfeed property pages	Tabs	Description
	Connection	Used to define the connection type: LAN or Dialup. If you are using Dialup, set the account, password, and connection information for Dial-Up Networking.
	Security	Used to set security features of the NNTP newsfeed. By default, security is not set up. You can require SSL connections and specify outbound user account and password information.
	Schedule	**Frequency:** Never—Disables connections. Always—Starts connections every 15 minutes. Selected Times—Starts the connection according to the times selected in the schedule grid. **Time Detail:** 1 Hour—Displays the schedule grid in 1-hour increments. 15 Minute—Displays the schedule grid in 15-minute increments.
	Inbound	Used to define newsgroups that will be available for inbound pull feeds. If you are configuring push feeds from another server, you can specify which newsgroups will be available.
	Outbound	Used to specify which newsgroups you will be sending to your newsfeed provider.
	Advanced	Used to mark all newsgroup messages as delivered to speed up the next set of messages waiting to be delivered. This allows your server to catch up on newsfeeds if your server is behind.

Using the Lightweight Directory Access Protocol

The Lightweight Directory Access Protocol (LDAP) allows Internet mail clients to access the Exchange Server directory. When you set access permissions on the LDAP container, users can make changes to their own directory entries.

Although the Microsoft objectives refer to LDAP as Local Directory Access Protocol, it is more commonly referred to as Lightweight Directory Access Protocol.

LDAP is enabled on a site by default; the administrator can modify LDAP properties on a server-by-server basis. To do so, follow these steps:

1. Start the Exchange Administrator program.

2. Select the Site Configuration object that contains the server you want to modify. Double-click the object to open the container.

3. Select the Server, and double-click the server object to open the container.

4. Select the Protocols Container.

5. Choose File ➤ Properties to open the LDAP Protocol property pages.

These property pages contain the following tabs and options:

General—Used to assign the display name and to enable the protocol.

Permissions—Used to define users to groups of users who have access to this object.

Authentication—Used to choose one or more of the following authentication types:

- Basic (Clear Text)
- Basic (Clear Text) Using SSL
- Windows NT Challenge/Response
- Windows NT Challenge/Response Using SSL
- MCIS Membership System

Anonymous—Used to determine if anonymous access is allowed for lookups.

Search—Used to define parameters for how searches will be performed:

- Treat "any" substring searches as "initial" substring searches (fast)
- Allow only "initial" substring search (fast)
- Allow all substring searches (slow)
- Maximum number of search results returned

Referrals—When a request for information is received from an LDAP client that cannot be resolved, this property provides a list of other servers to which to refer the request.

Idle Time-out—Used to define how long LDAP clients can remain idle before the Exchange server closes the connection.

Tracking Messages

With Exchange Server 5.5, you can track messages in order to troubleshoot mail-delivery problems. You can enable message tracking on the following components:

- MTA
- Information store
- Microsoft Mail Connector
- Internet Mail Service

To enable message tracking on the MTA or the information store, follow these steps:

1. Start the Exchange Administrator program.

2. Select the Site Configuration object for the site you want to modify, and double-click to open the container.

3. Select the Information Store site configuration to enable message tracking for the information store.

4. Choose File ➤ Properties.

5. To turn on message tracking, check the Enable Message Tracking checkbox.

To enable message tracking on the Microsoft Mail Connector, follow these steps:

1. Start the Exchange Administrator program.

2. Select the Site Configuration object for the site you want to modify, and double-click to open the container.

3. Select the Connections Container object and click once.

4. Select the Microsoft Mail Connector.

5. Choose File ➤ Properties to open the Microsoft Mail Connector property pages.

6. Select the Interchange tab.

7. To turn on message tracking for the connector, check the Enable Message Tracking checkbox.

To enable message tracking on the Internet Mail Service, follow these steps:

1. Start the Exchange Administrator program.

2. Select the Site configuration object for the site you are modifying, and double-click to open the container.

3. Select the Connections container to display the connectors configured for your site.

4. Select the Internet Mail Service.

5. Choose File ➤ Properties to open the Internet Mail Service property pages.

6. Select the Internet Mail tab.

7. To turn on message tracking for this service, check the Enable Message Tracking checkbox.

For much more information on tracking messages, see Unit 5.

Creating Public Folder Server Locations

To increase the efficiency of public folder access, you can create locations. *Locations* are groups of servers that will be used by default unless the public folder contents cannot be found. If a public folder is not found within a location, the information store searches outside the location.

Using this method, you can assign a group of high-bandwidth servers to perform as a subgroup that contains searches. You can also use locations to contain searches within a specific group; doing so lets you restrict users to a specific group of servers and no others.

In addition, you can create a default location. This default location is searched after the specified location found on the server's General property page. The default location is known by the asterisk symbol (*). Configuring servers with the location of asterisk assigns them to the default group.

With this default location, the search order for replicas is:

1. The server location specified on a server's General property page.

2. If you specify the default location of asterisk in your organization, the search continues on the servers in the default group.

3. If you have established no default location, the search continues on servers outside your location.

Configuring Security

As part of advanced security, Exchange Server 5.5 uses the Key Management (KM) Server to support message encryption and digital signatures. The KM Server provides a database of keys that are used to encrypt messages and the ability to digitally "sign" a message to ensure its authenticity.

Installing and Starting the KM Server

The KM Server is installed during the Exchange Server 5.5 installation when you choose the Complete/Custom installation type. To support the advanced security features of the KM Server, you must:

- Install the Exchange Policy Module

- Install and start the Microsoft Certificate Server

- Install and start the KM Server

To start the KM Server, you must configure the Service Startup properties to use the Site Service account in the Control Panel Services applet. When the service is started at system boot time, you will be prompted for the diskette that contains the KM password (created during the installation of Exchange). If you did not save the password onto a diskette during the Exchange installation, enter the password in the Startup Parameter field of the service.

Configuring the KM Server

To administer the KM Server, you must:

- Set the Security properties for the CA (Certificate Authority) object
- Set the properties for the Site Encryption Configuration object

Table 2.26 lists and describes the tabs for the CA object. To configure the CA Object, follow these steps:

1. Start the Exchange Administrator program.

2. Select the Site Configuration object that you want to modify. Double-click the object to open the container.

3. Select the CA object container.

4. Choose File ➤ Properties to open the CA property pages.

T A B L E 2.26	Tabs	Description
The tabs in the CA property pages	General	Used to assign a display name to the CA object.
	Permissions	Used to define users or groups of users who have access to this object.
	Administrators	Used to view the Windows NT accounts that have permissions to administer the KM Server, to add and remove administrators, and to change an administrator's password.
	Passwords	Used to set the number of passwords required to perform a specific task such as adding or deleting administrators, recovering a user's security keys, revoking a user's security keys, and importing or revoking the trust of another CA certificate.
	Enrollment	Used to set policies for transmitting temporary keys, to enroll large groups of users, and to set Exchange 4 and 5 compatibility features.
	Certificate Trust List	Used to define trust relationships with other organizations. This allows users to verify signatures from users in other organizations.

Table 2.27 lists the properties and values for the Site Encryption object. To configure the Site Encryption object, follow these steps:

1. Start the Exchange Administrator program.

2. Select the Site Configuration object that you want to modify. Double-click the object to open the container.

3. Select the Site Encryption object container.

4. Choose File ➤ Properties to open the Site Encryption property pages.

	Tabs	Description
T A B L E 2.27 The tabs in the Site Encryption property pages	General	Used to assign the display name for the object.
	Permissions	Used to define users or groups of users who have access to this object.
	Algorithms	Used to define which security algorithm to use when creating encryption keys for your users: CAST-64, CAST-40, or DES. You can also use this tab to define S/MIME encryption algorithms and the preferred security format.

Enabling Advanced Security on a Mailbox

After you configure the CA and Site Encryption objects, you are ready to enable advanced security for users. Table 2.28 lists and describes the options on the Security tab of the Mailbox property page. For instructions on how to open the Mailbox property page, see the "Creating Mailboxes" section earlier in this unit.

T A B L E 2.28 The options on the Security tab in the Security Mailbox property page

Option	Description
Enable Advanced Security	Used to create a temporary key for a user. Once users are given this key, they can enable advanced security through their clients.
Recover Security Key	Used to reissue security keys if a user loses their advanced security password or if the password becomes corrupt. This option removes the password from their account.

T A B L E 2.28 The options on the Security tab in the Security Mailbox property page *(continued)*

Option	Description
Revoke Advanced Security	Used to permanently disable the certificate for a specific mailbox. Used when the user leaves the company or when security has been compromised for that user.
Forget Remembered Password	Used to clear the previous security key password for the user, before assigning another security key.
Security Certificate Validation Dates	Used to list the valid dates of the security certificate.

Installing Exchange Server

1. True or False. To install Exchange Server, you should be logged on to your own account.

2. True or False. Microsoft NT Cluster software doesn't support Exchange Server 5.5.

3. The three types of Exchange Server Installations are _____/ _____, _____, and _____.

4. True or False. To create a new Exchange site, you must choose the Create a New Site option during installation.

5. True or False. To install the Exchange Administrator on NT Workstation 4, you must choose a Complete/Custom installation.

6. To add an Exchange server to an existing site, choose _____ _____ _____ _____ during installation

7. During installation, the Site Service account will be granted the Log On As a _____ right.

8. True or False. You should use the Adminstrator account when installing Exchange Server 5.5.

9. To ensure the efficiency of running Exchange Server 5.5 on your NT server, always run the _____ _____ after installation.

10. True or False. Whenever you change the hardware configuration or add additional software applications, always run the Performance Optimizer.

11. To allow Exchange administrators to create users and mailboxes, you must add the Admin permissions for these users to the _____ containers.

Configuring Exchange Server

12. True or False. Users' mailboxes can be created from two utilities: The Exchange Administrator program and the User Manager for Domains.

13. Mailboxes can reject messages from a specific address if you configure the _____ _____ property in the Mailbox property pages.

14. True or False. Using file and block quotas from Windows NT Server 4 can enforce storage limits in a user's mailbox.

15. A mailbox that describes a user but does not store messages on a server is known as a _____ recipient.

16. Public folder content that is _____ to another server is known as a replica.

17. Public folder content that is pulled onto a public information store is known as a/an _____.

18. True or False. You can set up a schedule to automate the replication of public folder contents.

19. The _____ property on the Public Folder property pages is used to assign access to users who need to work with the public folder.

20. True or False. Only a super user can create and modify distribution lists.

21. Exchange Server 5.5. creates three default address types:

_____

_____

_____

22. True or False. Whenever you add a connector, Exchange Server adds an address type for that connector in the Site Addressing container.

23. List the three recipient objects from which the Exchange Address Book is created.

_____

_____

_____

24. True or False. Address Book views are rules for grouping recipients by a common attribute or a list of attributes.

25. To control which users have access to Address Book views, use _____ _____ search controls.

Creating and Maintaining Exchange Server Connectors

26. True or False. Connectors are Exchange Server applications that convert a mail message from a foreign mail system data type to the Exchange native format.

27. The X.400 Connector uses an MTA _____ _____ to build upon the existing network type.

28. True or False. Unlike the MTA Site Connector, the X.400 Connector can be scheduled.

29. True or False. Whereas a Site Connector connects one or more dedicated communication links with another Site Connector, an X.400 Connector can use an existing connection on your network or can use an X.400 network as a backbone to connect two sites.

30. The Lotus cc:Mail Connector requires the cc:Mail _____ and _____ tool.

31. True or False. The Container property on the Import Tool property page is used to assign users to a specific recipient container.

32. The _____ _____ Connector provides mail and schedule data to be shared between Exchange and its postoffice.

33. The three major objects that make up the Microsoft Mail Connector are _____ _____ _____, Connector Interchange, and Connector MTA.

34.   True or False. To configure the Microsoft Mail Connector, choose Server ➤ Microsoft Mail Connector.

35.   True or False. The Microsoft Mail Connector Interchange is responsible for converting messages.

Synchronizing Directory Information

36.   The method of sharing recipient information with other mail systems is known as

_____ _____.

37.   True or False. The object used to perform the Dirsync is known as the Directory Synchronization Agent.

38.   True or False. The Dirsync Server and the Dirsync Remote Requestor are the same object.

39.   True or False. The Dirsync Agent performs in one of two modes, either as a Dirsync Server or as a Dirsync Requestor.

40.   True or False. The Dirsync Server compiles recipient lists and forwards the list to Remote Dirsync Requestors.

41.   A Dirsync _____ connects with a Dirsync Server to pull the newly compiled list over to the selected Exchange server.

42.   True or False. Directory synchronization can be performed manually to immediately update any changes to the Directory database instead of waiting until the next scheduled update.

Replicating the Exchange Directory

43.   True or False. Directory replication is done automatically within a site.

44.   Directory replication starts _____ after the last directory change.

45.   To share directory information across sites, you must configure a/an _____ _____ connector.

46.   In the following diagram, name the type of server used to connect two Directory Replication sites.

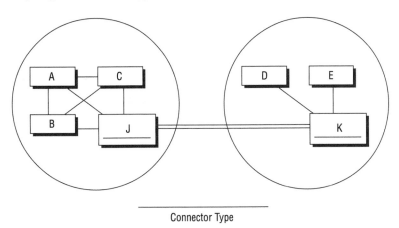

Connector Type

Importing Data from Foreign Mail Systems

47.   The three tools used in migration are known as Source Extractors, the Migration Wizard, and _____ _____ and _____ tools.

48. True or False. Developers can create Source Extractors by referring to and using the Exchange SDK.

49. The Exchange Migration Wizard imports to a _____ _____ _____ so that a user can still send messages to addresses used frequently.

Installing and Configuring Exchange Clients

50. True or False. Exchange Server provides a client for Apple Macintosh computers.

51. The minimum RAM requirement for Outlook on a Windows 95 computer is _____ MB.

52. True or False. The Outlook Web Access pages are always added as part of the Exchange Server installation if the Active Server Pages are installed as part of NT

53. True or False. Schedule+ 7.5 is included as part of the Exchange client distribution to allow users to send mail from an MS-DOS machine.

54. A collection of client configuration data is known as a _____ _____.

55. True or False. Outlook provides a personal management application that also supports messaging.

Using the Message Transfer Agent

56. The _____ is the core component responsible for delivering messages across sites.

57. True or False. The MTA delivers messages from the sender's mailbox to a recipient mailbox on the same server.

58. The MTA connects to another server's _____ component to deliver messages to another server on the same site.

59. True or False. The client notifies the MTA that a message needs to be sent to another server. The information store is not involved in intrasite communication.

60. True or False. A Site Connector is needed when intersite messaging transfer is required.

61. Associate the Site Connector type with its description.

Answer	Connector Type	Description
_____	Site	1. Used for dial-up connections between sites. You must have an asynchronous connection between sites. You can schedule this connector.
_____	Dynamic RAS Connector	2. Used for SMTP mail connectivity with an SMTP Mail Relay Host. Also used to connect two sites over an intranet or over the Internet.
_____	Internet Mail Service	3. Used for connection to a CCITT mail system. Also used to connect two sites over an existing CCITT network.
_____	X.400 Site Connector	4. Used for stable and high-bandwidth network connections. Used predominantly with a LAN.

62. True or False. To connect sites in separate domains, you must specify remote access information on the Override tab of the Site Connector property pages.

63. True or False. You can schedule the X.400 Connector.

64. True or False. You can schedule the Site Connector.

65. True or False. You can use the Dynamic RAS Connector in addition to many LAN connections between sites.

66. True or False. You can schedule the Internet Mail Service.

67. In the following diagram, identify the type of connector that should be used between the sites.

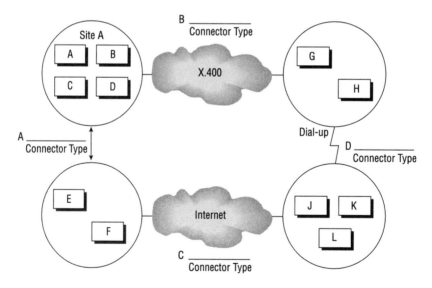

Understanding Internet Protocols and Properties

68. The protocol used for newsfeeds is _____.

69.   True or False. IMAP5 can only be used to retrieve inbox contents.

70.   Exchange Service provides Outlook Web Access to all Exchange users through a

_____ _____.

71.   True or False. POP3 provides full access to a user's mailbox and public folders.

72.   True or False. You can enable a user's mailbox to use protocols even if the server's protocol properties are disabled. The server properties are merely defaults.

Tracking Messages

73.   True or False. Exchange Server 5.5 message tracking is turned on by default.

74.   Circle Yes or No to choose which components support message tracking.

Component	Circle Choice
MTA	Yes or No
Information Store	Yes or No
System Attendant	Yes or No
Directory Database	Yes or No
Internet Mail Service	Yes or No
Microsoft Mail Connector	Yes or No
Server Container	Yes or No
cc:Mail Connector	Yes or No
Site Configuration Container	Yes or No
Connections Object	Yes or No

75. Message tracking is enabled whenever you need to _____ mail delivery.

Creating Public Folder Server Locations

76. True or False. Locations provide a search path for looking up public folders.

77. To provide a default location for public folder lookups, enter the _____ _____ character in the Location entry box.

78. True or False. The Public Folder location field is found on a server's General property page.

Configuring Security

79. To use advanced security, you must install the _____ _____ Server software.

80. True or False. Before you install the Key Management Server software, you must install the Exchange Policy Module and the Microsoft Certificate Server.

81. Before you configure the Key Management Server you must set the properties on the _____ object.

82. True or False. During the installation of the Key Management Server, you will be prompted for a diskette to save the KM password. You can choose to save this password on a diskette or enter the password manually.

83. You can use the following algorithms to create key encryption pairs: CAST64, CAST40, and

_____.

84. To create a build set of key pairs for users, use the _____
option on the CA Enrollment property page.

85. True or False. If a user forgets his encryption password, there is nothing that an administrator can do to reenable encryption for that user.

2-1 Which installation type would you select to install all connectors on an NT server or the Exchange Administrator program on an NT workstation?

    A. Typical

    B. Complete/Custom

    C. Minimum

    D. Laptop

2-2 When should you run the Performance Optimizer? Choose all that apply.

    A. After installation

    B. Before you shut down Exchange

    C. Whenever you change the hardware resources on the server and whenever you move Exchange components from one device to another

    D. Before installing Exchange Server

2-3 Which utility do you use to create distribution lists?

    A. Outlook Client for Windows 95

    B. Outlook Client for Windows NT 4

    C. Exchange Client for Windows 3.1

    D. The Exchange Administrator program

2-4 Which of the following is/are not a valid MTA transport stack?

    A. TCP/IP

    B. TP0/X.25

    C. IPX/IP

    D. TP4/CLNP

2-5 Choose the two modes in which Dirsync Agent will run.

    A. Dirsync Server

    B. Dirsync Requestor

    C. Dirsync Remote Requestor

    D. Dirsync Compiler

2-6 Ryan Rae has created and configured a Site Connector for intersite messaging and now wants to share directory information. What must she do to share directory information across sites?

    A. Nothing. The Site Connector will move the Directory Replication updates to the other servers automatically.

    B. Configure a Dynamic RAS Connector to transfer updates to other sites automatically.

    C. Create and configure a Directory Replication Connector to send updates to a bridgehead server in the remote site.

    D. Create and configure an X.400 Connector between sites.

2-7 Kathy Ree wants to migrate a large group of users from Microsoft Mail to Exchange Server 5.5. She wants all user information including scheduling information transferred to new mailboxes on an Exchange server. What would be the best tool for Kathy Ree to use?

    A. Exchange Server's 5.5 Source Extractors

    B. Directory Export

    C. Migration Wizard

    D. Exchange SDK

2-8   Marc is experiencing problems receiving mail on his server through the Microsoft Mail Connector. He has message tracking enabled on the information store. What other components should he track to troubleshoot this problem?

    A. Microsoft Mail Connector

    B. MTA

    C. System Atténdant

    D. All the above

2-9   Chris and Dan are system administrators at a large organization. They want to implement advanced security at the company. Chris has devised a plan to have four Certificate servers and four KM servers across the United States to handle their large site. Dan disagrees; he believes that only one Certificate server and one KM server should be installed in an organization. Who is right?

    A. Chris

    B. Neither of them

    C. Dan

    D. Both of them

2-10   When installing an additional Exchange server in an existing site, what other object must be available?

    A. A KM Server.

    B. You must install on a current PDC or BDC.

    C. A current Exchange server in the site to join.

    D. All the above.

SAMPLE TEST

2-11   Shannon wants a group of senior help desk employees to create Exchange mailboxes. She has reservations about giving these employees administrative permissions. What would be the best solution?

A. Grant the employees Admin permissions on the Site object.

B. Grant the employees Admin permissions on the Organization object.

C. Grant the employees Admin rights in User Manager for Domains.

D. Add the employees to the super user list.

2-12   What types of addresses are automatically created when Exchange Server is installed?

A. MS Mail

B. SMTP

C. X.400

D. X.25

2-13   Jesse needs to import the global address lists from several Microsoft Mail Post Offices. He has set up several requestors within his site to import addresses from each postoffice. Now the global address list has duplicate addresses. What went wrong?

A. Jesse should have connected to only one postoffice.

B. Jesse should have only one requestor per Dirsync Server.

C. The addresses that have been imported were duplicates to begin with.

D. The address list is corrupt.

2-14 Angie is in charge of security at her site. She is concerned about how secure connections to mailboxes are from POP3 and IMAP4 clients. Which options on the Authentication property page of the Site Encryption object provide encryption?

    A. Basic (Clear Text)

    B. Basic (Clear Text) Using SSL

    C. Windows NT Challenge/Response

    D. Windows NT Challenge/Response Using SSL

2-15 Taylor wants to make sure that her site doesn't receive mail from certain SMTP sites (company competitors), and she wants to make sure that no mail is sent to any of those sites as well. What properties can she use in the Internet Mail Service to exclude these sites from communication?

    A. Message Size Limits

    B. Delivery Restrictions

    C. Security Sites

    D. KM Server encryption pairs

2-16 Ruddy Enterprises wants to import a large group of users from Lotus cc:Mail to their new Exchange server. Anthony wants to organize the users into functional groups while he imports the users. What tools can he use to build the users into functional groups and then import them with predefined sets of properties?

    A. Microsoft Mail Migration Wizard

    B. Directory Import and Custom Recipients

    C. Source Extractors and Templates

    D. User Manager for Domains and Domain Groups

2-17   Choose the three tools provided in Exchange Server 5.5 that help in migrating users from foreign mail systems.

   A. Source Extractors

   B. NT Trust Relationships

   C. Migration Wizard

   D. Directory Export and Import

2-18   When installing Exchange Server, Theo could not successfully install the core components. The error message said that the Site Service account could not be accessed. What could be causing the problem?

   A. The User Manager for Domains could not be started.

   B. A BDC or PDC was not available.

   C. The KM Server was not installed.

   D. The server did not meet the hardware requirements for installation.

2-19   Emmy wants to roll out Outlook to several hundred users. She doesn't want to distribute the software to each of the users. She also wants to make sure each user runs Outlook from their own computer. Which installation choice should she make?

   A. Install Outlook on a shared network drive and have each user perform a shared network installation.

   B. Install Outlook on tape and have each user pass the tape along to the next person.

   C. Download the files from the Microsoft Web site and perform a local installation.

   D. Copy the files onto a shared network drive and have each user perform a local installation onto each user's computer.

2-20   When a user leaves the company and you want to delete the security keys associated with that user, which option would you use on the CA Server property page?

   A. Forget Remembered Password

   B. Enrollment

   C. Revoke a User's Security Key

   D. Import or Untrust Another CA Certificate

U N I T

3

Configuring and Managing
Resource Access

Test Objective: Configuring and Managing Resource Access

- **Manage site security.**

- **Manage users.**

- **Manage distribution lists.**

- **Manage the directory.**

- **Manage public information store databases. Elements include:**
  - Server locations
  - Homing of public folders

- **Manage private information store databases.**

- **Back up and restore the Exchange Server organization.**

- **Manage connectivity.**

Exam objectives are subject to change at any time without prior notice and at Microsoft's sole discretion. Please visit Microsoft's Training & Certification Web site (www.microsoft.com/Train_Cert) for the most current exam objectives listing.

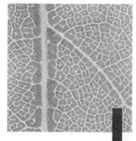

n the previous unit, we explored the configuration parameters of Exchange objects. In this unit, we're going to look at how you use these parameters to manage Exchange resources effectively. In particular, we'll look at how you do the following:

- Manage site security

- Manage users

- Manage distribution

- Manage the directory

- Manage the public information store database

- Manage the private information store database

- Back up the databases

- Manage connectivity

Managing Site Security

In Unit 2, we looked at how to configure and start the Certificate Authority and Key Management servers. In this section, we'll review the encryption algorithms. You'll have to become familiar with the U.S. export laws regarding software encryption if you are managing an organization that has sites outside the United States and Canada.

Maintenance is important in managing a secure site and keeping it up-to-date. Maintaining the encryption keys for your users may require that you create large groups of keys at one time. As users leave your organization, you have to revoke and remove keys from those accounts. As new users are added, you have to create and add the keys for their accounts.

Selecting Encryption Algorithms and Standards

Exchange Server 5.5 supports two types of encryption algorithms:

- Those compatible with Exchange Server 4 and 5
- Those compatible with S/MIME

You must decide which algorithms you'll support.

You'll want to use algorithms that are compatible with Exchange Server 4 and 5 if most of your users are on a 16-bit platform and you want to be backward compatible with previous versions of Exchange Server. These algorithms include the following:

CAST64: This algorithm is named for its creators, Carlisle Adams and Stafford Tavares, who worked at Northern Telecom Research. Because this algorithm uses 64 bits, you'll only be able to use this encryption algorithm inside the United States and Canada. It is illegal to export this algorithm.

CAST40: This algorithm, also created by Carlisle Adams and Stafford Tavares, uses shorter bits. U.S. export laws allow this encryption algorithm to be exported to countries other than the United States and Canada.

DES (Data Encryption Standard): IBM developed this 64-bit key algorithm, and it can be sold only in the United States and Canada.

The industry-preferred standard is algorithms that are compatible with S/MIME (Secure Multipurpose Internet Mail Extensions). If you have Outlook and Internet mail clients that will be using encryption, you'll want to use these algorithms, which include the following:

- DES
- 3DES
- RC2-40
- RC2-64
- RC2-128

After you decide which algorithm to use, you need to open the Site Encryption Configuration object and enter the choice in the Algorithms tab. The settings on this tab are used as site defaults, but your users can modify them in their mailbox's Advance Security tab. Follow these steps:

1. From the Exchange Administrator program, select the site where the KM server is located, and choose File ➤ Properties to open the Site Encryption Configuration property pages.

2. When you open these property pages, you will be prompted for the KM Server password. Because the KM password is initially saved on diskette, be sure that the KM diskette is in your floppy drive. On the other hand, if you choose to type the password manually, enter it in the Key Management Server Passwords text box.

3. Select the Algorithms tab:

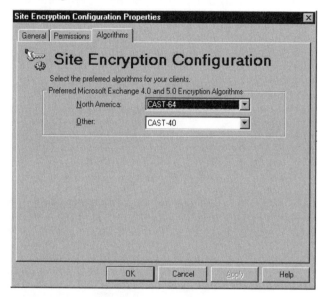

You have the following options:

Preferred Microsoft Exchange 4.0 and 5.0 Encryption Algorithms: Choose the algorithm for Exchange client users.

Preferred S/MIME Encryption Algorithms: Choose the algorithm for your Internet Mail users.

Preferred Security Message Format: Choose the format you want to use.

As you can see, these options don't appear in the Algorithms tab shown here. At the time of writing, Microsoft was in the process of releasing these features, which will be available in the version on which you will be tested.

Managing a Secure Site

One of your first tasks is to decide who will be KM administrators. Exchange Server administrators are not automatically allowed to manage security, so you'll have to assign KM privileges to those who will be doing so.

Whenever you open any of the objects that deal with security, you are prompted to enter your KM administrator password. This gets a little annoying when you're working on multiple screens. In the Key Management Server Password dialog box, you can check a checkbox so that your password is remembered for a maximum of five minutes. In general, this gives you plenty of time to perform your KM administration tasks.

To create KM administrators, follow these steps:

1. Open the Exchange Administrator program.

2. Double-click the Site Configuration container that hosts the KM Server.

3. Select the CA object, and choose File ➤ Properties to open the CA property pages.

4. Select the Administrators tab:

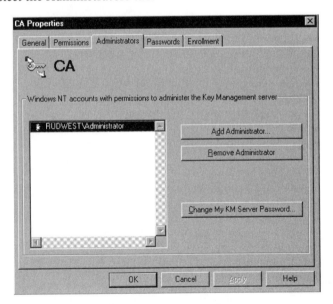

Managing KM Administrators

To add KM administrators, click the Add Administrator button, and select the user to whom you want to assign Key Management permissions. This administrator will be given the default password of password, which he or she should change as soon as possible.

To remove KM administrators, click the Remove Administrator button, and select the administrator you want to remove. When you remove an administrator, he or she no longer has access to your site's KM objects.

Changing the Administrator Password

In the Administrators tab, you'll notice another button, the Change My KM Server Password button. Click this button to change your KM administrator password.

Setting the Number of Passwords

If you will be the only person managing security, you probably need to authenticate only one password. If your site has multiple administrators, you may want to control when changes are made to security properties. To do this, you can configure security policies so that more than one administrator must enter their password before the CA and KM objects are modified.

To view the Password property page, follow these steps:

1. Open the Exchange Administrator program, and double-click the Site Configuration container that hosts the KM Server.

2. Select the CA object, and choose File ➤ Properties to open the CA property pages.

3. Select the Passwords tab:

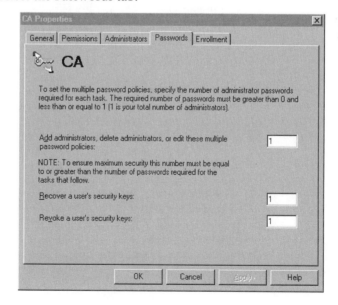

You have the following options:

- Add administrators, delete administrators, or edit these multiple password policies
- Recover a user's security keys
- Revoke a user's security keys
- Import or untrust another certification authority's certificate

As you can see, this fourth option is missing from the Passwords tab shown here. At the time of writing, Microsoft was in the process of releasing this feature, which will be available in the version of the software on which you will be tested.

Enter the number of passwords that you would require administrators to enter to make a change to any of the above properties.

The prompt on the CA Password property page is a little bit misleading. It lists the number of administrator passwords required, much like a quorum. In my humble opinion, this option should read *Number of administrator passwords required to make a change.* Each administrator must enter his or her password to reach the quorum.

Managing User Security

At this point, you've decided on your algorithm, and you've chosen your administrators. Now you're ready to assign user key pairs, which you can do in two ways:

- By individual user
- By bulk

Because enabling user security by individual user can be quite time-consuming, you might want to take a look at enabling security by bulk. Enabling users by bulk allows you to choose a group of users and assign temporary keys by group instead of by individual user.

Bulk enrollment of a large container or groups of containers can increase
message traffic to the KM server.

To enable security by bulk, you will want to work with the Enrollment tab
on the CA object. Follow these steps:

1. Open the Exchange Administrator program and double-click the Site
Configuration container that hosts the KM Server.

2. Select the CA object.

3. Choose File ➤ Properties to open the CA property pages.

4. Select the Enrollment tab:

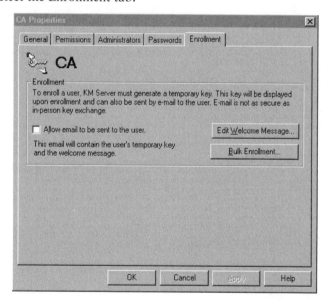

From this property page you can configure three options:

Allow E-mail to Be Sent to the User: Check this checkbox if you want to
mail all users their temporary keys. Users still must enter their temporary
key on their Mailboxes Advanced Security property page.

 Mailing temporary keys is less secure than giving them to users manually.

Edit Welcome Message: Click this button to create a welcome message to your users. You might give them instructions on how to use their key to enable Mailboxes advanced security, and you might want to include a warning about keeping this key secure and not giving the password to anyone.

Bulk Enrollment: Click this button to save yourself lots of time and work. Using this feature you can enable users to use advanced security. You must select each container individually. You can also choose to save the results of your bulk enrollment in a file to review later, and you can choose to mail temporary keys to your users. You have the following options on the Bulk Enrollment property page:

Microsoft Exchange 4.0 and 5.0 Compatibility: If your organization consists of mixed Exchange versions, you're going to have to choose which certificate version you will support.

Issue both V1 and V3 Certificates: Choose this option if you have a mixed Exchange client environment, running Exchange clients 4 and 5 or Outlook 8.0*x* and S/MIME compatible clients.

Issue X.509 V3 Certificates Only: Choose this option if all your users will be running an S/MIME compatible clients.

Issue X.509 V1 Certificates Only: Choose this option if you will be supporting Exchange clients 4 and 5 and Outlook 8. Choosing this option prevents users of S/MIME from choosing S/MIME security format.

Renew All Users: Whenever you change certificate types, you need to renew the certificates that users are using. Click this button to update the certificates whenever a change is made.

Managing Users

In the previous unit, we looked at how to create user mailboxes. Now we're going to look at how to manage them, which includes the following tasks:

- Deleting mailboxes
- Moving mailboxes
- Placing storage limits on mailboxes (See Unit 2 for details on this task.)
- Cleaning up mailboxes

Deleting Mailboxes

Although we want to think that our Exchange organization will only grow, you will inevitability end up deleting users through natural attrition.

Before you delete user mailboxes, always back up the contents, in case someone needs something for use later.

To delete a mailbox, follow these steps:

1. Open the Exchange Administrator program, and double-click the Site Configuration container for the site you are modifying.

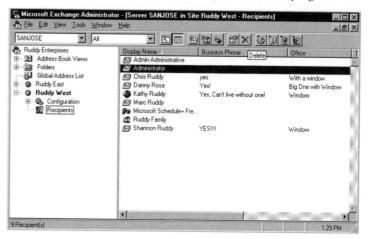

2. Select Recipients.

3. Select the mailbox or group of mailboxes you want to delete.

4. Choose File ➤ Delete. You can delete only the mailbox or the mailbox and the associated NT account.

Moving Mailboxes

As your Exchange organization grows, you will inevitability add servers to your sites and then add sites to your organization. All this growth will cause you to reevaluate the load of mailboxes on each server. Let's look at the options you have for moving mailboxes across servers in the same site and moving mailboxes between sites and recipient containers.

To move a mailbox or a group of mailboxes, follow these steps:

1. Open the Exchange Administrator program, and double-click the Site Configuration container for the site you are modifying.

2. Select Recipients.

3. Select the mailbox or group of mailboxes you want to move.

4. Choose Tools ➤ Move Mailbox.

5. In the Move Mailbox To box, select a server.

 If a user's mail is delivered to a personal folder file, all previously configured folder and message views are lost when the mailbox is moved.

To move mailboxes between sites and/or recipient containers, you need to do a little more work. Follow these steps:

1. If you are running Microsoft Outlook, use the Inbox Assistant to set up an AutoForward rule to forward all mail to the new mailbox.

2. Set up an auto reply, informing users that the mailbox has moved and giving them the new location.

3. Select the recipient from the specific recipient container, and modify the Advanced properties to enable the Hide from Address Book checkbox.

4. Ask the user to move all mail messages to a personal folder on their local computer.

5. Choose Tools ➤ Directory Export to export all the user's directory information to a file.

6. If the user is moving to another site, use the Directory Import tool to set up the mailbox on the new site. If the user is moving to a new recipient container, modify the export file to specify the new container, and then use the Directory Import tool to create the user in the new container.

 You can also use the Mailbox Migration tool available in the BackOffice Resource Kit, Part 2. You can download the tool from http://microsoft .com/exchange/reskit.htm.

Cleaning Up Users' Mailboxes

You can clean up a mailbox or a group of mailboxes to recover space in the private information store. You can also write a batch script that will clean up a group of mailboxes on a regular basis. In this section, we'll look at how to use the Exchange Administrator program to clean up a mailbox. Follow these steps:

1. Open the Exchange Administrator program and double-click the Site Configuration container for the site you are modifying.

2. Select Recipients.

3. Select the mailbox or group of mailboxes you want to clean.

4. Choose Tools ➣ Clean Mailbox to open the Clean Mailbox dialog box:

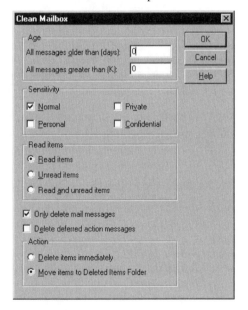

In the Clean Mailbox dialog box, you have the following options:

Age: Use these properties to delete messages based on their age.

All messages older than (days): Select this option to set the ages of messages. Any message older than this setting will be deleted.

All messages greater than (K): Select this option to set the size of a message in kilobytes. Any message larger than this property will be deleted.

Sensitivity: Messages marked with any of these settings will be deleted. You can choose more than one setting.

- Normal

- Personal

- Private

- Confidential

Read items: Use this setting to specify which inbox messages will be deleted.

- Read items

- Unread items

- Read and unread items

Only delete mail messages: You can choose to delete only mail messages or to delete messages pertaining to the user's calendar, contacts, and tasks.

Delete deferred action messages: When you select this option, all messages in the deferred action queue are deleted. *Deferred action messages* are commands that define the type of action to execute the next time the user logs on. A deferred action message can contain rules for moving messages from one folder to another or Inbox Assistant rules that your user has created.

Action: You can use this property to specify what action should be taken on messages that will be deleted during the mailbox cleaning.

Delete items immediately: Message are deleted immediately.

Move items to Deleted Items folder: Messages are moved to the Deleted Items folder where users can view, retrieve, and move them to other folders.

You use the Clean Mailbox dialog box to clean only user mailboxes recipients. You cannot clean other types of recipients such as distribution lists, custom recipients, and so on. You don't have to shut down the server to clean the mailbox, and you can clean the mailbox while the user is logged on.

Managing Distribution Lists

Distribution lists are simply lists of recipients; these lists don't store messages, calendar information, tasks, or even journal information. Although it is a good idea to keep these lists up-to-date, maintenance for distribution lists is minimal.

It's also a good idea to assign the ownership of distribution lists to your super users. A *super user* is an employee who is in touch with the day-to-day changes that may affect an organization and can make adjustments quickly.

You can do this in two ways:

Assign admin permissions on the Site object. When you assign administrator permissions to a user, he or she can manage recipients. Since a distribution list is considered a recipient, this user can create mailboxes for users and manage distribution lists.

Give ownership to a distribution list you created. Although the first approach is less time-consuming, you might not want users to manage recipients. You can change the ownership of distribution lists after you create them. Although the new owners cannot create distribution lists, they can manage their contents.

Setting the Distribution List Expansion Server

When a user in your site sends a message to a distribution list, Exchange has to expand the list and resolve all the names in it. Your server then determines the most efficient routing and sends the message on its way. You can imagine the load this places on a server that is already over worked.

Exchange allows you to specify a server in your site that will handle the expansion of the distribution list and the routing of the message. This property is on the distribution list's property page.

To change a distribution list expansion server, follow these steps:

1. Open the Exchange Administrator program, and double-click the Site Configuration container for the site you are modifying.

2. Select Recipients.

3. Select the distribution list you want to modify.

4. Choose File ➤ Properties to open the distribution list's property pages.

5. Select the General tab:

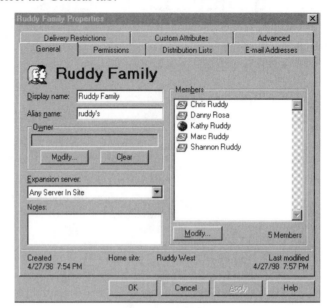

6. In the Expansion Server drop-down list, select the server in your site that you want to perform the expansion.

Managing the Directory

Managing the directory should be easy at this point. To do so, you need to know which configuration properties will affect the overall performance of the directory. Two of the most important properties are Tombstone Lifetime and Garbage Collection Interval.

To view the Directory Site Configuration object, follow these steps:

1. Open the Exchange Administrator program, and double-click the Site Configuration container for the site you are modifying.

2. Select the DS Site Configuration object.

3. Choose File ➤ Properties to open the DS Site Configuration property pages.

4. Select the General tab:

DS Site Configuration Properties

| Offline Address Book | Custom Attributes | Attributes |
| General | Permissions | Offline Address Book Schedule |

DS Site Configuration

Display name: DS Site Configuration

Directory name: Site-DSA-Config

Tombstone lifetime (days):   30

Garbage collection interval (hours):   12

Anonymous access

Anonymous account

Password:

Confirm Password:

Created   Home site: Ruddy West   Last modified
4/27/98 1:34 PM   4/27/98 1:34 PM

OK   Cancel   Apply   Help

Tuning Properties

A tombstone is a directory object that is marked for deletion. To specify a tombstone's lifetime, you set the number of days in the Tombstone Lifetime (days) text box. You need to make sure that the tombstone updates other copies of itself that may reside on other servers. Make the lifetime long enough so that Directory Replication can update all servers within your site and bridgehead servers in other sites.

Garbage collection is the task of deleting tombstones. By deleting tombstones, you decrease the amount of disk space used and make your Directory database searches more effective. You use the Garbage Collection Interval (hours) option to specify the number of hours between garbage collections.

Generating Offline Address Books

Offline Address Books are copies of recipient information that are downloaded to remote users of Exchange clients. If copies of the global address list are available to remote users, they can look up addresses for every recipient in your organization.

If you have a large enterprise, downloading the Offline Address Book can be time-consuming. Consider downloading the Address Book View containers for only a subset of users. The Offline Address Book that your users can download depends on the search permissions you assign to each view.

If you must support multiple Offline Address Books, you must set the Offline Address Book server to Exchange Server 5 or later.

To configure Offline Address Books, you use the DS Site Configuration properties. Follow these steps:

1. Open the Exchange Administrator program and double-click the Site Configuration container for the site you are modifying.

2. Select the DS Site Configuration object.

3. Choose File ➤ Properties to open the DS Site Configuration property pages.

4. Select the Offline Address Book tab:

You use the options on this property page to configure the Offline Address Book server and Address Books.

Configuring the Offline Address Book Server

To balance the processing load across your site, you can specify the least-used or most powerful server to generate Offline Address Books. After you change servers, manually create the Offline Address Books; if you do not, your users will not be able to download the Offline Address Book until a new one is created.

Configuring Address Book Containers

You can use any of the following containers to generate an Offline Address Book:

- Organization global address list
- The default recipient container
- Any recipient container
- Address Book View containers

Exchange Server 5.5 generates Offline Address Books for all Outlook and Exchange clients. If your site doesn't use Exchange clients earlier than version 5 or Outlook versions earlier than 8.03 (including 16-bit versions), you can disable Offline Address Book generation for these clients. This decreases the amount of processing required to generate the books. To disable Offline Address Book generation, clear the *Microsoft Exchange 4.0 and 5.0 compatibility* checkbox.

Ensuring Directory Consistency

To ensure that your directory is consistent across your site, run the Directory Consistency check on each server in your site. The Directory tables include information about each server in your site. Whenever a new server is added to your site, all servers are updated with information about the new server. The new Directory tables are scheduled to update across your site every three hours.

To force the Directory Consistency check, follow these steps:

1. Open the Exchange Administrator program and double-click the Site Configuration container for the site you are modifying.

2. Double-click the server whose Directory service settings you are modifying.

3. Select the Directory Service object.

4. Choose File ➤ Properties to open the Directory Service property pages.

5. Select the General tab:

Click the Check Now button to immediately run the Directory Consistency check on your server to update the Directory tables with information about new servers or objects.

By default, information from your server's Directory database is exchanged five minutes after the last transaction. If you want to force the replication to occur immediately, click the Update Now button.

Managing Public Information Store Databases

Public folders are objects that store information that is shared among your users. You need to manage the use of public folders carefully so that users aren't creating public folders for the wrong reasons. You may end up with more public folders than you know what to do with!

In the previous units, we looked at how to restrict the creation of top-level public folders. Now we need to take a look at some of the properties you can configure to handle the Public Information Store database.

Assigning a Public Folder Server

All top-level public folders are created on the Public Folder server, which is the first server searched when viewing public folders. By default, a user's Public Folder server is the server on which his or her mailbox resides.

You can isolate the public information store (Public Folder database) on a specific server in your site. You might want to do this if you have a server that has the capacity and power. Another benefit of separating your public and private information stores is that those servers without a public folder store will not incur system overhead managing a public information store.

In Figure 3.1, there is only one Public Folder server in the site. Whenever clients want to view the contents of a folder, all requests are forwarded to this Public Folder server.

FIGURE 3.1

An Exchange site that has only one Public Folder server

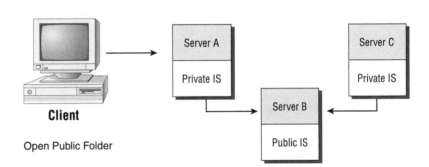

To set up a Public Folder server, you must modify the Private Information Store properties on all servers that will not host public folders. Follow these steps:

1. Open the Exchange Administrator program and double-click the Site Configuration container for the site you are modifying.

2. Double-click the server whose Public Folder settings you are modifying.

3. Select the Private Information Store object.

4. Choose File ➤ Properties to open the Private Information Store property pages.

5. Select the General tab:

6. In the Public Folder Server drop-down list box, enter the name of the Public Folder server you've chosen.

Setting Age Limits for Public Folders Contents

Using Public Information Store properties, you can set age limits for the contents of the following (in order of precedence):

- A replica in a public information store
- All folders in a public information store
- All replicas of a public folder in your organization

Setting Age Limits on a Replica

To set age limits on a replica in your public information store, follow these steps:

1. Open the Exchange Administrator program, and double-click the Site Configuration container for the site you are modifying.

2. Double-click the server whose Public Folder settings you are modifying.

3. Select the Public Information Store object.

4. Choose File ➤ Properties.

5. Select the Age Limits tab.

6. In the list box for all the folders, select the replica on which you want to set age limits.

7. Click the Modify button to open the Modify Age Limits dialog box:

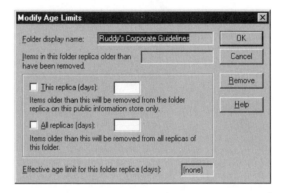

8. Check the This Replica (days) checkbox, and enter a value in the text box.

Setting Age Limits on All Folders

To set age limits on all folders in your public information store, follow these steps:

1. Open the Exchange Administrator program, and double-click the Site Configuration container for the site you are modifying.

2. Double-click the server whose Public Folder settings you are modifying.

3. Select the Public Information Store object.

4. Choose File ➤ Properties to open the Public Information Store property pages.

5. Select the Age Limits tab.

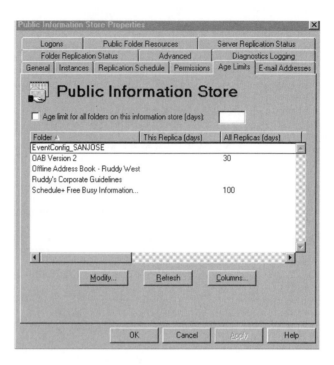

6. Check the *Age limit for all folders on this information store (days)* checkbox, and enter the number of days in the text box.

Exchange Server 5.5 deletes all messages in your public folder that are older than the number of days you enter.

Setting Age Limits for All Replicas

To set an age limit for all replicas in a public folder, follow these steps:

1. Open the Exchange Administrator program, and double-click the Site Configuration container for the site you are modifying.

2. Double-click the server whose Public Folder settings you are modifying.

3. Select the Public Information Store object.

4. Choose File ➤ Properties to open the Public Information Store property pages.

5. Select the Age Limits tab.

6. In the list box for all the folders, select the replica on which you want to set age limits.

7. Click the Modify button to open the Modify Age Limits dialog box.

8. Select All Replicas, and type a value in the text box.

Scheduling Information Store Maintenance

By default, the Exchange Server 5.5 Information Store (IS) maintenance job runs automatically every 15 minutes. It takes care of the following:

- Cleaning up "Deleted ItemRetention"

- Deleting expired folder contents

- Synchronizing the server's public information store version with other servers

- Removing expired public folder conflicts

If the IS maintenance jobs are causing too much processing overhead during the day when your users are connected to their mailboxes, you can change this schedule. Follow these steps:

1. Open the Exchange Administrator program, and double-click the Site Configuration container for the site you are modifying.

2. Select the server whose IS maintenance job settings you are modifying.

3. Choose File ≻ Properties to open the property pages for this server.

4. Select the IS Maintenance tab:

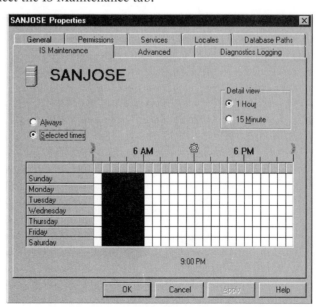

You now have the following options:

Always—Runs the IS maintenance job at 15-minute intervals.

Selected Times—Runs the IS maintenance job at the times you specify in the schedule grid.

Rehoming Public Folders

When working with public folders, you may need to move a folder from one server to another. For example, if a server in your site is performing poorly, you might want to move its public folders to another server in your site. The process of moving public folders from one server (home server) to another server in your site is known as *rehoming public folders* (see Figure 3.2).

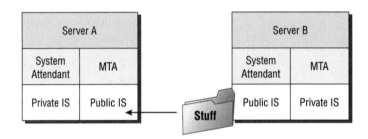

F I G U R E 3.2

Rehoming a public folder

You can use two tools to rehome a public folder:

- PFAdmin
- PST file

The PFAdmin utility is part of the Microsoft BackOffice Resource Kit, Part Two. To use PFAdmin, you must have the BackOffice Resource Kit for Exchange installed. Using this utility is the least cumbersome way to rehome a public folder.

If you don't have the BackOffice Resource Kit installed on your system, you can rehome a public folder using a PST file. Follow these steps:

1. Create a personal folder from the Administrator's mailbox in Outlook.

2. Choose the public folder you want to move, and copy the entire contents (including subdirectories) to the personal folder.

3. Delete the public folder from the public folder structure. (You can use the Exchange Administrator program to do so.) Deleting your public folder will also mark all public folder replicas for deletion.

4. Allow replication to take place so that this deleted public folder is replicated to all other sites within your organization.

5. Log on to a mailbox on the new server where you want to home the public folder.

6. Create a new public folder. This folder will become your rehomed public folder; name the folder accordingly.

7. Copy the folder contents from your PST file to the new folder and assign permissions.

Only rehome a public folder if absolutely necessary. If you make a mistake, you can accidentally propagate the changes across your site and inadvertently cause a complete loss of data!

Managing Private Information Store Databases

With Exchange Server 5.5, you can allow users to recover deleted documents. Before enabling this feature, however, you need to define the properties for recovering deleted documents. Enabling this feature for all users requires a lot of disk space; so think about which users really need it.

Setting Storage and Retention Time Limits

Before you set storage limits for users, you need to set default storage limits on the private information store. Doing so sets the defaults that all users inherit. To change those defaults for a specific user, you modify the user's advanced properties to set an override limit.

In addition to setting storage limits, you will need to configure the time limit for retaining deleted documents. Both these settings are used unless you specify specific storage and retention settings for individual mailboxes.

To set the information store defaults, follow these steps:

1. Open the Exchange Administrator program, and double-click the Site Configuration container for the site you are modifying.

2. Double-click the server whose Private Information Store settings you are modifying.

3. Select the Private Information Store object.

4. Choose File ➤ Properties to open the Private Information Store property pages.

5. Select the General tab:

In the Item Recovery section, you have the following options:

Deleted item retention time (days): Sets the number of days that deleted items are retained before they are permanently deleted.

Don't permanently delete items until the store has been backed up: Select this option if you want to ensure that all items are backed up before they are deleted. In this way, you can keep deleted documents even though the retention period has been exceeded.

In the Storage Limits section, you have the following options:

Issue warning (K): Set a value in kilobytes to represent the maximum space that mailboxes can occupy before a warning message is sent.

Prohibit send (K): Set a value in kilobytes to represent the maximum space that mailboxes can occupy before Exchange prevents the owner of the mailbox from sending further messages. The value you set here should be higher than the value for the Issue Warning property.

Prohibit send and receive (K): Set a value in kilobytes to represent the maximum space that mailboxes can occupy before Exchange prevents owners from sending and receiving mail. The value you set here should be higher than the value for the Prohibit Send property.

In the Public Folder Server section, you specify a server on which to store public folders.

For more information on configuring this property, see the earlier section "Managing Public Information Store Databases."

Backing Up and Restoring

One of your most important maintenance tasks is backing up the Exchange Server databases and your NT server. In this section, we'll look at how to formulate a backup strategy and how to restore Exchange components in the event of a failure.

Backup Strategies

When planning a backup strategy, you have several options. Before you select one, though, you need to understand how transaction logs work on an Exchange server.

Exchange uses write-ahead logging to improve performance of your server and to provide fault-tolerance for your core components. As each transaction is completed, it is written synchronously to memory cache and to a transaction log. Each transaction log is always 5MB in size, even if it is not full. You can use normal or circular logging.

WARNING If you notice that one of your transaction logs is not exactly 5MB, you have a corrupted transaction log. Never edit, delete, or rename the transaction log files. Exchange keeps the names of the transaction log files in the Registry. If the files are renamed or deleted, Exchange logs an error.

Using Normal Transaction Logging

In this type of logging, Exchange creates a new transaction log file as the previous log becomes full. Each prior version is kept until you do a full or an incremental backup. During the backup, Exchange deletes the transaction logs of all transactions committed to the databases.

Advantage

With each transaction file saved on disk, you can recover to the last transaction written, in case of a catastrophe.

Disadvantage

Normal logging can use as much as 100MB of disk space, in addition to the overhead your servers will require to maintain the transaction files on disk.

Using Circular Logging

If normal transaction logging uses too much disk space, you might want to consider circular logging. Circular logging overwrites the parts of a transaction log file that has already committed transactions to the database.

Advantages

- You can reuse each of your log files instead of creating a new transaction log when the previous one becomes full.
- You can save as much as 100MB of disk space.

Disadvantages

- You can recover only to the last full backup and not to the last transaction. This is the default setting for Exchange Server 5.5.
- Microsoft discourages the use of circular logging.

Choosing a Backup Type

After you decide which transaction logging method to use, you are ready to decide on the backup type. In the following sections, we'll look at the three types of backups—Full, Incremental, and Differential. Each copies the Directory and Information Store databases.

Full (Normal) Backup

Advantages

- Easy to schedule
- Easy to restore
- Deletes transaction logs
- Works with circular logging

Disadvantages

- Affects server performance
- Takes a lot of time
- Requires the most tapes and tape replacements

Incremental Backup

Advantages

- Does not affect server performance as much as a Full backup
- Deletes transaction logs
- Requires fewer tape resources

Disadvantages

- Must be used in addition to a Full backup strategy
- Does not work with circular logging

Differential Backup

Advantages

- Does not affect server performance as much as a Full backup
- Easy to restore data
- Requires fewer tape resources

Disadvantages

- Does not delete transaction log files

- Does not work with circular logging

- Requires more tapes than an Incremental backup but fewer than a Full backup

Running Backups

When you install Exchange Server on your Windows NT server, Exchange adds an application component to the Backup utility. With this additional component, you can back up Exchange databases using NT Backup. The main benefit is that you can back up Exchange databases across all the servers in your site (see Figure 3.3).

FIGURE 3.3

Backing up across a site

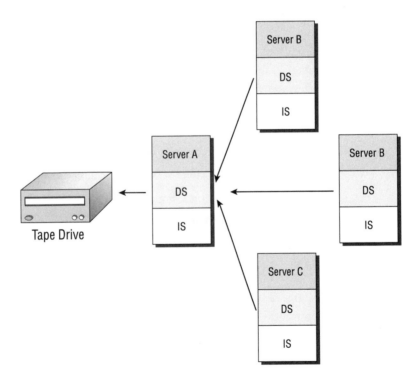

Exchange Server 5.5 provides three ways to back up:

- Online
- Offline
- Automatically at a specific time

Running an Online Backup

You can back up your Exchange server while the database and transaction files are open. To do so, choose Start ➢ Programs ➢ Administrative Tools ➢ Backup.

Running an Offline Backup

To ensure that all files are closed and that all transactions are backed up, you can run an Offline backup. Before you do so, you must shut down the services using the Services applet in Control Panel. Table 3.1 lists the files and default locations of the databases.

If Exchange has been stopped, you must back up each database file separately.

T A B L E 3.1 Exchange databases, filenames, and locations	Database	Filename	Default Location
	Directory	Dir.edb	Exchsrvr\Dsadata
	Private Information Store	Priv.edb	Exchsrvr\Mdbdata
	Public Information Store	Pub.edb	Exchsrvr\Mdbdata
	Microsoft Mail Directory Synchronization	Xdir.edb	Exchsrvr\Dxdata
	KM Server	Kmsmdb.edb	Exchsrvr\Kmsdata

Running Automatic Backups

You can use the Windows NT Server AT utility to schedule jobs to run at a specific time. Follow these steps:

1. Create a batch file with your backup commands.

2. Save the file.

3. Submit the file using the AT utility.

The syntax of the NT backup utility for Exchange is as follows:

```
Ntbackup backup { DS servername | IS servername} {type of backup}
```

For example, to execute a full backup of the Directory and Information databases on server host SANJOSE, the command is:

```
Ntbackup backup DS \\SANJOSE IS \\SANJOSE /t:normal
```

Restoring Files

Using the operations we'll look at next, you can restore a single user's mailbox or all your database files.

Restoring Data for a User

You may need to restore a user's mailbox for a couple of reasons.

- A user has left the company and you want to give the mailbox to a new user.

- You have accidentally deleted a user's mailbox.

To do so, follow these steps:

1. Open the Exchange Administrator program, and double-click the Site Configuration container for the site you are modifying.

2. Select Recipients.

3. Select the mailbox that you are restoring.

4. Give yourself ownership permissions for the mailbox.

5. Log on to a client and open the mailbox.

6. Copy the mailbox to a personal folder (PST) file.

7. Give the file to the user. Ask the user open the mailbox and restore the personal folder to the server.

Restoring an Information Store to the Same Server

Before you restore an information store to the same server, stop all Exchange services (choose Start ➤ Settings ➤ Control Panel ➤ Services). Now, follow these steps:

1. Choose Start ➤ Programs ➤ Administrative Tools ➤ Backup.

2. In the Tapes window, select the sets you want to restore.

3. Choose Restore.

You now have the following options:

Erase All Existing Data: Choose this option if you want to restore the entire database and delete all the previous contents. You would do this if you have a corrupt database or if you want to use the last full backup.

Private: You must select both Private and Public, even if the backup contains only one database.

Public: You must select both Private and Public.

Start Service after Restore: Choose this option if you want the services to start after the restore operation.

Verify after Restore: Choosing this option verifies the restore operation and logs any exceptions.

Destination Server: The server to which you are restoring.

Restoring an Offline Backup

Whenever you are restoring a backup offline, you must stop all the Exchange services (follow the steps in the previous section). Use the NT Backup utility to restore the database files.

After you restore an information store from an offline backup, run the ISINTEG using the –patch switch, restart the services, and run the Directory Consistency check. For information on this tool, see Unit 5.

Managing Connectivity

Managing connectivity is a little bit of this and a little bit of that. Let's start with how the MTA communicates.

Setting MTA Message Defaults

To set message defaults, follow these steps:

1. Open the Exchange Administrator program, and double-click the Site Configuration container for the site you are modifying.

2. Select MTA Site Configuration.

3. Choose File ➤ Properties to open the MTA Site Configuration property pages.

4. Select the Messaging Defaults tab:

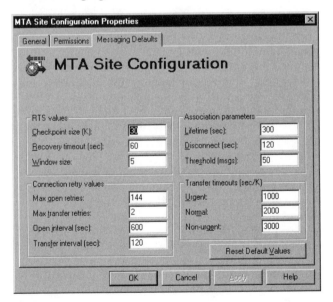

In the RTS Values section, you determine how often you want to verify messages that are being transferred:

RTS is an abbreviation for Reliable Transfer Service.

Checkpoint Size (K): Enter the amount of data to be sent before a checkpoint is entered. A *checkpoint* is a pause in the transmission to allow for an acknowledgment of data sent. If you enter zero, no checkpoint is set. The default is 30.

Recovery Timeout (sec): Enter the amount of time after an error that the MTA will wait for a reconnection. If the time expires, the MTA will delete the checkpointed information and restart the transfer.

Window Size: Enter the number of checkpoints that can go unacknowledged before data transfer is stopped. The greater the window size, the more data are transmitted. Use this value only if the checkpoint size is greater than zero.

You use the Connection Retry Values section to determine how many times you want to try to open a connection and send a message:

Max Open Retries: The number of times the system attempts to open a connection before it sends an NDR (nondelivery report). The default is 144.

Max Transfer Retries: The maximum number of times that MTA tries to send a message across an open connection. The default is 2.

Open Interval (sec): The time to wait before the MTA attempts to reopen a connection after an error is reported. The default is 600.

Transfer Interval (sec): The time the MTA waits before attempting to resend a message over an existing connection.

Associations are paths that are open to other systems, much like a circuit. In the Association Parameters section, you can specify how long you want to keep an association open as well as other options that allow you to manage associations:

Lifetime (sec): The time to keep an association open to another server after a message is sent. The default is 300.

Disconnect (sec): The time to wait for a response from another server's MTA before closing the connection. The default is 120.

Threshold (msgs): The maximum number of waiting messages to be sent to a specific server. When this value is reached, another association is created, and that association attempts to send messages. The default is 50.

In the Transfer Timeouts (sec/k) section, you specify the time to wait before sending an NDR:

Urgent: The time in seconds, before the MTA sends an NDR for urgent messages. The default is 1000.

Normal: The time in seconds, before the MTA sends an NDR for a normal message. The default is 2000.

Non-Urgent: The time in seconds, before the MTA sends an NDR for a non-urgent message. The default is 3000.

Rebuilding the Routing Table

The Routing table is rebuilt once each day or after a change. A change could involve adding a connector, deleting a gateway, or adding a server to your site. Each of these events triggers the rebuilding of the Routing table. If you want changes to take place immediately instead of waiting until the Routing table is updated (approximately five minutes), you can rebuild the Routing table manually. Follow these steps:

1. Open the Exchange Administrator program, and double-click the Site Configuration container for the site you are modifying.

2. Double-click the server whose Routing table you are rebuilding.

3. Select the Message Transfer Agent object to open the Message Transfer Agent property pages.

4. Select the General tab:

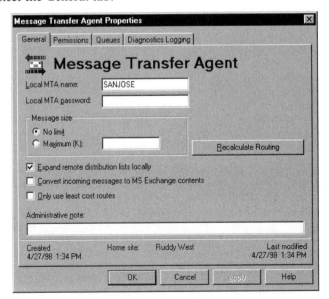

5. Choose Recalculate Routing.

By default, the server whose Routing tables are being modified is the server that will run your recalculation job. If your server is overloaded as is, you can specify another server to perform all routing recalculations. To specify the Routing Calculation server, follow these steps:

1. Open the Exchange Administrator program and double-click the Site Configuration container for the site you are modifying.

2. Select the Site Addressing object.

3. Choose File ➤ Properties to display the property pages for this object.

4. Select the General tab.

5. In the Routing Calculation Server box, select a server.

Managing Site Security

1. True or False. Exchange Server 5.5 supports two types of encryption for messaging.

2. True or False. Exchange is compatible with S/MIME encryption.

3. True or False. CAST64 can be used in European Exchange sites for an organization that is headquartered in the United States.

4. To configure any security properties, you need to enter the _____ _____ password.

5. True or False. Exchange administrators are automatically granted permissions to manage security objects.

6. To add security administrators, use the _____ object property pages.

7. Using the CA Password Policy property page, for which tasks can you set minimum password required policies?

_____

_____

_____

_____

8. What are the two methods for passing a temporary key to a user?

_____

_____

9. True or False. Exchange does not support bulk enrollment for large groups of users.

10. What two security actions can a user perform?

_____

_____

11. What types of certificates for messages does Exchange Server 5.5 support?

_____

_____

Managing Users

12. True or False. To delete a user's mailbox, you must log on using a client and delete the mailbox.

13. True or False. User mailboxes can be renamed.

14. True or False. You can use the Exchange Administrator program to move a group of mailboxes to another server.

15.   Which tools can you use to move a large group of users to another site or to another recipient container?

_____

_____

16.   What tool can you use to purge messages from users' mailboxes?

_____

17.   What criteria can you use to choose which messages will be purged from a user's mailbox?

_____

_____

_____

_____

18.   True or False. With Exchange, you can purge messages for all recipient types.

19.   What tool would you use to remove a user's deferred-action messages?

_____

Managing Distribution Lists

20.   What are the two methods of assigning a super user the ability to manage a distribution list?

_____

_____

21. True or False. Distribution lists must be expanded on the server on which they are stored.

Managing the Directory

22. Which two Directory Services properties affect the clean-up of old directory objects?

_____

_____

23. What is a tombstone?

_____

_____

24. Which property controls how often tombstones are cleaned up?

_____

25. True or False. Multiple Offline Address Books have been supported since Exchange Server 4.

26. Offline Address Books are created for what type of users?

_____

27. True or False. With Outlook 8.03, users can download only the objects that have been modified since the last download of the Offline Address Book.

28. What types of containers can be used to build Offline Address Books?

_____

_____

_____

_____

29. What maintenance job can you run if you suspect your directory contains invalid entries across the site?

_____

_____

30. What Directory Service maintenance job can you run to replicate information across a site immediately instead of waiting for the next scheduled run?

_____

31. Directory replication will occur _____ minutes after the last transaction has been recorded.

Manage Public Information Store Databases

32. All top-level public folders are created and stored on the _____ _____ _____.

33. True or False. Exchange Server 5.5 allows you to separate public and private information stores across several servers.

34. To specify a Public Folder server, you must edit the _____
Information Store General property page.

35. Which default server stores public folders as they are created?

_____

36. What criteria can you use to purge public folder contents?

_____

37. To which three objects can you assign age limits?

_____

_____

_____

38. What does the IS maintenance job do?

_____

_____

_____

_____

39. IS maintenance jobs run every _____ minutes by
default.

40. Which option can you use on the Public IS Maintenance Job property page to run the IS maintenance job at specific intervals?

_____

41. True or False. Rehoming a public folder is defined as moving a public folder back to its original server after a client moved it to the wrong server.

42. What are the two tools that you can use to rehome a public folder?

_____

_____

43. Where can you get a copy of the PFAdmin utility?

44. True or False. You can delete a public folder using the Exchange client software.

Managing Private Information Store Databases

45. True or False. Users must use Outlook 8.03 client software to recover deleted documents.

46. What tool can you use to control user mailbox disk space?

47. What properties can you use to specify the maximum age of a file to recover?

_____

48. What are the three storage limit properties?

_____

_____

_____

49. Which storage limit should be set to the highest value?

_____

50. Which storage limit should be set with the lowest value?

_____

51. Can your users set a higher storage limit?

_____

52. Mark the order precedence of these storage limits.

_____ Mailbox Storage Limits

_____ Private Information Store Limits

53. Which Exchange clients support recovering a deleted document?

A. Exchange Client V4.0 for DOS

B. Exchange Client V5.0 for Windows 95 and Windows NT

C. Outlook 8.03

D. Exchange Client for Windows 3.1

Backing Up and Restoring

54. What is a transaction log?

_____

_____

55. True or False. Circular logging is not recommended because of the large amount of disk space it consumes.

56. True or False. Transaction log files are always 5MB in size.

57. What type of transaction logging method creates more than one transaction file?

_____

58. What is the benefit of using normal transaction logging?

_____

59. True or False. With normal transaction logging, log files are kept until a Full or Incremental backup is done. After the backup, the files are automatically deleted.

60. True or False. With circular logging, you can restore only to the last incremental backup.

STUDY QUESTIONS

61.   List and describe the three backup types.

_____

_____

_____

62.   True or False. Full backups typically take longer than Incremental backups.

63.   True or False. To perform an Offline backup of the Exchange database files, you must stop all Exchange services.

64.   What must you do after restoring a Public Information Store database file?

_____

_____

65.   True or False. When Exchange Server 5.5 is installed, a component is added to NT Backup that allows you to back up your own database only.

66.   What option can you specify to overwrite all existing data when you restore the Exchange database files?

_____

_____

67.   True or False. If you want to restore a private information store and nothing else, choose Private on the Restore options.

68. What is the filename of the Directory database?

_____

69. What is one of the default locations for the Exchange database files?

_____

70. What is the filename of the public information store?

_____

71. What is the full location and filename for the KM Server database files?

_____

Managing Connectivity

72. Describe a checkpoint.

_____

73. True or False. The MTA Message Default Window Size property is used to size messages between two servers.

74. True or False. Associations are communication links between two MTAs.

75. Which option in the Messaging Defaults property page controls how many times the MTA attempts to open a connection to send a message?

_____

76. What does the term NDR stand for?

_____

77. Which option in the Messaging Default property page controls how long the MTA waits before sending an NDR?

78. When is the Routing table updated?

_____

_____

79. True or False. You can force the recalculation of a Routing table by clicking the Recalculate Routing button on the MTA property pages.

80. By default, which server rebuilds the Routing table?

_____

81. If resources are unequal across the servers in a site, you can specify the most powerful server as the _____ _____ server.

SAMPLE TEST

3-1 Michael is the senior administrator and works with Frankie, a junior administrator. Michael wants to manage the changes made to the Exchange Security objects. How can he approve the changes Frankie has made to the Security objects?

    A. Require two administrator passwords whenever a change is made to any security setting.

    B. Do not give Frankie any NT account access.

    C. Give Frankie a computer-generated random password.

3-2 Lisa wants to move a group of mailboxes to another site. What tool or options must she use?

    A. Move mailbox in the site container.

    B. Move the NT account; Exchange mail will follow.

    C. Use the Directory Export and Import tool, and copy the user files to a PST file.

    D. Use the Migration Wizard, and forward all mail to a user's new mailbox.

3-3 When a user sends a mail message to a distribution list, which servers will Exchange use to expand and process it?

    A. The server to which the user is connected

    B. The first server configured in the site

    C. The Distribution List container server

    D. The Distribution List expansion server

3-4 Daniel has modified the Directory Service objects on a server within a site. After completing his changes, he wants the changes sent to all other servers immediately. Which job should he run?

    A. Directory Knowledge Consistency Check

    B. IS maintenance job

    C. NTBackup

    D. Directory Update Now replication job

SAMPLE TEST

3-5   On which public folder objects can you set age limits?

    A. A replica in a public information store

    B. All folders in a public information store

    C. All replicas in a public information store

    D. All the above

3-6   Exchange Server 5.5 supports a new option that allows users to recover deleted documents. In order for this option to work, what property on the private information store must be configured?

    A. Item Recovery

    B. Storage Limits

    C. Public Folder Server

    D. Information Store Maintenance

3-7   Alan and Alexander want to use the Windows NT Server AT utility to submit an Ntbackup job to batch. Which of the following is the correct command and syntax to do an Incremental backup of the Directory database on Server FS01 and the information store on FS02?

    A. `ntbackup backup DS \\FS02 IS \\FS01 /t:d`

    B. `ntbackup backup DS \\FS** /t:I`

    C. `ntbackup backup DS \\FS01 IS \\FS02 /tIncremental`

    D. `ntbackup backup DS \\FS001 /t:d`

3-8 On the MTA Advanced property page, what is the default timeout setting (in seconds) for an NDR report sent on a normal message?

    A. 1000

    B. 2000

    C. 3000

    D. 200

3-9 Which are valid encryption algorithms supported by Exchange Server 5.5?

    A. DES-128

    B. CAST40

    C. DES

    D. CAST64

3-10 Shannon is the site security manager for a DOD site. She wants to make sure that users know the security rules for encryption and digital signatures. She has agreed to let the security temporary keys be e-mailed to each user. What Exchange property can be configured to send the security rules to each user as their temporary security key is sent?

    A. CA User property pages

    B. CA Object Enrollment property page, Welcome Message button

    C. File attachment

    D. Cannot be done

3-11 Which of the following is not an option in the Clean Mailbox dialog box?

  A. Age

  B. Read Item

  C. Sensitivity

  D. Distribution List

3-12 What are the two important properties that will affect the performance of the directory?

  A. Tombstone Lifetime

  B. Tombstone Pizza

  C. Garbage Collection Interval

  D. Compression Settings

3-13 Where is information that is shared among users stored?

  A. Public mailboxes

  B. Public folders

  C. Private folders

  D. Chain letters

3-14 Logan and Devin are co-administrators of an Exchange enterprise. Devin has noticed that IS maintenance jobs are causing a lot of processing overhead during the day. Logan wants to change the maintenance job so that it runs only at night, when few users are on the system. What option can he use?

  A. Run the job after mail transfer

  B. Run the job manually at 3 AM

  C. Use the Selected Time property on the IS Maintenance property page

  D. All the above

3-15   Exchange uses write-ahead logging to provide fault-tolerance for core components. During a normal system review, Shannon notices that one of the older transaction log files is 7.3MB. Is this OK?

    A. Yes, the size of these files will change as backups are done.

    B. Yes, the size of all transaction files will be 7.3MB.

    C. No, all transaction files will be 5MB.

    D. No, all transaction files must be 50MB in size.

3-16   Which are determining factors in your decision to use normal or circular logging?

    A. Disk space

    B. Processor overhead

    C. Speed of your processor

    D. Backup strategies

3-17   Bernadette noticed that a server has a corrupted Public Information Store database. She has restored the file associated with the public information store. What maintenance tasks must she perform to ensure the public information store's integrity?

    A. Run ISINTGEG with the –patch option.

    B. Run the Directory Knowledge Consistency Check.

    C. Nothing. The backup will cause the public information store to resync itself.

    D. You cannot recover from a Public Information Store database loss.

3-18 Chris is an Exchange administrator without security administrative permissions. Danny is the Exchange security administrator and is on vacation, but has left the KM administrator password for Chris should he need it. Chris needs to recover a user's key and types the password when prompted. He receives an "Access Denied" message. What is the problem?

A. Caps Lock is turned on.

B. Chris is not an NT administrator.

C. Chris has not been authorized as an Exchange security administrator.

D. The moon is in the wrong phase.

3-19 What are the two ways to authorize users to use advanced security?

A. NT User Manager for Domains

B. NT Server Manager

C. Enable security by individual user, using the Security property pages

D. Bulk Enrollment on the CA security property pages

3-20 Kathy, the Exchange administrator, wants to know how to delete a user who is leaving her organization. What tools can she use?

A. User Manager for Domains

B. Exchange Administrator

C. NT Server Manager

D. PFAdmin Tool

UNIT

4

Monitoring and Optimization

Test Objectives: Monitoring and Optimization

- **Configure a link monitor and a server monitor.**

- **Optimize Exchange Server. Tasks include:**
  - Hardware optimization
  - Operating system optimization

- **Optimize foreign connections and site-to-site connections.**

- **Monitor and optimize the messaging environment.**

- **Monitor server performance by using SNMP and MADMAN MIB.**

As any experienced Exchange administrator can tell you, monitoring and tuning your Exchange organization is an ongoing task. Personally, I think it's the most rewarding task. In the previous units, we reviewed the steps for planning, installing, and managing Exchange components. In this unit, we'll look at how to monitor your Exchange environment. The next logical step is to take a look at how you can tune your server environment to ensure that Windows NT Server and Exchange Server 5.5 are running efficiently and effectively. There's a lot to review here, so let's begin.

Configuring Link and Server Monitors

As part of monitoring, you will check the status of the communication links to your site servers and to your foreign connectors. You'll also be checking the status of servers within your site and within your organization. Exchange Server 5.5 provides two easy-to-use monitors that you can configure to automatically start and alert you whenever predefined Exchange link or server events occur:

- Link monitor
- Server monitor

In this section, we'll look at how to configure and start each of these monitors, and I'll discuss which works best for a particular situation.

Using the Link Monitor

You use the link monitor to check your communications links between servers and connectors. It doesn't check the status of the server, just the link to a server or to a connector. If the information returned to you indicates a problem, you can then investigate to determine why the link is unavailable. If your link is available, you can check whether it's performing as expected. If the link is slow, you will receive information to help determine the cause of the delay.

The link monitor configuration settings are used across multiple connections. If you want to use different settings for different servers, you must create another link monitor and specify which servers or foreign mail systems to monitor.

A link monitor checks communication paths by sending a "ping" message. This message is sent as part of the Exchange application to test the communication. Don't confuse it with the TCP/IP network-troubleshooting tool ping.

Creating a New Link Monitor

The Exchange Administrator program creates link monitors from the Monitors object in the Site Configuration object. To create a link monitor, follow these steps:

1. Open the Exchange Administrator program, and double-click the Site Configuration container for the site you are modifying.

2. Select the Monitors object.

3. Choose File ➢ New Other ➢ Link Monitor to display the Link Monitor property pages open at the General tab:

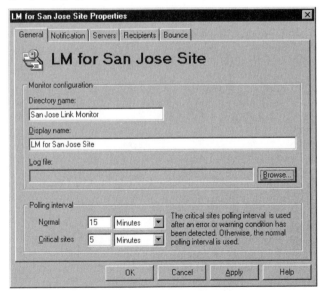

Configuring the Link Monitor

In the Monitor Configuration section of this property page, you have the following options:

Directory Name: Assign a directory object name to the link monitor. Once this name is set, it *cannot* be changed. Use a descriptive name that indicates the links that this monitor watches. The maximum name length is 64 alphanumeric characters.

Display Name: This name can be a maximum of 256 Unicode characters, and it can be modified.

Log File: Specify a log file that records information about the connection and notification status. You will find that logging your link monitor's actions will help troubleshoot your communication links. If no argument is assigned, a log file will not be created. You can use any path, including a path to a network share.

In the Polling Interval section of this property page, you have the following options:

Normal: Use this setting to specify how often to send a ping message from this Exchange server to the other Exchange servers and connectors. A typical value is 15 minutes.

Critical Sites: Use this setting to specify how often to send a ping message to those sites that have been in a warning or an alert state. The default is 5 minutes.

Monitoring the Links within a Site

As part of monitoring your intersite connections, it is a good idea to collect normal link communication data. Being familiar with this data will help you identify abnormal connections, for example, high network traffic or that links to a particular server are down. Either way, to identify the problem, you must know what constitutes normal operations.

Setting Bounce Properties   In Exchange Server 5.5, you use the Bounce property page to configure the acceptable time it takes a message to make a round trip from the initiating server to the target server and back. To set the Bounce property on an existing link server, follow these steps:

1. Open the Exchange Administrator program, and double-click the Site Configuration container for the site you are modifying.

2. Double-click the Monitors object.

3. Select the link monitor you want to update.

4. Choose File ➤ Properties to open the Link Monitor property pages.

5. Select the Bounce tab:

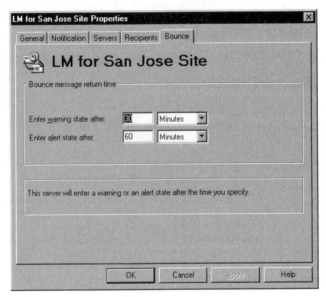

You can set the following properties from this page:

Enter Warning State After: Set the time after which a return ping message will be considered late. This setting can be in seconds, minutes, or hours. The default is 30 minutes.

Enter Alert State After: Set the time after which you consider a return ping message very late. This setting can be in seconds, minutes, or hours. The default is 60 minutes.

Choosing Servers for the Link Monitor   At this point, you must specify the servers to which you will send ping messages. These servers must be in your organization, but you can monitor links to servers in other sites.

To configure the list of servers to monitor, follow these steps:

1. Open the Exchange Administrator program and double-click the Site Configuration container for the site you are modifying.

2. Double-click the Monitors object.

3. Select the link monitor you want to update.

4. Choose File ➤ Properties to open the Server Monitor property pages.

5. Select the Servers tab:

6. Select a server, and click Add to add the selected server to the list of monitored servers.

 To remove a server from the list, select it and click Remove.

Using the Server Monitor

Exchange Server 5.5 provides a server monitor to check Exchange and dependent Windows NT 4 services running on servers within your site. The server monitor differs from the link monitor in that it doesn't check the links; the server monitor checks the services running on Exchange servers.

In addition to checking the status of services, you can specify an action to take if a specific service has stopped. For example, if the System Attendant has stopped, you can specify that your server monitor restart it.

Configuring the Server Monitor

To configure the server monitor, follow the steps in the previous section for configuring the link monitor, and in step 3, choose File ➢ New Other ➢ Server Monitor to display the Server Monitor property pages open at the General tab:

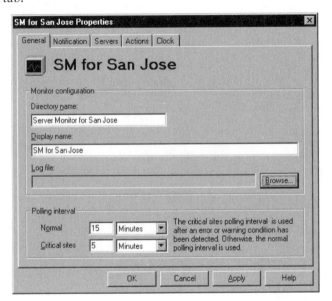

In the Monitor Configuration section of this page, you have the following options:

Directory Name: Assign a directory object name to the server monitor. Once this name is set, it *cannot* be changed. Use a descriptive name that indicates the servers that this monitor watches. The maximum name length is 64 alphanumeric characters.

Display Name: This name can be a maximum of 256 Unicode characters, and it can be modified.

Log File: Specify a log file that records information about the connection and notification status. You will find that logging your server monitor's actions will help troubleshoot your servers when an Exchange service fails. If you don't enter a valid filename in this box, a log file will not be created. You can use any path as part of the filename, including a path to a network share.

You have the following options in the Polling Interval section of this page:

Normal: Setting this property specifies the interval between each check of the servers you will be monitoring. The default is 15 minutes.

Critical Sites: Setting this property specifies the interval to check on servers that are in a warning or an alert state. The default is 5 minutes.

Monitoring Servers within Your Organization

As I mentioned earlier, server monitors check servers in other sites (if connected with RPCs) and check the status of services. Without specific permissions, a server monitor will not be able to synchronize clocks or restart services.

Use the Servers property page to choose which servers will be scanned. To set the server list, follow these steps:

1. Open the Exchange Administrator program, and double-click the Site Configuration container for the site you are modifying.

2. Double-click the Monitors object.

3. Select the server monitor you want to update.

4. Choose File ➤ Properties to open the Server Monitor property pages.

5. Select the Servers tab.

6. Select the server, and click Add to add the selected server to the list of monitored servers.

To remove a server, select it and click Remove.

Synchronizing Clocks   This feature allows you to initiate an alert if a monitored server's clock is off by a specific number of seconds. You can also specify that the monitored server synchronize its clock with the monitoring server's clock. Follow these steps:

1. Open the Exchange Administrator program, and double-click the Site Configuration container for the site you are modifying.

2. Double-click the Monitors object.

3. Select the server monitor you want to update.

4. Choose File ➤ Properties to open the Server Monitor property pages.

5. Select the Clock property tab.

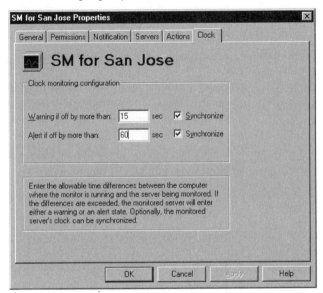

You can set the following properties on this page:

Warning If Off by More Than: Setting this value specifies the amount of time that a monitored server's internal clock can be different from your server's clock. Enabling the Synchronize checkbox forces a synchronization of time with the monitoring server's clock.

Alert If Off by More Than: Setting this value specifies the amount of time that a monitored server's internal clock can be different from your server's clock. Enable the Synchronize checkbox to force a synchronization of time with the monitoring server's clock.

Monitoring Server Status   You can use the Server Status property page of a server monitor to check the last-known status of monitored services. From the Actions property page, you can also change the status of the services. The state of the services reflects the state when the server monitor last ran. To view server status, follow these steps:

1. Open the Exchange Administrator program, and double-click the Site Configuration container for the site you are modifying.

2. Double-click the Monitors object.

3. Select the server monitor you want to update.

4. Choose File ➤ Properties to open the Server Monitor property pages.

5. Select the Actions property tab:

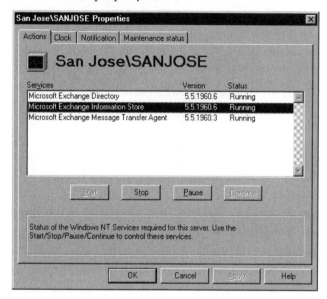

This property page displays the following information:

Services: The components and connectors that are monitored.

Version: The version of the services.

Status: The last-known status as known by the last monitor.

You can click the following buttons to manipulate services:

Start: Starts a service that was previously stopped.

Stop: Stops a running service.

Pause: Temporarily stops a service until you continue.

Continue: Restarts a service that had been paused.

Configuring Common Monitor Properties

You configure the following properties and settings the same on both link and server monitors.

Setting Notification Properties

At this point, we need to specify who will be notified whenever a monitor goes into a warning or an alert state. There is no limit to the number of notifications that you can configure for a single link monitor. For example, mail notifications can send messages to users, or programs can page a group of individuals. Notifications can be delivered as the following items:

- Notification applications, such as pagers, cellular phones, and so on.

- Mail messages to an individual or a distribution list.

- Network alerts that are broadcast on specified computers, if they are up. If the computer you choose is not up, nothing will occur.

To specify notifications, follow these steps:

1. Open the Exchange Administrator program, and double-click the Site Configuration container for the site you are modifying.

2. Double-click the Monitors object.

3. Select the link monitor you want to update.

4. Choose File ➤ Properties to open the Link Monitor property pages.

5. Select the Notification tab.

Running Notification Applications   Whenever you want to alert users who are not logged in of a warning or an alert state, you can run a program that will generate a notification. This program can be a pager program or a cellular call with a specific voice message. To use the program as a notification application, it must be installed on your Exchange server.

To configure a launch process, follow these steps:

1. On the Notification property page, click the New button.

2. Select Launch a Process, and click OK to open the Escalation Editor (Launch Process):

3. Configure the properties as shown in Table 4.1.

TABLE 4.1 The properties in the Escalation Editor	**Property**	**Description**
	Time Delay	Set the time to wait after a monitor enters either a warning or an alert state. After this time has expired, your notification program begins.
	Alert Only	Select this checkbox if you want to specify that this notification will occur only if the monitor is in an alert state. Clear this checkbox if you want the notification to occur during both a warning and an alert state.
	Launch Process	Enter the name of the program file to run whenever the monitor goes into a warning or an alert state.
	Command Line Parameters	Enter your monitor specific parameters (for example, a phone number to dial and the message to send) if your notification program requires any.
	Append Notification Text to Parameter List	Specify a text message to send in addition to the text message your specific notification program sends.
	Test	Click this button to test your notification.

Configuring Mail Message Notifications   To configure mail message notifications, follow these steps:

1. On the Notification property page, click the New button.

2. Select Mail Message, and click OK to open the Escalation Editor (Mail Message):

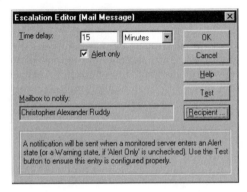

3. Configure the properties as shown in Table 4.2.

T A B L E 4.2	Property	Description
The properties in the Escalation Editor (Mail Message)	Time Delay	Sets the time delay after a monitor enters either a warning or an alert state. After this time delay, the mail message is sent.
	Alert Only	Select this checkbox if you want to specify that this mail message notification will occur only if the monitor is in an alert state. Clear this checkbox if you want the mail message notification to occur during both a warning and an alert state.
	Mailbox to Notify	Select the name of a recipient. This recipient will be sent a mail message whenever the monitor goes into a warning or an alert state.
	Test	Click this button to see if your notification works like it should.

Configuring Network Alerts   You can use network alerts to broadcast messages to network users who are currently logged on. This will not work if users are not logged on or if the Windows NT Messaging Service is not started. This feature works best for operator workstations that are staffed at all times.

To configure network alerts, follow these steps:

1. On the Notification property page, click the New button.

2. Select Windows NT Alert, and click OK to open the Escalation Editor (Windows NT Alert):

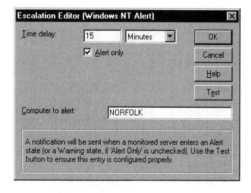

3. Configure the properties as shown in Table 4.3.

TABLE 4.3	Property	Description
The properties in the Escalation Editor (Windows NT Alert)	Time Delay	Set the time to wait after a monitor enters either a warning or an alert state. After this time expires, a broadcast message is sent.
	Alert Only	Select this checkbox if you want to execute this alert only if the monitor is in an alert state. Clear this checkbox if you want the alert to occur during both a warning and an alert state.
	Computer to Alert	Enter the name of the computer to receive the alert.
	Test	Click this button to test your alert.

Monitor Specific Services

Exchange Server 5.5 monitors only the directory, the information store, and the MTA. If you want to monitor any other server service, you must add that service to the list. To view or add services, follow these steps:

1. Open the Exchange Administrator program, and double-click the Site Configuration container for the site you are modifying.

2. Select the server you want to change.

3. Choose File ➤ Properties to open the Server property pages.

4. Select the Services tab:

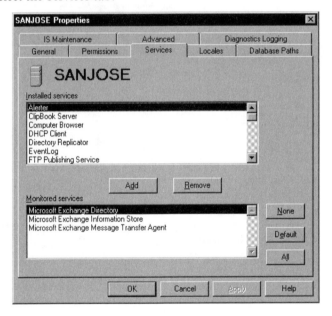

To add an installed service, select it in the Installed Services list and click Add.

To add an Exchange Server service, select it in the Monitored Services list and click Default.

To add all installed services, select them and click All.

Starting a Monitor

You can start Exchange Server 5.5 monitors manually, or they can be started automatically whenever an NT server is started up. If your server is only up during the week and only available for messaging during business hours, you can manually log on to the NT server and start the Exchange Administrator program. Starting the program automatically starts any monitors that were running when you last exited the Exchange Administrator program.

If your work site is a 7×24 shop (7 days a week, 24 hours a day), you can have an account automatically log on and run the monitors if the NT server is rebooted for any reason. In this section, we will go through the steps to start the monitors manually and automatically.

Starting a Monitor Manually

If you choose to monitor your servers or links part of the time, you must manually start the monitors when you want them to run. To start a monitor, follow these steps:

1. Start the Exchange Administrator program.

2. Double-click the Site Configuration object that hosts the monitor you want to start.

3. Double-click the Servers container.

4. Select the server that hosts your monitor to open the container and display a list of the objects associated with this server.

5. Select Monitors, and then chose the monitor you want to start.

6. Choose Tools ➤ Start Monitor to open the Monitor window:

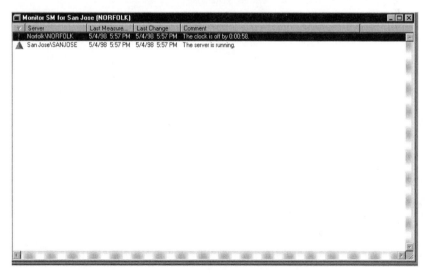

As you can see, the Monitor window has five columns:

- State

- Server

- Last Measure

- Last Change

- Comment

The State column displays one of four symbols for each server:

- The question mark indicates that the status of your monitor is unknown. When a monitor has just started and has not completed its check, the monitor will usually be in this state. It will change when the first check is completed.

- The green up arrow indicates that the monitor checks are completing normally.

- The red exclamation point indicates that your server is in a warning state. Check this monitor for more information, or check the monitor log file if you have turned on logging.

- The red down arrow indicates that your monitor has moved into an alert state. Check your monitor for more information, and definitely check your monitor log if you have turned on logging.

Starting a Monitor Automatically

There may be times in a 7×24 shop when your Exchange servers shut down and reboot due to power outages or system crashes. If no one is in the area to log on and start the Exchange Administrator program, your monitors will not start. You can use some features of Windows NT Server 4 to include some instructions in the Registry to automatically log on to an account with permissions to start the monitors.

You must create the account and set the Exchange administrator permissions to allow this account to start monitors and to restart services if Exchange services stop for any reason. This account should also be able to synchronize server clocks. (See the BackOffice Resource Kit (BORK) Part One for instructions on how to configure an autologon account.)

The second part of automatically starting monitors is to customize the Start menu of the account you created for autologon. Adding the Exchange

Administrator program to the Startup folder of the taskbar will automatically start the Exchange Administrator program whenever this account logs on to Windows NT Server.

To customize the Startup folder, log on to the autologon account and then follow these steps:

1. Choose Start ➢ Settings.

2. Select Taskbar to open the Taskbar Properties dialog box.

3. Select the Start Menu Programs tab:

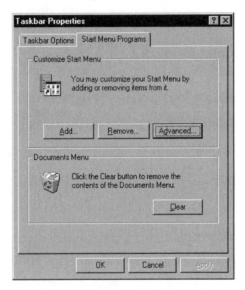

4. Click the Add button, and choose Browse to select the program to add.

5. Browse through your file structure, and select the Exchange Administrator program's icon. You can find the program in the \Exchsrvr\bin subdirectory.

6. Click Open to display the command line dialog box.

7. Add the instruction to start the monitor, using the following syntax:

```
path\admin.exe /m[site name]\monitor name\server name
```

You can start multiple monitors by appending additional /m arguments.

8. Click the Next button, and double-click the Startup folder.

9. Enter a name for this Start menu item, and click Finish.

10. In the Taskbar Properties dialog box, click OK.

Optimizing Exchange Server

Optimizing your Exchange servers is an ongoing process. In this section, we will review the two areas where optimizing can make the most difference:

- Hardware
- Windows NT Server

Optimizing Your Hardware

Exchange Server 5.5 includes a tool for optimizing existing hardware—the Performance Optimizer. You normally run Performance Optimizer after installing Exchange Server and after making any change in your hardware configuration.

The Performance Optimizer does the following:

- Analyzes your hard disk configuration to determine which device has the fastest access time. The Performance Optimizer reserves the disk that has the fastest access time for Exchange's transaction logs.

- Analyzes your hard disk configuration to determine which device has the fastest random access time. This drive becomes the location of your public information store.

- Analyzes physical memory against the number of users and how the server will be used and then determines the optimal size of the directory and information store caches.

The Performance Optimizer inspects logical drives, analyzing each partition and moving database files onto different partitions. The Performance Optimizer cannot determine whether a device is a logical drive or a physical drive.

The Performance Optimizer is an Administrative Wizard that will display several screens on which you enter options. Before you run the Performance Optimizer, be sure you have the information shown in Figure 4.1.

Identifying Your Hardware Resources

The performance of your server is determined by your hardware resources:

CPU: To run Exchange Server 5.5, you need at minimum a 90 MHz Pentium processor. This processor is sufficient for very small sites that process a minimal number of messages outside the organization. But a Digital Alpha computer with multiple processors will outperform any 90 MHz Pentium. It's important to have a processor that can handle your transactions, but it's more important to have a well-balanced system.

Memory: Windows NT Server 4 uses a virtual memory model. You need to ensure that your system pagefile is big enough to handle all the movement of data between physical memory and your server's disk. If the pagefile is too small for all the data that needs to be in physical memory, excessive paging (known as *thrashing*) will occur. Adding more physical memory to your system is better than adding disk space. You can use the

Windows NT Server Performance Monitor to monitor your page fault rate and CPU utilization.

IO Subsystem: The transaction logs used in Exchange Server 5.5 use sequential writes. Sequential disk access is faster than random disk access. Keep the Exchange Server 5.5 transaction log files on one disk, and keep the databases on another because Exchange databases are usually random access reads and writes.

Network Hardware: Network performance is adversely affected by loading unnecessary protocols. Load only the network protocols and services that will be used. In addition, use one or more high-performance network adapters to handle the traffic and increase the speed of transmissions.

Optimizing the Operating System

To check on how the Windows NT Server operating system is performing, run the NT Performance Monitor to track operating system resources. The NT Performance Monitor uses counters to watch objects. The counters are compiled to show a trend that identifies how resources are being used on your NT server.

To start the Windows NT Performance Monitor, choose Start ➤ Programs ➤ Administrative Tools ➤ Performance Monitor:

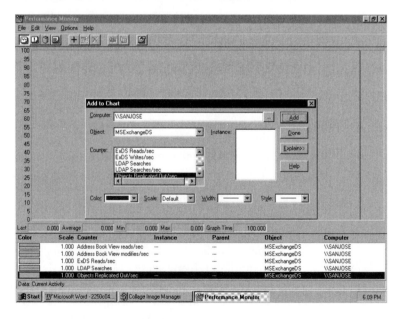

After monitoring your NT Server over time, you can use the results to optimize the performance of your system. Table 4.4 lists and explains those counters that directly affect Windows NT Server performance:

T A B L E 4.4   Windows NT performance counters

Object	NT Counter	Description
Redirector	Bytes Total/sec	Records the number of bytes transferred per second. Compare this value against the speed of your network adapter to determine whether the network traffic on this server is a problem.
Redirector	Network Errors/sec	Records the number of network errors the Redirector has reported. Count this object if you suspect a network problem.
Process	Elapsed Time	Records how long a process has been running. Use this counter to determine whether a process has been restarted.
Memory	Pages/sec	Reports on memory utilization. If this counter reports a high average, your server is low on memory. Ignore infrequent high values because you will encounter spikes when the server is started or when a process is started.
LogicalDisk	% Disk Time	Records the percentage of time a hard drive is performing I/O. A value of more than 90% indicates this hard drive is experiencing a bottleneck.
Processor	% Processor Time	Records the percentage of time that your processor is executing non-idle threads. Anything more than 90% indicates your processor is overworked.

Optimizing Foreign Connections

Y̲ou can use several Exchange Server 5.5 tools to monitor performance across sites or between foreign systems.

Monitoring Links to a Foreign Mail System

Now that we've looked at how to monitor servers in the same Exchange site, we need to look at how to monitor communication links to foreign mail systems.

Exchange Server 5.5 sends ping messages to nonexistent recipients at foreign mail addresses; you use the reply to determine whether the link is working. Because the link monitor expects an NDR, you must send the message to a non-existent recipient. If an existing user receives the message, the message will be delivered, and the ping message won't be returned to your link monitor.

Before you configure the link monitor, test it to see what the foreign system returns in the NDR. If the foreign mail system creating the NDR sends back a message with the original text of the message in the body of the NDR, choose the *Message subject or body returned from* option. If the foreign mail system returns an NDR with the original message text in the body of the message, choose the *Message subject returned from* option.

To configure the link monitor, follow these steps:

1. Start the Exchange Administrator program.

2. Double-click the Site Configuration object that hosts the monitor you want to configure.

3. Double-click the Servers container.

4. Select the server that hosts your monitor to open the container and display a list of the objects associated with this server.

5. Select Monitors, and choose the monitor you want to modify

6. Select the Recipients tab:

To specify a recipient that returns subjects only, follow these steps:

1. In the *Message subject returned from* section, click Modify.

2. Select the names of the recipients, and then click Add.

To specify recipients that return the subject or message body, follow these steps:

1. In the *Message subject or body returned from* section, click Modify.

2. Select the names of the recipients, and then click Add.

Create a custom recipient's container for invalid recipients used by the link monitor. Set this recipient's advanced mailbox properties to Hide from Address Book. This keeps the address hidden from your users.

Monitoring the Microsoft Mail Connector

Use the NT Performance Monitor to track the state of the Microsoft Mail Connector on your Exchange server. Monitoring this connector will give you some data on what is normal and help you quickly identify those areas that can be tuned to increase performance. Table 4.5 lists and explains the counters associated with the Microsoft Mail Connector.

T A B L E   4.5   Counters associated with the Microsoft Mail Connector

Object	NT Counter	Description
MSExchange MSMI	Messages Received	Records the number of messages received by Exchange from the connector. If this number doesn't change, either no mail is being sent, or there is a problem with your connector or network.
MSExchange PC MTA	File contentions/ hour	Records the number of reads and writes to the Microsoft Mail Connector MTA and any other Microsoft Mail (PC) MTA and MS Mail Clients, to the Microsoft Mail and Microsoft Mail Connector postoffices. A few file contentions will occur with this activity. If you notice an increase in this counter, a file may be locked, or network traffic may be heavy.

T A B L E 4.5   Counters associated with the Microsoft Mail Connector *(continued)*

Object	NT Counter	Description
MSExchange PC MTA	LAN/WAN Messages Moved/hour	Indicates how the Microsoft Mail Connector (PC) MTA is performing. Monitor this counter to record the average number of messages moved. If this number drops or increases dramatically, check the connector for problems.

Monitoring the Internet Mail Service

Use the NT Performance Monitor to track the state of the Internet Mail Service on your Exchange server. Monitoring this connector will give you some data on what is normal and help you quickly identify those areas that can be tuned to increase performance on this connector. Table 4.6 lists and describes the counters associated with the Internet Mail Service.

T A B L E 4.6   Counters associated with the Internet Mail Service

NT Counter	Description
Queued MTS-IN	Records the number of messages waiting to be delivered to the Exchange Server MTA.
Bytes Queued MTS-IN	Records the size of messages in bytes that have been converted and are waiting to be delivered to the Exchange Server MTA.
Messages Entering MTS-IN	Records the number of converted messages waiting to be delivered to the Exchange Server MTA after conversion from Internet mail format.
Queued MTS-OUT	Counts the number of messages waiting to be converted to Internet mail format.
Bytes Queued MTS-OUT	Records the size in bytes of messages that have been converted and are waiting to be delivered to the Internet Mail Service.
Messages Entering MTS-OUT	Records the number of converted messages waiting to be delivered to the Internet Mail Service after conversion from Exchange mail format.

T A B L E 4.6 Counters associated with the Internet Mail Service *(continued)*

NT Counter	Description
Messages Leaving MTS-OUT	Counts the messages entering the outbound queue.
Connections Inbound	Counts the number of connections from SMTP hosts to the Internet Mail Service.
Connections Outbound	Counts the number of connections from the Internet Mail Service to other SMTP hosts.
Connections Total Outbound	Counts the number of successful connections from the Internet Mail Service to other SMTP hosts since the service was started.
Connections Total Inbound	Counts the number of successful connections from SMTP hosts to the Internet Mail Service since the service was started.
Connections Total Rejected	This counter is used to count the number of rejected connections from SMTP hosts since the service was started.
Connections Total Failed	Counts the number of SMTP connections that failed since the service was started.
Queued Outbound	Counts the number of messages from the Exchange MTA that are queued for delivery to the Internet Mail Service.
Queued Inbound	Counts the number of current messages destined for the Exchange server.
NDRs Total Inbound	Counts the number of NDRs for incoming mail.
NDRs Total Outbound	Counts the number of NDRs for outbound mail.
Total Inbound Kilobytes	The number of kilobytes of incoming messages to the Exchange server.
Total Outbound Kilobytes	The number of kilobytes of outgoing messages from the Exchange server.
Inbound Messages Total	The total number of messages delivered to the Exchange server.
Outbound Messages Total	The total number of messages delivered to SMTP hosts.

Monitoring and Optimizing the Messaging Environment

As part of monitoring your connections and servers, it's important to monitor the components that handle messaging. In this section, we'll look at how to monitor the messaging environment, which consists of the MTA, the directory, and the information store.

Reviewing the Status of Messages

The MTA on each server contains queues for each message target. It's important to review these queues to ensure that the messages are passing through each MTA and/or connector. There are two types of queues:

Secured: These queues are for the Microsoft Mail Connector and the Internet Mail Service. The queue remains empty until the connector or the service sends messages or tries to retrieve messages.

Unsecured: These queues are for the MTA and associated connectors. You can change the priority of these messages.

To view the MTA queues, follow these steps:

1. Start the Exchange Administrator program.

2. Double-click the Site Configuration object that hosts the MTA you want to configure.

3. Double-click the Servers container.

4. Select the server that hosts your MTA to open the container and display a list of the objects associated with this server.

5. Select the MTA.

6. Choose File ➤ Properties to open the Message Transfer Agent property pages.

7. Select the Queues tab:

8. Select the queue from the list of message queues on this server.

For information on troubleshooting the MTA, see Unit 5.

Monitoring the Message Transfer Agent

You can monitor the MTA using the Windows NT Performance Monitor, which will report counts on the MSExchange MTA object. Paying attention to these counters will help you determine the average number of messages waiting to be delivered and other items. Once you understand what is normal, you can use the MTA Advanced property pages to set the messaging parameters.

For information on how to start the NT Performance Monitor, see the "Optimizing the Operating System" section, earlier in this unit. Table 4.7 lists and describes the counters that monitor the MTA.

	NT Counter	Description
T A B L E 4.7 Counters associated with monitoring the MTA	Messages/sec	Records the average number of messages the MTA sends and receives each second. Use this setting to monitor messages going to other servers.
	Work Queue Length	Records the number of messages waiting to be delivered to other servers or waiting to be delivered to this server. If this counter spikes, there could be a problem with the MTA.
	Queue Size	Records the number of objects in queues to and from each connection.

Monitoring the Directory Service

You can monitor the Directory Service to ensure that your messages are directed to the correct destinations and that addresses are updated quickly. Using the counters in Table 4.8, you can build averages of the transmission of updates. You can then tune the Directory Service Advanced properties.

For information on how to start the NT Performance Monitor, see the "Optimizing the Operating System" section, earlier in this unit.

	NT Counter	Description
T A B L E 4.8 The counters associated with the Directory Service	Pending Replication Synchronization	Records the current synchronization requests sent by the Directory Service that have not been returned. Select the Update Now option, and check this value. The counter should start high and slowly decrease as the sync messages arrive.
	Remaining Replication Updates	Tracks the number of current sync updates waiting to be written to your server's directory.

Monitoring the Information Store

Monitoring your server's information store can give you an idea of how incoming and outgoing messages are being handled. If the information store becomes a bottleneck, you might want to add another Exchange server in your site and move users from this information store to the new server.

For information on how to start the NT Performance Monitor, see the "Optimizing the Operating System" section, earlier in this unit. Table 4.9 lists and describes the counters associated with the information store.

T A B L E 4.9	NT Counter	Description
The counters associated with the information store	Average Time for Delivery	Tracks the average length of time the last 10 messages waited before being picked up by the MTA for delivery. A high value might indicate a problem with your MTA.
	Average Time for Local Delivery	Tracks the average length of time the last 10 messages waited in the queue before being delivered to their mailbox. A high value might indicate a problem with the information store.
	Logon Count	Use this counter to build an average of the number of clients logged on to this information store.
	Logon Active Count	Use this counter to determine the average number of clients who have initiated server activity within the last 10 minutes.
	Messages Delivered/min	Setting this counter gives you a average number of messaged delivered to your information store per minute.
	Message Recipient Delivered/min	This counter gives you a great picture of the actual number of messages delivered. The calculation used here is the number of messages sent divided by the number of recipients.
	Messages Sent/min	This counter gives you a clear picture of the number of messages sent per minute to the information store to be sent by the MTA to other servers' MTAs or connectors.

Monitoring Server Performance with SNMP and MADMAN MIB

As part of a fully functional TCP/IP network application, Exchange Server provides *SNMP (Simple Network Management Protocol)* in the form of a *MIB (Management Information Base)*. This protocol works with an SNMP management console application. You can use any SNMP management console software (Version 1) to manage your Exchange organization's network load and traffic.

The Exchange Server 5.5 MIB complies with TCP/IP RFC (Request for Comment) 1566. The MIB is known as the *MADMAN (Maintenance and Directory Management)* MIB. In addition to providing SNMP support, the Exchange Server 5.5 MIB also adds counters to the NT Performance Monitor as MIB objects.

To install and configure SNMP support, you must install the SNMP service from the network Control Panel before installing and configuring the Exchange Server 5.5 MADMAN. For specifics on how to install and configure the SNMP, see the Windows NT Server 4 documentation. In the following sections, we'll go through the steps for installing and configuring the Exchange Server 5.5 MIB and MADMAN. In addition, we'll look at the counters for use with the NT Performance Monitor.

Be sure you reinstall the Windows NT 4.0 Service Pack 3 after installing the Windows NT 4.0 SNMP from Control Panel.

Installing MADMAN MIB

You can install the Exchange MADMAN MIB in two ways:

- Automatically
- Manually

If you have not installed any MIB other than those installed with Windows NT, you can run a batch file to automatically install a compiled version of the MIB. If you have already installed any MIB other than the NT MIB, you must manually install the Exchange Server 5.5 MIB.

Installing the MIB Using a Batch File

To install the MIB using the batch file, follow these steps:

1. From the Desktop, choose Start ➤ Programs ➤ Command Prompt to open the NT Command Prompt window.

2. From the command prompt, type:

   prompt> *<cdrom drive>*\Support\Snmp*platform*\Install.bat

Installing the MIB Manually

If you've installed MIBs other than those provided with Windows NT, you must do the following to install the Exchange Server 5.5 MIB:

- Run the Perf2mib.exe to compile Performance Monitor counters into a new MIB for Exchange Server.

- Run Mibcc.exe to rebuild your current Mib.bin with the new MIB you just created.

To install the Exchange Server 5.5 MIB, follow these steps:

1. At the command prompt, run the Per2mib.exe command to create the Perf2mib.mib and the Perfmib.ini files:

   <cdrom drive>\Support\Snmp*platform*\Perf2mib Perfmib.mib
   ➡Perfmib.ini MSExchangeMTA 1 MTA "MSExchangeMTAConnections"
   ➡2 "MTA Connection" MSExchangeIMC 3 *<counter name>* *<index>*
   ➡*<description>*

   In this case, *counter name*, *index*, and *description* are additional Performance Monitor counters that you want to make available in the MIB.

2. Run the Mibcc command to create Mib.bin:

   <cdrom drive>\Support\Snmp*platform*\Mibcc –Omiv.vin –n –t
   ➡–w2 Smi.mib LMMIB2.MIB Mib_II.mib Perfmib.mib

3. Copy Perfmib.dll, Perfmib.ini, and Mib.bin to the <drive letter>:\<winnt>\System32 directory.

4. Run the regini command to install the values to support the Performance MIB:

   Regini perfmib.bin

5. Restart the SNMP service by stopping and restarting the service in the Services applet in Control Panel.

Configuring SNMP Service for Exchange

As I mentioned, you can use any SNMP management console to view the MADMAN MIB. You can read and set the SNMP objects in the following sections using the management console.

Viewing the MIB Using the SNMP Management Console

Use the following object to view the MTA values:

```
.iso.org.dod.internet.private.enterprises.microsoft.software
➡.systems.os.winnt.performance.MSExchangeMTA.1.3.6.1.4.311.1
➡.1.3.1.1
```

Use the following object to view the MTA connection values:

```
.iso.org.dod.internet.private.enterprises.microsoft.software
➡.systems.os.winnt.performance.MSExchangeMTA.1.3.6.1.4.1.311
➡.1.1.3.1.1.2.x
```

Use the following object to view the Internet Mail Service values:

```
.iso.org.dod.internet.private.enterprises.microsoft.software
➡.systems.os.winnt.performance.MSExchangeIMC.1.3.6.1.4.1.311
➡.1.1.3.1.1.3
```

Viewing the MIB Using the SNMP Utility

If you don't have an SNMP management console, you can view these counters using the snmputil tool available in the Windows NT Resource Kit.

The following command displays the value for the mtaInboundBytes-Total object:

```
Snmputil get <server name> public .iso.org.dod.internet.
➡private.enterprises.microsoft.software.systems.OS.WinNT.
➡Performance.1.38.0
```

The following command displays the value for the mtaOutboundBytes-Total object:

```
Snmputil get <server name> public .iso.org.dod.internet.
➡private.enterprises.microsoft.software.systems.OS.WinNT.
➡Performance.2.1.32.0
```

The following command displays the value for the imsQueuedMTS-IN object:

```
Snmputil get <serer name> public
➡.iso.org.dod.internet.private.enterprises.microsoft.software
➡.system.OS.WinNT.Performance.3.1.0
```

Viewing the MIB Counters in the NT Performance Monitor

Table 4.10 lists the MIB objects defined in RFC 1566 and their corresponding Exchange NT Performance Monitor counters. The MIB object supports both MTA and IMC Exchange objects.

T A B L E 4.10   NT Performance counters associated with MIB objects

MIB Object	MSExchangeIMC Counter	MSExchange MTA Counter
MtaReceivedMessages	Inbound Messages Total	Inbound Messages Total
MtaStoredMessages	Total Messages Queued	Work Queue Length
MtaTransmitted Messages	Outbound Messages Total	Outbound Messages Total
MtaReceivedVolume	Inbound Bytes Total	Inbound Bytes Total
MtaStoredVolume	Total Bytes Queued	Work Queue Bytes
MtaTransmittedVolume	Outbound Bytes Total	Outbound Bytes Total
MtaReceivedRecipients	Total Recipients Inbound	Total Recipients Inbound
mtaStoredRecipients	Total Recipients Queued	Total Recipients Queued
mtaTransmittedRecipients	Total Recipients Outbound	Total Recipients Outbound
mtaSucessfulConverted Messages	Total Successful Conversions	Total Successful Conversions
mtaFailedConverted Messages	Total Failed Conversions	Total Failed Conversions
mtaLoopsDetected	Total Loops Detected	Total Loops Detected

Configuring a Link Monitor and a Server Monitor

1. What types of monitors does Exchange Server 5.5 include?

_____

_____

2. True or False. You use a link monitor to test communication links between servers.

3. True or False. You use a server monitor to test communication links between servers.

4. A link monitor uses a/an _____ _____ _____
message to test communication links.

5. True or False. Link and server monitors are created in the Site Configuration container only.
Monitors are not set up in Server containers.

6. True or False. Monitors cannot use log files to track events.

7. List the two polling intervals used in a server monitor's configuration.

_____

_____

8. What is the default time for both polling intervals?

_____

_____

9. True or False. The Bounce property is used to bounce user messages back and forth between multiple servers.

10. Which monitor would you use to monitor a server that is used only as a public folder server?

11. Which Monitor Server property can you set to readjust any server's internal clock that is off more than three minutes?

_____

12. True or False. A server monitor can reboot your system if your server's services are stopped.

13. Which property page do you use to view the status of any server that is being monitored by your server monitor?

_____

14. Which two properties can you configure to take action whenever your server has a problem?

_____

_____

15. True or False. An Exchange administrator can add NT services to monitor in addition to Exchange Server services on the Server Monitor property page.

STUDY QUESTIONS

16. Which three types of notifications are available for each monitor type?

_____

_____

_____

17. True or False. You can assign only one notification per server.

18. True or False. The valid recipient types for a server monitor Mail Message notification are custom recipients.

19. Network alerts broadcast messages to users who are logged on and to _____.

20. The two methods for monitor start up are:

_____

_____

21. What are the four states of any monitor, as identified by the following symbols?

Question Mark (?) _____

Red Exclamation Point (!) _____

Green Up Arrow (↑) _____

Red Down Arrow (↓) _____

STUDY QUESTIONS

22. True or False. To configure Exchange Server to automatically restart after a reboot, you must set up an NT autologon account to log on and autostart the Exchange Administrator program

Optimizing Exchange Server

23. You optimize Exchange Server's hardware configuration by running the Exchange

_____ _____.

24. True or False. The Performance Optimizer can tell the difference between a physical and a logical disk.

25. The Exchange Performance Optimizer measures the amount of physical memory against the number of users and then sizes the _____ and the

_____ database caches.

26. What is the minimum processor recommended for use with Exchange Server 5.5?

_____

27. True or False. While monitoring memory, you notice that your processor is experiencing disk thrashing. The best solution is to add more physical memory.

28. The Exchange transaction logs use _____ writes.

29. True or False. It is best not to add unnecessary protocols to your network adapter.

30. To monitor Exchange performance, use the Windows NT Server _____

_____.

31. True or False. During the Exchange Server installation, setup installs Exchange Server–specific counters in the Windows NT Performance Monitor.

32. List the NT Performance objects used to measure general Windows NT Server performance.

_____

_____

_____

_____

_____

33. Which two counters measure network performance for general Windows NT Server performance?

_____

_____

34. Which counter tracks the percentage of time that a hard drive is performing I/O?

_____

35. Which counter tracks how long a process has been started?

_____

36. Which counter tracks memory utilization?

_____

37. True or False. Whenever you change your hardware configuration, you should run the Exchange Server Performance Optimizer.

Optimizing Foreign Connections and Site-to-Site Connections

38. True or False. The Exchange link monitor cannot monitor communication links outside your Exchange organization.

39. To test a foreign mail system's connection, you must send the ping message to a _____ recipient.

40. True or False. It's a good idea to create a container for your link monitor recipients and to hide the container.

41. If you are not sure whether a foreign mail system will return the subject of a message or the body of a message, use the _____ property.

42. The NT Performance Monitor counter that records the number of messages received from the Microsoft Mail connector is:

_____

STUDY QUESTIONS

43. True or False. Exchange Server 5.5 does not provide NT Performance Monitor counters for monitoring purposes; you must use the SNMP MADMAN MIB for queries.

44. The counter that tracks the number of messages waiting to be converted to SMTP format is the _____.

45. The counter that tracks the number of successful connections from the Internet Mail Service to other SMTP hosts is the _____.

46. True or False. The counter that tracks the number of messages entering the Internet Mail Service outbound queue is Messages Entering MTS-OUT.

47. The counters that represent the total number of messages passing through the Internet Mail Service to and from Exchange are _____ and _____.

Monitoring and Optimizing the Messaging Environment

48. MTA message queues are divided into two types: _____ and _____.

49. True or False. MTA secured queues allow you to modify, delete, and change the priority of a message.

50. Building a performance baseline for Exchange involves monitoring the MTA using _____ counters.

51. To monitor the Directory Service's counter for the number of messages received since the last update waiting to be applied to the Directory database, use the _____ _____ _____ counters.

52. What types of foreign mail system messages appear in the Secured queue on the Server MTA Queue property page?

_____

_____

53. Which counter records the average time spent for delivery of messages for the Internet Mail Service?

_____

_____

Monitoring Server Performance Using SNMP and MADMAN MIB

54. True or False. Exchange Server 5.5 provides SNMP support if the Windows NT Server SNMP Service and Agent are installed.

55. The Exchange Server 5.5 MADMAN MIB complies with RFC _____ of the TCP/IP Standards and Recommendations.

56. The Exchange Server 5.5 MIB is called the MADMAN MIB. What does MADMAN stand for?

_____

57. List the two methods for installing the MADMAN MIB:

_____

_____

58. True or False. If you've already installed a nonstandard MIB, you can still use a batch file to install the Exchange MIB.

59. True or False. You must reinstall the Windows NT Server 4.0 Service Pack 3 after you install the Windows NT Server SNMP Service and Agent.

60. Which two executables must you run to install the Exchange MADMAN MIB manually?

_____

_____

61. True or False. You can only view the MADMAN MIB values by using an SNMP management console application.

62. Finish entering the SNMP MIB code for the MTA object:

```
iso.org.dod.internet.private.enterprises.microsoft.software.systems.os.winnt
.performance.MSExchangeMTA.1.3.6._____.
```

63. Finish the command line to read the MTA value for the mtaInboundBytes Total object:

```
snmputil get <server name> public  .iso.org.dod.internet.private.enterprises.
microsoft._____.OS.WinNT.Performance.1.
_____.0
```

64. True or False. When you install the Exchange MADMAN MIB, you also install the MIB NT performance counters.

65. What is the MSExchange MTA NT performance counter for the MIB mtaLoopsDetected object?

_____

66. What is the MSExchange IMC NT performance counter for the MIB mtaTransmitted-Volume object?

_____

4-1 Theo wants to monitor multiple connections between different servers. He also wants to observe the state of the link on a foreign mail server in his company. What tool must he create to watch over these systems?

  A. Server monitor

  B. NT sniffer

  C. HP Openview

  D. Link monitor

4-2 Emmy has installed an Exchange server monitor on her system. During a normal service check of the monitored servers, she notices that the System Attendant is not running on a server. Emmy is getting tired of having to log on to different servers and start services that have stopped. What can she do to avoid this task?

  A. Configure an NT Performance Check to execute a batch file to start the services on the service

  B. Use the command prompt command `Net start \\server\exchangesitename service_name`

  C. Configure a server monitor's action to restart the service if it has failed

  D. Configure a batch procedure to watch when the server is rebooted and restart the service

4-3 After configuring two link monitors, you realize the names of the monitors are too much alike for you to easily tell the difference between them. What can you do to change the directory name of a link monitor?

  A. Select the monitor and choose rename.

  B. You cannot change the directory name of an object, but you can change the display name.

  C. Edit the Windows NT Registry and select the object. Delete the object name and restart.

  D. Edit the name property.

S A M P L E   T E S T

4-4   Logan is the system manager of an Exchange server at a legal corporation. He wants to set the critical polling interval on both his link and server to 5 minutes. Does he need to make any changes to the default polling interval?

    A. Yes, the default polling interval is 10 minutes.

    B. Yes, the default polling interval is 25 minutes

    C. No, the default polling interval is 5 minutes.

    D. No, the default polling interval is 10 minutes

4-5   Kathlyn has configured a link server to send ping messages to a nonexistent user on a foreign system. The ping message was not returned, and the link monitor went into a warning state. What could be the problem?

    A. Kathlyn did not use TCP/IP.

    B. Kathlyn used IPX/SPX and TCP/IP.

    C. Kathlyn sent her message to a distribution list.

    D. Kathlyn sent a ping message to an existing user instead of a nonexistent user.

4-6   Vicky wants to configure a link monitor to test the communication links of a foreign mail system. Which property page should she configure to send a message to the nonexistent user and set the timeouts?

    A. Server

    B. Link Monitor Bounce

    C. NT Performance Monitor

    D. Monitor and Warning

SAMPLE TEST

4-7 Alex has configured a server monitor to resynchronize the clocks if they are off by more than two minutes. He has set the alarms correctly, and the monitor does run at specific intervals. He notices that if a clock is off, it does not reset even though he has a valid instruction in the Action field. What could be the problem?

A. Alex does not have permissions on the monitored server's system to modify system time.

B. Alex did not specify AM or PM on the server monitor.

C. Alex did not configure the link monitor.

D. Alex did not enter the magic word.

4-8 Choose the three types of notifications that can be set whenever a monitor goes into an alert state.

A. Notification Printouts

B. Notification Programs

C. Network Alerts

D. Notification Mail Messages

4-9 Which two conditions must be met before a user will receive a network alert?

A. The user must be logged on.

B. The NT Messenger Service must be running.

C. The NT Performance Counter must be configured.

D. The link monitor must be in a paused state.

4-10   Ryan Tapia is a system manager in a 7×24 shop. The previous system manager would manually start all the Exchange Server 5.5 monitors whenever a server went down and rebooted itself. What can Ryan do to automatically start the monitors?

    A. Nothing—you cannot autostart monitors.

    B. Edit the Registry entries for the monitors, and set the value for those monitors to autostart.

    C. Create an auto logon account using Windows NT Server 4, and configure the StartUp to automatically start the Exchange Administrator program with the monitors.

    D. Install SMS version 5.

4-11   While Jesse is checking his Exchange monitors, he notices a red exclamation point (!) in the first column. What, if anything, is the problem?

    A. The server is in an alert state.

    B. The monitor is in a warning state.

    C. The server is in a warning state.

    D. The monitor is in an alert state.

4-12   Chili has added three more hard drives to his Exchange server. He runs the Performance Optimizer after he boots up his servers. The Performance Optimizer has determined that drive J has the fastest sequential access time. This drive will be used for what type of file storage?

    A. Database caches

    B. Transaction logs

    C. Information Store databases

    D. Event Viewer logs

```
┌────────────┤ S A M P L E   T E S T ├────────────┐
```

4-13 Danny has been monitoring his Windows NT server resources for the last two months. He has noticed quite a lot of paging activity on his server. He has increased the pagefile size on his hard disks, but the server performance has still not increased. What would increase performance on his Exchange server?

    A. There is nothing that Danny can do.

    B. Make smaller pagefiles.

    C. Run the Exchange Performance Optimizer.

    D. Add memory.

4-14 Marc wants to monitor his links to a foreign mail system. In order to constantly monitor this link, he must create a custom recipients container for invalid recipients. How can Marc keep the addresses from showing up in the global address list?

    A. Select the Hide from Address Book property on the Mailbox Advanced Mailbox property page.

    B. Make a distribution list, and add those invalid addresses. Make the distribution list read-only.

    C. Create the invalid recipients as custom recipients.

    D. None of the above.

4-15 Chris is an Exchange administrator at a small company using the Internet Mail Service on his Exchange server. He is using the NT Performance Monitor to monitor the Internet Mail Service. Chris wants to know how many of his outbound connections are successful and how many fail. Which counters can he monitor?

    A. Queued MTS-IN and Bytes Queued MTS-OUT

    B. Inbound Messages Total and Outbound Messages Total

    C. Connections Total Outbound and Connections Total Failed

    D. Queued MTS-OUT and Bytes Queued MTS-Out

SAMPLE TEST

4-16   Which three core components should be monitored as part of the Messaging Environment?

    A. System Attendant

    B. Message Transfer Agent

    C. Directory Service

    D. Information Store

4-17   Shannon has a fully functional TCP/IP network with a network management console application. She wants to monitor her Exchange server with SNMP support. What can she install that will support SNMP monitoring for Exchange Server 5.5?

    A. MADMAN MIB

    B. INFOMAN MIB

    C. EXCH MIB

    D. MADMIB MIB

UNIT

5

Troubleshooting

Test Objectives: Troubleshooting

- **Diagnose and resolve upgrade problems.**

- **Diagnose and resolve server installation problems.**

- **Diagnose and resolve migration problems.**

- **Diagnose and resolve connectivity problems. Elements include:**
  - Foreign connectivity
  - Site-to-site connectivity
  - Internet connectivity
  - Connectivity within a site

- **Diagnose and resolve problems with client application connectivity.**

- **Diagnose and resolve information store problems.**

- **Diagnose and resolve server directory problems.**

- **Diagnose and resolve server resource problems.**

- **Diagnose and resolve message delivery problems.**

- **Diagnose and resolve backup problems and restore problems.**

- **Diagnose organization security problems.**

Exam objectives are subject to change at any time without prior notice and at Microsoft's sole discretion. Please visit Microsoft's Training & Certification Web site (www.microsoft.com/Train_Cert) for the most current exam objectives listing.

Of all the topics we look at in this book, this unit on troubleshooting will be the most intensive. Here, we'll tie together all the subjects and all the tools we reviewed in previous units. Troubleshooting Exchange Server 5.5 involves knowing your product, understanding your environment, and *practice*.

Troubleshooting the Exchange Server Installation and Upgrade

First, let's take a look at some areas in which you'll encounter the most common problems during the installation of Exchange Server 5.5.

Permissions

Be sure you are using a Windows NT account that has permissions on the site to add new servers to a site. If you are using an account in a different domain to add a server to a site, use trust relationships between domains.

Always use the Administrator account when installing Exchange. If you are going to use an account other than the Administrator account, be sure you use that account for every installation and that it has administrative permissions on the existing Exchange server.

Copying Files

You may run into problems while trying to copy files onto the server during installation. Here are a couple that are common and what you can do about them:

Problem	Resolution
You are running applications that are currently locking or using the files.	Closing all other applications will resolve this problem. Be sure that your Startup group on the Start menu is cleared so that no programs will autostart at logon.
Windows NT Event Viewer displays the error "The system cannot find the file specified."	Closing all applications and clearing the Startup group will fix this problem. The problem is that the ESE97 key in the Registry was not created. This will happen if you are running a program that is also writing to the Registry.

Network Configuration

You must use the same network protocol within a site and across sites for Exchange Server 5.5 to communicate and add servers to sites. If you cannot join another, you'll see this message: "Unable to connect to Server *ServerName.*"

Here are two problems that may be the cause and their resolutions.

Problem	Resolution
The account you are using to install Exchange does not have permissions for the other server.	Grant Administrator permissions for the other server at the site and for configuration objects.
The two servers do not have RPC network connectivity.	Check your network for errors. Be sure you have installed a common network protocol on both servers.

Exchange Services

If Exchange services do not start after installation, there may not be enough virtual memory configured. To solve this problem, use the System applet in Control Panel to create more pagefile space.

Troubleshooting Exchange Connectivity

In this section, we're going to review all the components that allow one Exchange server to communicate with another—the MTA, Site Connectors, the Directory Replication Connector, the Internet Mail Service, and foreign system connectors. Before we begin, though, let's review some general troubleshooting tools.

General Troubleshooting Tools

Some tools work with all connectors and all components. You should have worked with these tools already or at least have run them to see what they do. Some are part of Windows NT Server, and others are part of Exchange Server 5.5.

Windows NT Event Viewer

The Event Viewer is an NT tool that logs events registered by the System, Security, and Application classes. The Event Viewer is especially helpful in diagnosing problems in Windows startup. It lists the services that recorded error events.

Exchange Server 5.5 uses the Windows NT Event Viewer to list critical and fatal application events. To view the Event Viewer application log, follow these steps:

1. From the Desktop, choose Start ➤ Programs ➤ Administrative Tools to open the Event Viewer, displaying the default System log.

2. To view the application log, choose Log ➤ Application.

Event Viewer - Application Log on \\SANJOSE						
Log View Options Help						
Date	**Time**	**Source**	**Category**	**Event**	**User**	**Co**
⬤ 5/10/98	2:00:26 AM	ESE97	Online Defragmer 180		N/A	
⬤ 5/10/98	2:00:26 AM	ESE97	Online Defragmer 179		N/A	
⬤ 5/10/98	1:15:00 AM	ESE97	Online Defragmer 180		N/A	
⬤ 5/10/98	1:15:00 AM	ESE97	Online Defragmer 179		N/A	
⬤ 5/10/98	12:15:00 AM	ESE97	Online Defragmer 180		N/A	
⬤ 5/10/98	12:15:00 AM	ESE97	Online Defragmer 179		N/A	
⬤ 5/10/98	12:03:25 AM	MSExchangeSA	General	5004	N/A	
⬤ 5/10/98	12:03:19 AM	MSExchangeSA	General	5003	N/A	
⬤ 5/10/98	12:00:26 AM	ESE97	Online Defragmer 180		N/A	
⬤ 5/10/98	12:00:26 AM	ESE97	Online Defragmer 179		N/A	
⬤ 5/9/98	11:15:00 PM	ESE97	Online Defragmer 180		N/A	
i 5/9/98	11:15:00 PM	ESE97	Online Defragmer 179		N/A	
⬤ 5/9/98	11:01:24 PM	MSExchangeSA	General	5000	N/A	
⬤ 5/9/98	10:15:01 PM	ESE97	Online Defragmer 180		N/A	
⬤ 5/9/98	10:15:01 PM	ESE97	Online Defragmer 179		N/A	
⬤ 5/9/98	10:15:01 PM	ESE97	Online Defragmer 180		N/A	
⬤ 5/9/98	10:15:01 PM	ESE97	Online Defragmer 179		N/A	
⬤ 5/9/98	10:15:01 PM	MSExchangeIS Priv General		1207	N/A	
⬤ 5/9/98	10:15:01 PM	MSExchangeIS Pub General		1207	N/A	
⬤ 5/9/98	10:15:01 PM	MSExchangeIS Pub General		1206	N/A	
⬤ 5/9/98	10:15:01 PM	MSExchangeIS Priv General		1206	N/A	
⬤ 5/9/98	10:00:26 PM	ESE97	Online Defragmer 180		N/A	
⬤ 5/9/98	10:00:26 PM	ESE97	Online Defragmer 179		N/A	
⬤ 5/9/98	10:00:00 PM	ESE97	Online Defragmer 180		N/A	

By default, Exchange Server 5.5 writes critical and error events to the Event Viewer application log, but you can specify which events Exchange writes to the application log. Exchange writes to the application log in groups known as *categories*. You determine which categories you want to log and select them from the Diagnostic Logging property page for the following objects:

- MTA
- Directory
- Information Store
- Internet Mail Service
- Microsoft Mail Connector
- Microsoft Schedule+ Free/Busy Connector
- Microsoft Exchange Connector for Lotus cc:Mail

The categories are listed in Appendix A of the "Maintenance and Trouble-shooting Guide" of the Exchange Server 5.5. documentation.

To modify the diagnostic logging settings for the MTA, follow these steps:

1. Start the Exchange Administrator program and double-click the Site Configuration object that contains the site you want to modify.

2. Double-click the Server that you want to modify.

3. Select the MTA object.

4. Choose File ➤ Properties to open the Message Transfer Agent property pages.

5. Select the Diagnostics Logging tab:

Table 5.1 lists the properties for the Diagnostics Logging property page and their possible values.

Choosing Maximum for all categories will cause your hard disk to fill quite quickly. Choose Maximum only if you know the category that is presenting the problem.

TABLE 5.1 The MTA Diagnostics Logging property page	Property	Description
	Services	This section displays the services that are associated with the MTA. You can't modify this field.
	Category	This section lists the category of events and the current logging level.
	Logging Level	**None**–Logs only critical and errors events. This is the default.
		Minimum–Logs only high-level events. Use this setting when you're not sure which object is causing the problem.
		Medium–Logs steps taken to run a task. Use this setting when you've narrowed the problem to a service or a group of categories.
		Maximum–Logs all events, which is a lot of information. Choose this level only if you have narrowed the category or groups of categories causing the problem.

Message Tracking

The Message Tracking tool tracks a message from one location to another and records the stops along the way. If the message is rejected because of an error, this information is recorded, and you can review it to troubleshoot the MTA or connector causing the problem. You can enable Message Tracking on the Site objects of the MTA, on the information store, and on the Microsoft Mail Connector.

Enabling tracking on each component creates a log that contains the entries for that day. At midnight a new log is created for the new day.

Enabling Message Tracking on the MTA   To enable Message Tracking on the MTA, follow these steps:

1. Start the Exchange Administrator program.

2. Double-click the Site Configuration object that contains the site you want to modify.

3. Select the MTA Site Configuration object.

4. Choose File ➤ Properties to open the MTA Site Configuration property pages:

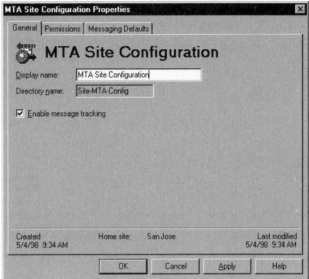

5. Select the General tab, and check the Enable Message Tracking checkbox.

You must restart the Exchange MTA to begin Message Tracking.

Enabling Message Tracking on the Microsoft Mail Connector   To enable Message Tracking on a Microsoft Mail Connector, follow these steps:

1. Start the Exchange Administrator program.

2. Double-click the Site Configuration object that contains the site you want to modify.

3. Double-click the Site Connector object.

4. Select the Microsoft Mail Connector.

5. Choose File ➤ Properties to open the Microsoft Mail Connector property pages.

6. Select the General tab, and check the Enable Message Tracking checkbox.

You must restart the Microsoft Mail Connector to begin Message Tracking.

Enabling Message Tracking on the Information Store   To enable Message Tracking on the information store, follow these steps:

1. Start the Exchange Administrator program.

2. Double-click the Site Configuration object that contains the site you want to modify.

3. Select the Information Store Site Configuration object.

4. Choose File ➤ Properties to open the Information Store Site Configuration property pages:

5. Select the General tab, and check the Enable Message Tracking checkbox.

You must restart the information store to begin Message Tracking.

Enabling Message Tracking on the Internet Mail Service   To turn on Message Tracking for the Internet Mail Service, you must configure each instance of the Internet Mail Service separately. If, for example, you have seven Internet Mail Service connectors in your site, you must configure each one to enable Message Tracking. It's a good idea to determine which Internet Mail Service you want to enable and turn on Message Tracking from one Internet Mail Service at a time. Turning on Message Tracking for all Internet Mail Services in your site will fill up your hard disk quickly.

To enable Message Tracking on the Internet Mail Service, follow these steps:

1. Start the Exchange Administrator program.

2. Double-click the Site Configuration object that contains the site you want to modify.

3. Double-click the Connections object.

4. Select the Internet Mail Service.

5. Choose File ➤ Properties to open the Internet Mail Service property pages:

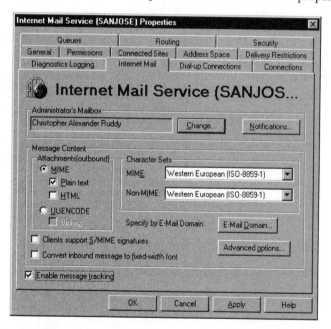

6. Select the Internet Mail tab, and check the Enable Message Tracking checkbox.

You must restart the Internet Mail Service to begin tracking messages.

Tracking a Message

After you've turned on Message Tracking, you're ready to start tracking messages. You must first select the server whose recipient is on the message you want to track.

To track a message, follow these steps:

1. Start the Exchange Administrator program.

2. Double-click the Site Configuration object that contains the site.

3. Double-click the Server object.

4. Select the server whose message you want to track.

5. Choose Tools ≻ Track Message to open the Select Message to Track dialog box:

6. Click the From button, select the sender from the global address list, and then choose Add. (Repeat this step to select additional senders.)

7. Click the Sent To box, select the name of a recipient in the global address list, and then choose Add. (Repeat this step to select additional recipients.

8. In the Look Back box, specify the number of days to search in the past.

9. Click Find Now.

Table 5.2 lists the options and the values associated with each option.

T A B L E 5.2 The options in the Select Message to Track dialog box	Option	Value
	From	Choose a mailbox that created the message you want to track. You can select only one mailbox to search.
	Sent To	Choose the mailbox or mailboxes to which the message was sent. If you leave this field blank, all recipients are found.
	Look Back	Set this box with the number of days in the past during which to search the message logs.
	Start Date	This box will appear with the date of the first log searched. This property will be calculated automatically based on the Look Back property.
	Search on Server	Set this box with the name of the server to be searched. Your home server will be selected by default.
	Time	After your search is complete, the searched list box will display this column with the time the message was sent. The symbol in the first column identifies the type of event.
	Size	This column displays the size of the message in bytes.
	No. Recp.	This column displays the number of recipients to which the message was addressed.
	Recipients	This column lists the first recipient in the recipient list. If you want to see the entire recipient list, click the Properties button.

You can use Message Tracking to do the following:

- Follow a message from one information store to another
- Track a ping message from one link monitor to another link monitor across sites

In this unit, we'll review how to use Message Tracking to diagnose and resolve problems with specific Exchange components. You can track messages from the following Exchange objects:

- MTA
- Directory Service Replication Messages
- Information Store
- Internet Mail Service
- Microsoft Mail Connector
- cc:Mail Connector

Tracking Log

The tracking log is stored in the `<drive letter>`: `\Exchsrvr\tracking.log` directory. The log name is the date the log was created in the format *yyyy-ddmm.log*. You can use any text editor to search this log directory. I prefer a text editor that has a Find option, such as WordPad or Microsoft Word.

NOTE For information on the event classes for each component and the actual event numbers, see Chapter 4 in the "Maintenance and Troubleshooting Guide" of the Exchange Server 5.5 documentation set.

We will look at the tracking log entries for specific components in this unit. You can find more detail and examples of the tracking log entries in the sections on the individual components.

Checking Message Queues

Each connector or communication object within Exchange Server 5.5 contains a Queue property page that lists messages waiting for some type of action. The queues have separate categories that reflect the action that needs to be taken on that message. For example, the MTA contains the following queues:

- Inbound messages waiting to be delivered
- Outbound messages waiting to be transferred

To view the Queue property page, follow these steps:

1. Start the Exchange Administrator program.

2. Double-click the Site Configuration object that contains the site you want to modify.

3. Double-click the Server object.

4. Select the server whose MTA queues you want to view. This opens the container for the server.

5. Select the MTA object.

6. Choose File ➤ Properties to open the Message Transfer Agent property pages:

7. Select the Queues tab.

8. To display the specific queues, click the Queue Name drop-down box and select the queue you want to view.

You can use the buttons on this property page to manipulate the queue:

Details: Click this button to see details about the selected message.

Refresh: The queue is constantly changing because messages are moving through the MTA at a fast rate. Click this button to refresh the queue to see the current messages.

Priority: You can change the order in which messages are delivered by changing the priority of messages. Your choices are high, normal, and low. To change the priority of a message, select it, click the Priority button, and choose the new priority of the message.

Delete: I use this button to delete messages that I know are either bad or blocking the queue or to delete messages going to a destination that no longer exists. You can delete any message in the queue using this button.

Foreign Connectivity

You can use a number of tools and utilities to diagnose and resolve problems with foreign mail systems. Some are available with Exchange Server 5.5, and others are available from third-party vendors. In this section, we'll look at the resources you have to troubleshoot problems with the Microsoft Mail Connector and cc:Mail Connector.

Diagnosing and Resolving Problems with the Microsoft Mail Connector

Let's begin by reviewing the tools that you use to diagnose problems with the Microsoft Mail Connector.

Diagnostics Logging: This tool tracks all events that occur with the Microsoft Mail Connector and writes them to the Windows NT Event Viewer application log. You then use the Event Viewer to view this log. Be careful to log only the events associated with a connector problem; tracking all events will affect your disk space.

Windows NT Performance Monitor: Review your Microsoft Mail Connector performance by using the Windows NT Performance Monitor. Become familiar with the normal operation of the connector by creating a baseline log of connector transactions.

Message Queues: Use the Microsoft Mail Connector Queues property page to find out if mail is moving in and out of this connector.

Message Tracking: Enabling Message Tracking for the connector creates a log file of all the events associated with the delivery of a message. Use this feature when you want to track the failure of a message to find out which component is causing the problem.

You'll find instructions on how to start most of these tools in the "General Troubleshooting Tools" section earlier in this unit, and you'll find information on using NT Performance counters for the Microsoft Mail Connector in the "Monitoring the Microsoft Mail Connector" section in Unit 4.

Let's review some of the problems that can occur with the Microsoft Mail Connector and their possible solutions.

Symptom: Mail isn't moving.

Problem	Resolution
Messages are stalled in the MS Mail queues.	Return or delete some of the oldest messages in the queue. If you can't, the outbound mail queue may be failing.
The MS Mail Interchange Service is not running.	Check the Windows NT application log for event problems. If there aren't any, restart the Interchange service using the Services applet in Control Panel.
The connector mail database is corrupted.	Check that the connector postoffice directories exist and that their contents are intact.
You do not have permissions for the postoffice share or volumes.	Have an MS Mail administrator grant Read, Write, and Delete permissions to the PC MTA.

Symptom: You can't create an instance.

Problem	Resolution
An instance with the same name previously existed and was incorrectly removed.	Use a different name or choose Apply three times and ignore the messages.
You don't have permission to create instances.	Have the site administrator grant you permissions.

Symptom: Some or all mail from MS Mail (PC) to Microsoft Exchange Server recipients is returned as nondeliverable.

Problem	Resolution
The address space is incorrect.	Check your address space for the recipients against the address space for the connector.
The Routing table was not rebuilt after the last changes.	Recalculate the Routing table in the MTA General property page.

Diagnosing and Resolving Problems with the cc:Mail Connector for Lotus

You can use a couple of tools to diagnose problems with the cc:Mail Connector.

Diagnostics Logging: This tool tracks all events that occur with the cc:Mail Connector and writes them to the Windows NT Event Viewer application log. You then use the Event Viewer to view this log. Be careful to log only the events associated with a connector problem; tracking all events will affect your disk space. (See the section "General Trouble-shooting Tools" for instructions on how to start the Event Viewer.)

Windows NT Performance Monitor: Review your cc:Mail Connector performance by using the Windows NT Performance Monitor. Become familiar with the normal operation of the connector by creating a baseline log of connector transactions. (You'll find information on the NT Performance counters in the "Monitoring the Microsoft Mail Connector" section in Unit 4.)

Site-to-Site Connectivity

Before we look at the tools you can use to troubleshoot site-to-site connectivity, let's review why you use one type of site connector over another. Table 5.3 lists the site connectors and their uses.

T A B L E 5.3 Comparing site connectors	Site Connector	Uses
	Site Connector	Use this site connector if your connections are stable and permanent across a LAN. You cannot schedule this connector, and therefore it will report errors if the network connections are not up. Use this connector when you have a fast link across sites.
	X.400 Connector	Use this connector when you want to schedule connections across a LAN or across an X.400 network. This connector converts messages from the Exchange message format to X.400 format.
	Dynamic RAS Connector	Use this connector if the network connections across the sites are not permanent and you must use a dial-up connection to connect the two sites. You can schedule this connector.
	Internet Mail Service	Use this connector when you want to connect two sites across a TCP/IP network. You can also use this connector to connect two sites across the Internet, using the Internet as your connection backbone. You can schedule this connector.

Diagnosing and Resolving Site Connector Problems

You can use the following tools to help track and resolve problems with site connectors:

Diagnostics Logging: This tool tracks all events that occur with your site connector and writes them to the Windows NT Event Viewer application log. You then use the Event Viewer to view this log. Be careful to log only the events associated with a connector problem; tracking all events will affect your disk space.

Windows NT Performance Monitor: Review your connector's performance by using the Windows NT Performance Monitor. Become familiar with the normal operation of the connector by creating a baseline log of connector transactions.

Message Queues: Use the MTA Queues property page to find out if mail is moving in and out of this connector.

Message Tracking: Enabling Message Tracking for the connector creates a log file of all events associated with the delivery of a message. Use this feature when you want to track the failure of a message to find out which component is causing the problem.

Now let's look at some problems that can occur with the connectors across sites and the possible solutions.

Symptom: You can't view servers in another site. If the servers have never been visible, either directory replication was not configured or the replication was unsuccessful. You can resolve this problem in a couple of ways:

- Start and run a link monitor to check your connections. If connections are present, check the directory replication connector at the other site.

- Trace the path of a message in the Message Tracking log to find out which error message was received when attempting to connect to the other site.

Symptom: There are problems with mail between sites.

Problem	Resolution
The address space is incorrect.	Run the Exchange Administrator program and check the address space for the connection.
One of the MTAs is down.	Run and start a server monitor or the Performance Monitor to check the status of the connector. You can also use Message Queues to check the connection.

Problem	Resolution
Mail messages aren't scheduled to be delivered across your sites at this time.	Check the Schedule property page for the specific connector.
Site-to-site communication is configured correctly, but the transport is not routed between sites on the WAN.	Check your network connections, and verify that you are using the correct network protocol across your sites. If you are using bridgehead servers, check the status of the servers.
Mail is returned to sender because of its size.	Read the NDR to determine the exact cause of the error. If it is size, check the Connector property pages to determine if there is a size limit for this connector. If there isn't, check the sender's Mailbox Advanced property page to see if the sender has a size limit.
Message transfer was working, but it stopped after a change in network configuration.	The symptoms indicate a problem with the network. Use your Windows NT Server network tools to diagnose and correct any network protocol or hardware problems.

Diagnosing and Resolving Directory Replication Connector Problems

As you recall, changes in the directory within a site are propagated automatically, but you must configure replication across sites using a Directory Replication Connector. You can use the following tools to help diagnose and troubleshoot problems with replication across sites:

Diagnostics Logging: This tool tracks all events that occur with the Directory Replication Connector and writes them to the Windows NT Event Viewer application log. You then use the Event Viewer to view this log. Be careful to log only the events associated with a connector problem; tracking all events will affect your disk space.

Windows NT Performance Monitor: Review your Directory Replication performance by using the Windows NT Performance Monitor. Become familiar with normal operations of the connector by creating a baseline log of connector transactions.

Message Queues: Use the MTA Queues property page to find out if mail is moving in and out of this connector.

Message Tracking: Enabling Message Tracking for the connector creates a log file with all the events associated with the delivery of a message. Use this feature when you want to track the failure of a message to find out which component is causing the problem.

Now, let's look at one of the problems that can occur with the Directory Replication Connector and the possible solutions.

The Directory Replication Connector depends on the messaging site connectors that exist between sites. If the site connector is unavailable, you will have problems with Directory Replication across sites. First, check the Site connector. If everything with the site connector is fine, troubleshoot the Directory Replication Connector.

Symptom: Your Exchange Administrator program does not reflect the new sites you've added.

Problem	Resolution
The directory has not yet been replicated.	Check the replication schedule in the Schedule property page for this connector. You can accelerate the replication by clicking the Update Now button on the General property page of the connector.
	If your problem persists, increase the diagnostic logging level on the directory, and review the events in the Windows NT application log.

Problem	Resolution
Replication between sites has failed.	Check the Directory events in the Windows NT application log. Run the Consistency Knowledge Check available on the General property page of the Directory Replication connector.
	Create and run a server and Performance Monitor to make sure that directory information in both sites is being replicated.

Diagnosing and Resolving Internet Mail Service Problems

Troubleshooting the Internet Mail Service can be confusing, especially if you don't know if the problem resides with your Exchange server, your TCP/IP network, or your connection to the Internet. In this section, we'll review the problems with the Exchange server and your TCP/IP network.

You can use the following tools to troubleshoot the Internet Mail Service:

Diagnostics Logging: This tool tracks all events that occur with your Internet Mail Service and writes them to the Windows NT Event Viewer application log. You then use the Event Viewer to view this log. In addition, your Internet Mail Service can create a TCP/IP-compliant SMTP protocol log based on RFC 821. If you are familiar with troubleshooting from an SMTP protocol log, you can use the same troubleshooting methods on the Internet Mail Service.

For more information on the SMTP protocol log, see RFC 821. For information on how to get an RFC, see the Microsoft Windows NT 4 documentation.

Windows NT Performance Monitor: Review your Internet Mail Service performance by using the Windows NT Performance Monitor. Become familiar with normal operations of the connector by creating a baseline log of connector transactions.

Message Queues: Use the Internet Mail Service Queues property page to find out if mail is moving in and out of this connector.

Message Tracking: Enabling Message Tracking for the Internet Mail Service creates a log file of all events associated with the delivery of a message. Use this feature when you want to track the failure of a message to find out which component is causing the problem.

Let's look at some of the problems that can occur with the Internet Mail Service.

Symptom: The Internet Mail Service will not start.

Problem	Resolution
TCP/IP is not installed.	Install TCP/IP from the Windows NT Service 4 CD. You will need to reinstall NT Service Pack 3.
The delivery route of an e-mail domain can't be resolved. At least one name in the Email Domain box is incorrect.	Check and verify that the e-mail address is correctly spelled or if it appears at all in the Internet Mail Service Connections property page. If the domain name is correct, verify that DNS is configured correctly on your server.
The domain name of the Internet Mail Service host is missing.	Add the host domain name to the DNS Configuration box in the Network property page for this server.
A Messaging Application Programming Interface (MAPI) initialization error occurred.	Stop and restart all Exchange Server services.
	Stop and restart the Internet Mail Service. From the Services applet in Control Panel, select the Internet Mail Service, and verify that the startup parameters are the same as those for the other services.

Symptom: No messages are being sent or received.

Problem	Resolution
An Internet Mail Service or the MTA on the Internet Mail Service's server is not running.	Use a server monitor or Performance Monitor to confirm that the services are running. Restart the Internet Mail Service if the service is not running.
The Internet Mail Service is not on the network.	Send a TCP/IP ping command to the Internet Mail Service host or try to telnet to port 25 to see if the connection is working. If not, use your network diagnostic tools to determine the error.

Symptom: You can't send outbound messages through the Internet Mail Service.

Problem	Resolution
The MTA is down.	Restart the MTA.
The address space is not configured.	Check the Internet Mail Service Address Space property page to verify that the address space is correct and is defined on this page.
The MTA is returning the message.	Check the Internet Mail Service Address Space property page and enter an asterisk (*) in the Email Domain box so that all SMTP message traffic is pushed through the Internet Mail Service.
The address for the DNS server is incorrect.	Check the DNS server address using the Network Control applet in Control Panel.
The domain address for Exchange Server users is invalid.	Verify that the SMTP site is in the Site Addressing property page.

Symptom: Changes in the Exchange Administrator program aren't taking effect. The problem here is that all changes for the Internet Mail Service take effect only when you restart the service. To resolve this problem, try the following:

- Restart the Internet Mail Service.

- If your Exchange server is slow, the information may not have replicated. Wait a few minutes to ensure that the changes have been propagated. If the changes don't propagate, stop and restart the service.

Symptoms: You can't send mail to a user on the Internet.

Problem	Resolution
Mail doesn't arrive because the server is down or the Internet Mail Service is down.	Configure Message Tracking on the Internet Mail Service and track a message to locate the problem.
Mail is returned because the sender's mailbox contains delivery restrictions that prevent the sender from using the Internet.	Change the delivery restrictions on the Internet Mail Service.
An address in the user's Personal Address Book is incorrect.	Use the client global address list to address mail.
Mail is returned as undeliverable.	Track the message using the Message-Tracking log. You need to follow the path of the message and find the point at which the message is returned. The entry for the NDR will indicate where the transfer of the message failed.

Symptom: Mail sent from Microsoft Exchange Server is received with garbled text or extra attachments. The problem here is that the message was formatted with rich text and could not be resolved by the receiving systems. To resolve this problem, remove the rich text formatting by changing the option in one of the following objects:

- From the Internet Mail Service's Internet Mail property page, choose Interoperability. Uncheck the Send Microsoft Exchange Rich Text Formatting checkbox.

- For a custom recipient, uncheck the Allow Rich Text in Messages checkbox.

- From a user's Personal Address Book, double-click the recipient to open the property page for the recipient. Select the Address tab, and uncheck the *Always send to this recipient in Microsoft Exchange rich text format* checkbox.

Troubleshooting the Exchange Client

Diagnosing and resolving Exchange client problems is an involved process. A user reports the simple problem that he or she is having trouble connecting. You then must find the area that is causing the connection problem. Here are some questions to ask:

- Is the Exchange server down or is the network experiencing problems?

- If the server is up, are the network connections to the client computer the problem?

- If the network checks out, is the problem with the client's computer?

- If the problem involves the client computer, is it only the Exchange client or is it all network applications?

If the problem involves only the Exchange client, here are some further avenues to explore.

Symptom: You can't connect to a server.

Problem	Resolution
The profile is not configured correctly.	Check the server and mailbox name assigned to the client.
The server is unavailable.	Use the `net view` command from a command prompt to see if the server is running. If you are running a NetWare client, use the `ping` command.
The server is using a different network protocol.	If a large number of clients are using a specific protocol, update the server. If only a few clients are using a specific protocol, add the server protocol to the client.
The common network protocol is not routed between LAN segments.	Move the client to the server computers to the correct LAN segment. It may be easier, however, to add the network protocol to the router or bridge.
You do not have user permission for the mailbox.	Check the Mailbox Permission property page and modify the permission list if necessary.

Symptom: Mail sent to a user never arrives.

Problem	Resolution
There is a problem on a foreign system	Use the Message Tracking log to trace messages. Check the Windows NT application log for errors. If it is an Internet message, use the SMTP protocol log to troubleshoot.

Problem	Resolution
The message is still in the Outbox because the information store or MTA is not running.	Check the information store with the Windows NT Performance Monitor. Check that the originator can send e-mail to other Exchange Server mailboxes. If so, the problem is with that specific mailbox.
The message stopped at an intermediate server or system.	Use Message Tracking to determine which server or system is the problem.

Troubleshooting the Information Store

Problems with the information store are different from those with the connectors. The information store is a database, and you probably know from personal experience that databases become corrupt from time to time. In this section, we'll look at the tools you can use to diagnose and resolve problems with the information store.

Obtaining Information Store Status Data

You can quickly check the status of your information store by using the status information property pages of the private and public information stores. To display these pages, follow these steps:

1. Start the Exchange Administrator program.

2. Double-click the site whose information stores you want to check.

3. Select the server whose information store you want to view; this displays the objects contained within the server.

4. Double-click the public or private information store to open the container and display the status pages.

5. Select the view object for the specific view you need.

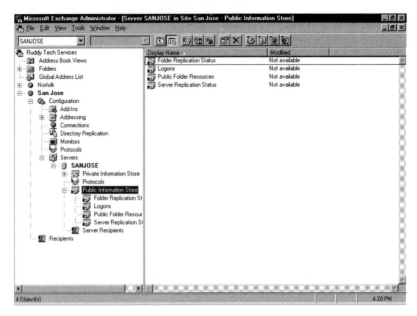

The Logon status view displays information about the logons to your server's information store. By default, the Logon status view displays two columns—User Name and Mailbox Name. You can customize the columns to view additional properties and values. Table 5.4 lists the columns available for the Logon view for the public/private information store.

	Column	Description
T A B L E 5.4 Public/private information store Logon status view	User Name	Displays the Windows NT username of the user currently logged on. This column is included in the default view.
	Mailbox	Displays the mailbox display name. This column is used in the default view.
	Windows NT Account	Displays the Windows NT username of the last user who logged on to use this mailbox or public folder. This column is used in the default view.
	Logon Time	Displays the last time that a user logged on. This column is used in the default view.

TABLE 5.4 *(cont.)*	Column	Description
Public/private information store Logon status view	Last Access Time	Displays the date a user last logged on. This column is used in the default view.
	Client Version	Used when you want to know the version of the client software that was used in the last logon. This column is used in the default view.
	Code Page	Displays the code page of the client.
	Folder Ops	Displays the total number of folder operations in the last minute. Opening, closing, or accessing a folder is considered a folder operation.
	Full Mailbox Directory Name	Displays the full e-mail address of the mailbox being accessed (only used for the private information store).
	Full User Directory Name	Displays the full user name of the mailbox that is being displayed.
	Host Address	Displays the IP address of the client.
	Locale ID	Displays the local language that the client is using.
	Messaging Ops	Displays the total number of messaging operations in the last minute. Creating, sending, reading, or deleting a message is considered a messaging operation.
	Open Attachments	Displays the total number of open attachments.
	Open Folders	Displays the total number of open folders.
	Open Messages	Displays the total number of open messages.
	Other Ops	Displays the total number of miscellaneous operations in the last minute.
	Progress Ops	Displays the total number of progress operations in the last minute. Progress operations tell the user how long a task will take.

	Column	Description
T A B L E 5.4 (cont.) Public/private information store Logon status view	Stream Ops	Displays the total number of stream operations in the last minute.
	Table Ops	Displays the total number of table operations. A table operation displays the contents of a folder.
	Total Ops	Displays the total number of operations in the last minute.
	Transfer Ops	Displays the total number of transfer operations in the last minute. Moving a message and associated data in and out of a folder is considered a transfer operation.

To view mailbox resources, select the Mailbox object in the Private information store status object list:

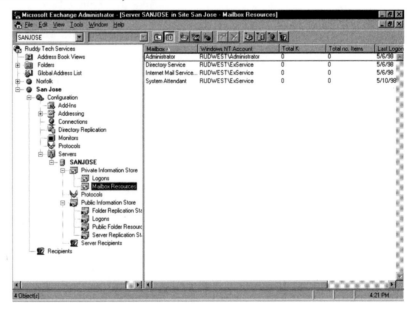

Table 5.5 lists and describes the columns available for view.

TABLE 5.5	Column	Description
Information store mailbox resource column descriptions	Mailbox	Displays the name of the mailbox. This column is used in the default view.
	Windows NT Account	Displays the Windows NT Account name of the last user to log on to this mailbox. This column is used in the default view.
	Total K	Displays the total amount of disk space used by this mailbox. This field reports on all objects associated with the mailbox, including attachments, messages, and hidden system information. This column is used in the default view.
	Total Number of Items	Displays the total number of nonassociated messages that are stored in the mailbox. This column is used in the default view.
	Last Logon Time	Displays the last time a user logged on to this mailbox. This column is used in the default view.
	Last Logoff Time	Displays the last time a user logged off this mailbox. This column is used in the default view.
	Deleted Items K	Displays the total amount of disk space used by deleted items that have been retained.
	Full Mailbox Directory Name	Displays the full e-mail address of the mailbox you are viewing.
	Storage Limits	Displays the status of the mailbox's storage limits.
	Total Number of Associated Messages	Displays the total number of associated messages in the mailbox, including forms, view, reply templates, and deferred action messages.

To view a folder's replication status, select the Folder Replication Status view in the Public Information Store status view list:

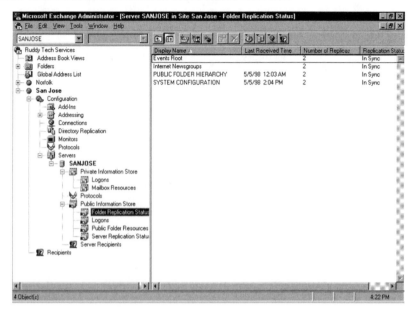

Table 5.6 lists the columns available for view.

	Column	Description
T A B L E 5.6 Information Store folder replication status view column descriptions	Display Name	Displays the name of the public folder as it appears in the Address Book. This column is used in the default view.
	Last Received Time	Displays when the last update was received. This column is used in the default view.
	Number of Replicas	Displays the total number of replicas of this folder that have been copied in your site. This column is used in the default view.
	Replication Status	Displays the status of the folder. *In sync* indicates that the folder is in synchronization across the site. *Local modified* indicates that your current server's replica has been modified and that the modifications have not been propagated across the site. This column is used in the default view.
	Folder	Displays the public folder name.

To view pubic folder resources, select the Public Folder Resources view in the Public Information Store status view list:

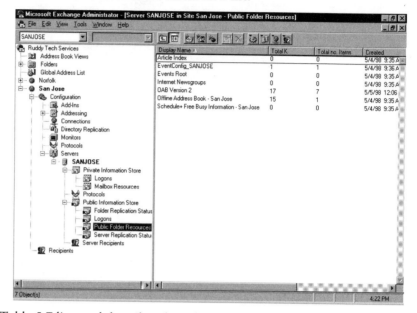

Table 5.7 lists and describes the columns available for view.

TABLE 5.7	Column	Description
Information store public folder resource column descriptions	Display Name	Displays the name of the public folder. This column is used in the default view.
	Total K	Displays the total amount of disk space this folder (including messages, attachments, and associated messages) occupies on this public information store. This column is used in the default view.
	Total Number of Items	Displays the total number of nonassociated items. This column is used in the default view.
	Created	Displays the date this folder was created. This column is used in the default view.
	Last Access Time	Displays the date that this folder was last accessed. This column is used in the default view.

	Column	Description
TABLE 5.7 *(cont.)* Information store public folder resource column descriptions	Number of Owners	Displays the number of Exchange users who have owner permissions on this folder. This column is used in the default view.
	Number of Contacts	Displays the number of Exchange users who have been assigned contact permissions. This column is used in the default view.
	Folder	Displays the name of the folder.
	Folder Path	Displays this folder's path.
	Total Number of Associated Messages	Displays the number of associated folder items.
	Deleted Items K	Displays the total amount of disk space currently being used by retained deleted items.

To view the server's replication status, select the server Replication Status view in the Public Information Store view list:

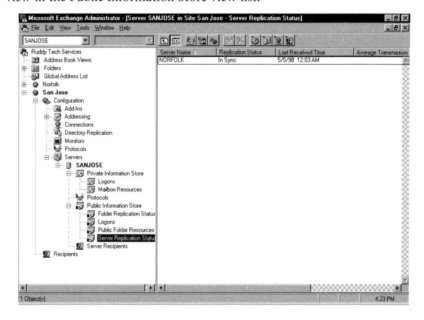

Table 5.8 lists the columns available for view.

TABLE 5.8	Column	Description
The information store server replication column descriptions	Server Name	Displays the name of the current server. This column is used in the default view.
	Replication Status	Displays the status of the folder. *In sync* indicates that the folder is in synchronization across the site. *Local modified* indicates that your current server's replica has been modified and that the modifications have not been propagated across the site. This column is used in the default view.
	Last Received Time	Displays the last time this local server received updates from the selected server. This column is used in the default view.
	Average Transmission Time	Displays the average time to send updates from the local server to the selected server. This column is used in the default view.
	Last Transmission Time	Displays the time for the last transmissions from the local server to the selected server. This column is used in the default view.

Running the Information Store Integrity Checker (ISINTEG)

Exchange Server 5.5 includes ISINTEG (Information Store Integrity Checker), a utility that can report and fix common errors with your information store databases. If you restore any of the Exchange information store databases from backup, ISINTEG can correct any inconsistencies between the information in the restored database and the information about the database in the Registry.

Run ISINTEG whenever errors are preventing the information store from starting or preventing your users from connecting to the information store.

The ISINTEG utility runs in one of three modes:

Check: Use this mode whenever you want to diagnose errors in the information store database, including incorrect reference counts, table errors, and unreferenced objects. ISINTEG writes these errors out in a log and displays them on the screen.

Check and Fix: Use this mode only on the advice of Microsoft Technical Support. Check and Fix runs in Check mode but also fixes any errors it finds. Be sure to back up your information store before running this utility.

Patch: Exchange Server 5.5 maintains a *GUI (Global Unique Identifier)* on the information store. If this GUI doesn't match the GUI for the information store databases stored in the Registry, the information store will not start. This will happen whenever you have restored your information stores from a backup. In Patch mode, ISINTEG replaces GUIs and patches the information used to backfill your information store. Patching this information prevents the backfill process from running on your information store. After running ISINTEG in Patch mode, you will be able to start your information store.

To run the ISINTEG utility, follow these steps:

1. Stop the information store services from the Services applet in Control Panel.

2. Start a command prompt session and type the following at the command line:

   ```
   <drive letter>:\exchsrvr\bin\ISINTEG -<store>
   ➡-<option list> -l<log name>
   ```

The options for the ISINTEG utility are:

Option	Description
-?	Help.
-pri	Checks the private information store.
-pub	Checks the public information store.

Option	Description
-fix	Runs the utility in Fix mode. Run this only on the advice of Microsoft Technical Support.
-verbose	Prints a report on all activity and verifies the information store.
-l	Changes the name of the log file. The default is isinteg.pri or isinteg.pub.

Resolving Problems with the Information Store

Use the following tools to help diagnose problems with the information store:

Diagnostics Logging: This tool tracks all events that occur with your information store and writes them to the Windows NT Event Viewer application log. You then use the Event Viewer to view this log. Be careful to log only the events associated with a problem with a public folder or a user mailbox; tracking all events will affect your disk space.

Windows NT Performance Monitor: Review your information store performance by using the Windows NT Performance Monitor. Become familiar with the normal operations of the public and private information stores by creating a baseline log of connector transactions.

Message Tracking: Enabling Message Tracking creates a log file of all events associated with the delivery of a message. Use this feature to track the failure of a message when you suspect that the information store is causing the problem.

ISINTEG Utility: Use this utility when restoring an information store from backup.

Public Folder Status Information: Use this tool when you suspect that public folders are not being replicated. Also, use this to view the status of mailboxes and public folders.

Let's look at some common problems associated with the information store.

Symptom: You can't access a public folder.

Problem	Resolution
The server with the replica of the public folder is not running.	Check to see if the home server of the public folder is running.
A replica of the public folder is on a server that the client network protocol can't reach.	This indicates that your network is having problems. Verify that your network is up by checking the status of your routers, bridges, and/or gateway. If a common protocol is missing, add it using the Network applet in Control Panel.
A replica of a public folder is on a server in a site where affinities have not been established.	Check the Information Store Site Configuration for Public Folder Affinity checkbox to set the affinity for this public folder.
You do not have permissions to access the folder.	Use the e-mail client to grant permissions to access the public folder.
You have lost the connection to the server.	Restart your client.

Troubleshooting the Directory Service

Diagnosing and resolving problems with the Directory Service involves monitoring and knowing how your Directory Service performs under a normal load. The following tools are available to help you diagnose and resolve problems that occur with your Directory Service:

Diagnostics Logging: This tool tracks all events that occur with your Directory Service and writes them to the Windows NT Event Viewer application log. You then use the Event Viewer to view this log. Be careful to log only the events associated with a problem with the Directory Service; tracking all events will affect your disk space.

Windows NT Performance Monitor: Review your Directory Service performance by using the Windows NT Performance Monitor. Become familiar with the normal operation of the Directory Service by creating a baseline log of connector transactions.

Message Tracking: Enabling Message Tracking for the Directory Service creates a log file of all the events associated with the delivery of Directory Replication messages. Use this feature when you want to track the failure of a message to find out which component is causing the problem.

Now, let's look at some common problems that can occur with the Directory Service and how to resolve them.

Symptom: Directory information isn't the same between servers within a site.

Problem	Resolution
Directory Replication within a site has failed or is delayed.	Check the Windows NT Server application log and use filtering to display those messages associated with replication.
	Use a server monitor to verify that both servers are running normally.
The network is down between servers.	Use the ping or the Net Use command between servers to see if they communicate. If not, use your network management tools to locate the break.

Symptom: Directory information isn't the same between servers in different sites.

Problem	Fix
The directory has not yet been replicated.	Use the Directory Replication Connector property pages to determine if the schedule is set to Never. Click the Update Now button on the General property page to start the replication.
	If the problem persists, use an elevated diagnostic logging level to help determine which component is causing the problem.

Problem	Fix
Replication between sites has failed.	Check your Windows NT application log for events that indicate a problem with the Directory Service.
	Configure and start a server monitor session to verify that servers are transferring replication information normally.
	Track replication messages between sites to identify which component is causing the error.

Troubleshooting Exchange Resource Problems

Your Exchange server will not perform well if the operating system and hardware are not performing well. In this section, we'll look at some of the tools you can use to monitor and resolve problems with your hardware and software.

Diagnostics Logging: This tool tracks all events that occur with your Exchange Server and writes them to the Windows NT Event Viewer application log. You can then use the Event Viewer to view this log. Be careful that you log only specific events; tracking all events will affect your disk space.

Windows NT Performance Monitor: Review your Exchange Server's performance by using the Windows NT Performance Monitor. Become familiar with the normal operation of the server by creating a baseline log of connector transactions.

Let's look at some of the problems that can occur with your resources.

Symptom: The hard disk is busy more than 90 percent of the time.

Problem	Resolution
There is not enough RAM; Windows NT is using virtual memory.	Use the Windows NT Performance Monitor to check the number of page faults per second. Add more physical memory, or build another Exchange server and move half the load to the new server.
Public folders are busy.	Use the Windows NT Performance Monitor to check the rate of open message and folder operations. Consider moving the public information store to another hard drive or moving public folders to a server that is not being fully utilized.
Private folders are busy.	Use the Windows NT Performance Monitor to check the rate of message submissions and delivery. Consider moving the mailboxes with the most activity to a server where the majority of those mailbox recipients are located.
The gateway or connector is constantly busy.	Use the Windows NT Performance Monitor to check the rate of inbound and outbound messages and their sizes. Consider adding a second gateway to balance the load and to increase the scheduled interval for this job to run.

Troubleshooting Message Delivery

Diagnosing and resolving message-delivery problems usually involves your network or the MTA. In this section, I'll give you some tips to help you troubleshoot message delivery.

You can use the following tools to track message delivery:

Diagnostics Logging: This tool tracks all events that occur with the MTA and the components involved with messaging and writes them to the Windows NT Event Viewer application log. You then use the Event Viewer to view this log. Be careful to log only the events associated with an MTA problem; tracking all events will affect your disk space.

Windows NT Performance Monitor: Review your MTA performance by using the Windows NT Performance Monitor. Become familiar with the normal operation of the MTA by creating a baseline log of message delivery transactions.

Message Queues: Use the MTA Queues property page to find out if mail is moving in and out of this server.

Message Tracking: Enabling Message Tracking for the server creates a log file of all events associated with the delivery of a message. Use this tool when you want to track the failure of a message to find out which component is causing the problem.

Reading and Understanding Your Tracking Log

As I mentioned, a Message Tracking log is built in the exchsrvr\tracking.log directory, when you turn on Message Tracking in any component that supports Message Tracking. You can track a message using the Message Tracking tool in the Exchange Administrator program, but you can search this log if you want a detailed report.

Open the log using any text editor such as Notepad or WordPad. Table 5.9 defines the fields in the tab-separated records. Table 5.10 defines the events that appear in the records.

T A B L E 5.9:   Message Tracking log fields

Field #	Name	Contents
1	Message ID	The message ID, which is a unique number assigned by Exchange Server. You can use this ID to track a message from origination to delivery.
2	Event #	The event type. Table 5.10 contains a list of the events used for troubleshooting.

T A B L E 5.9: Message Tracking log fields *(continued)*

Field #	Name	Contents
3	Date/Time	The date and time of the event.
4	Gateway Name	The name of the gateway or connector that generated the event. If no connector was used in the delivery of this message, this field is empty.
5	Partner Name	The name of the MTA or the messaging service associated with the event.
6	Remote ID	The message ID used by the connector or the gateway.
7	Originator	The unique distinguished name of the originating mailbox, if known.
8	Priority	Priority set by sender: 0=Normal, 1=High, -1=Low.
9	Length	The message length in bytes.
10	Seconds	The total transport time in seconds.
11	Cost	The cost per second for message transfer. Exchange Server does not use this field; therefore, the cost is always 1.
12	Recipients	The number of recipients.
13	Recipient Name	The distinguished name of the recipient. There is one field for each recipient.
14	Recipient Report Status	A number indicating the result of an attempt to deliver a report to the recipient: 0=Delivered; 1=Not Delivered.

T A B L E 5.10: Tracking Log Event Group List

Event #	Name	Contents
0, 2, 3	Incoming Messages	Information about message, probe, and report transfer in. The MTA completed the transfer of responsibility from a gateway, from an X.400 link, or from the MTA into the local MTA.
4, 5	Submission	Information about how a message or a probe was submitted to the MTA.

T A B L E 5.10: Tracking Log Event Group List *(continued)*

Event #	Name	Contents
6, 7, 8	Outgoing Messages	Information about message, probe, and report transfer out. The MTA completed the transfer of responsibility to a gateway, to an X.400 link, or from the MTA to a remote MTA.
9, 10	Delivery	Information about the successful delivery of a message or a report.
43, 50, 51, 52	Message Deleted	Information about messages that were deleted by an administrator.
1000	Local Delivery	Information on messages for which the sender and recipient are on the same server.
1001, 1002	Backbone Transfers	Information about transfers from another MAPI system across a connector.
1003 through 1007	Gateway Transfers	Information about transfers in and out by messages and reports.
1010 through 1018	SMTP Protocol events	Information about SMTP transfers of messages and reports, both incoming and outgoing.

For a detailed listing of the event groups, see the "Maintenance and Troubleshooting Guide" in the Exchange Server 5.5 documentation.

Using MTACHECK to Repair the MTA

Whenever messages stop moving through your message queues, run the Exchange Server 5.5 MTACHECK. The MTACHECK looks for objects that are corrupt and that interfere with the processing of messages through your server's MTA.

Run the MTACHECK whenever messages stop and whenever you want to check your MTAs integrity. To run the MTACHECK, follow these steps:

1. From the Services applet in Control Panel, stop the MTA.

2. Empty the `<drive letter>:\exchsrvr\Mtadata\Mtacheck.out\*.*`.

3. Open a command prompt and enter:

   `<drive letter>:\exchsrvr\bin\mtacheck [-f] filename [-v]`

The –**f** option in the command allows you to specify a log file in which to record the output of the MTACHECK command. The –v option in the command gives you more verbose information regarding the processing of the MTACHECK.

Diagnosing and Resolving Message Delivery

In this section, we'll take a look at some of the problems that prevent messages from being delivered.

Symptom: The MTA queue is growing.

Problem	Resolution
There is not enough bandwidth to support the traffic.	Run a network analyzer to check network traffic and utilization.
The destination MTA is down.	Run a server monitor and Performance Monitor to determine if services are running and mail is being processed.
The network is down between MTAs.	Run the `ping` or `net use` command from the working server to the server that is down.

Symptom: There are problems with mail between sites. If one of the MTAs is down, you can run a server monitor or Performance Monitor to check the status of the remote MTA. You can also use message queues to determine if the MTA is down or if the mail queue is slow. A long queue can indicate a problem with an incorrectly configured connector

Symptom: The recipient was not found.

Problem	Resolution
There is no such address in the network or in the domain of the gateway host.	Verify the address and the mapping of the address to the host.

Problem	Resolution
The address was not unique.	Check the address. Be sure that all addresses in your organization are unique. Check for duplicate user names across sites.
The address was a phrase in several address, but not an entire address of any mailbox.	Check the address by sending a message and pressing Ctrl+K to verify the address before the message is sent.

Symptom: The host is unreachable.

Problem	Resolution
The receiving host is not operating.	Run a link monitor to verify that the remote host is operational.
There is no such host in the domain, or the domain does not exist.	Check your DNS server for errors and misspellings. Verify that the local host is assigned a DNS server in the Network properties from Control Panel.

Troubleshooting Advanced Security

Most problems associated with advanced security have to do with the startup of the KM Server. The one other area that causes problems is the assignment and revocation of user security tokens. The Windows NT Event Viewer is valuable in tracking down problems with the KM Server. Exchange Server provides Diagnostics Logging for the KM Server but supports only the logging of critical and error events. Use the Windows NT Event Viewer to display messages pertaining to the KM Server in the Windows NT Security log.

Now, let's look at a couple of problems that can occur with advanced security.

Symptom: A mailbox user cannot use the encryption feature.

Problem	Resolution
The user is not authorized to use Advanced Security.	Check the Security tab on the user's mailbox and enable Advanced Security.
The user's security token has been revoked.	Enable the security token by choosing Recover Security Key on the Mailbox Security property page for this user.

Symptom: Mailbox users are unable to decrypt or verify the signature on messages sent from users in another site. The problem is that there are two KM servers in your organization. Remove one server and reinstall it as a slave server to the main KM server. You must re-enroll each user in the affected site into the main KM server and assign new tokens.

Troubleshooting the Exchange Server Installation and Upgrade

1. True or False. When installing Exchange Server 5.5 in a new site, you must install from your own account and add yourself to the Windows NT Server Administrator group.

2. True or False. The Exchange Site Services account must be a Windows NT User account that is dedicated to the Exchange Server 5.5 application.

3. While installing Exchange on the first server in a site, you receive the following error message: "The system cannot find the file specified." The installation fails, and you must reinstall. What caused the problem?

_____

4. While installing Exchange Server on the second server, the installation fails. The error message you receive is "Unable to connect to Server *<first server>*." Why did this installation fail?

_____

_____

_____

_____

_____

_____

5. After successfully installing Exchange Server, you reboot the server and notice that the Exchange services are not starting. What is the probable cause?

_____

_____

6. You are trying to install the Exchange Administrator program on a Windows NT workstation and have chosen the typical setup. The installation fails, and you get the following error message: "You must install Exchange Server 5.5 on an NT Server." What is the problem?

_____

_____

_____

Troubleshooting Exchange Connectivity

7. List the tools that you can use to diagnose and resolve Exchange connectivity problems.

_____

_____

_____

_____

8. On which Exchange components can you enable Diagnostics Logging?

_____

_____

_____

_____

_____

_____

9. What are the four levels of Diagnostics Logging?

_____

_____

_____

_____

10. To what does Diagnostics Logging write and which tool can you use to view the events?

_____

_____

11. True or False. To enable Message Tracking on the MTA, you must issue the following command at the MS-DOS prompt:

```
C:\> Enable_message_trk Exchange_MTA
```

12. When you enable Message Tracking, all events are written to a log file with the filename

_____.

13. True or False. To view the message queues for the MTA, you must stop the MTA and use the MTA property pages.

14. While viewing the MTA message queue, you notice a message that is corrupt and that is blocking the MTA's message queue for incoming messages. What command button can you use to delete the message?

15. True or False. To view the queues for the Microsoft Mail Connector, you must use the command line.

16. While checking the status of all the connectors, you notice that messages are stalled in the Microsoft Mail Connector queues. What can you do to fix this problem?

_____

_____

_____

_____

17. While configuring an instance of the Microsoft Mail Connector, you discover that you can't create an instance. What is the problem?

_____

_____

_____

_____

18.   True or False. Whenever you experience problems with the Microsoft Mail Connector, turn on Diagnostics Logging to view the events associated with the connector.

19.   True or False. The Exchange Server 5.5 Site Connector is used for fast high-bandwidth network connections.

20.   True or False. You have a large enterprise and are using TCP/IP as the network protocol, but since you are not connected to the Internet, you can't use the Internet Mail Service.

21.   Which four types of connectors can you use to connect sites?

_____

_____

_____

_____

22.   You want to connect two sites, but the two networks are not currently connected. You don't want to spend the extra money to build a permanent network connection. Which connector type would you choose for this site connector?

_____

23.   While running the Exchange Administrator program, you notice that you can't view servers in another site. What could be the problem?

_____

_____

_____

_____

24. After checking the components affecting the problem in question 23, which tool can you use to track the Directory Replication messages across the network?

_____

_____

_____

25. While checking your message queues, you notice that messages are not being forwarded to a server in the same site. How would you diagnose and resolve the problem?

_____

_____

_____

_____

26. After configuring several servers within a site, you notice that the Directory Service was updated automatically with information from the servers. You configure an X.400 Connector to communicate across sites. After a day of successful messaging between sites, you notice that the Directory Service has not been updated with the data from the other site. What is the problem?

_____

_____

27. True or False. Exchange Server 5.5 supports SMTP protocol logging in compliance with TCP/IP RFC 821.

28. True or False. Before troubleshooting your Internet Mail Service, you must build a baseline performance chart of the activities of the Internet Mail Service. If you do not, you will not be able to run Message Tracking.

29. True or False. Before any changes take effect on the Internet Mail Service, you must restart the service.

_____

_____

30. Mail is being returned to some of your users from the Internet Mail Service. The problem cannot be narrowed down to a segment or to a specific client. After checking the Message Tracking log, you see that the Internet Mail Service is denying access to those users who reported the problem. What can you do to resolve this problem?

_____

31. Messages to Internet Mail users come up garbled. It seems that the users' Internet Mail Client doesn't support Rich Text Format. What can you do to fix the problem?

_____

_____

Troubleshooting the Exchange Client

32. True or False. New Exchange users must configure their client with a profile that contains a list of Information Services that they will use.

33. A new user in another domain wants to use your Exchange server. What must you set up for this user to use the local domain?

_____

_____

34. What would you check if users complain that their mail is not leaving their Outbox?

_____

_____

_____

Troubleshooting the Information Store

35. Which tools can you use to diagnose problems with the information store?

_____

_____

_____

_____

_____

36. You want to view the status of a specific public folder in your information store. Which tool do you use?

_____

_____

STUDY QUESTIONS

37.   True or False. You cannot customize the information store status views.

38.   Using the private information store login status view, which column displays the version of the software that the user is running to connect to their mailbox?

_____

39.   Using the private information store login status view, which column can you use to display the last time a user logged on?

_____

40.   Using the information store mailbox resource column views, which column reports information on the total amount of space used by a specific mailbox?

_____

41.   Using the information store folder replication status view, which column displays the number of times a folder has been replicated?

_____

42.   Using the information store public folder resource view, which column displays the amount of space currently being used by retained deleted items?

_____

43.   Which tool can you use to verify and fix your information store?

_____

44. True or False. Whenever you restore an information store database from a backup, you must run the ISINTEG utility in Patch mode.

45. Which option would you add to the following command line to repair the private information store?

```
c:\exchsrvr\bin\ISINTEG
```

_____

Troubleshooting the Directory Service

46. Which tools can you use to diagnose and troubleshoot the Directory Service?

_____

_____

_____

_____

47. While examining the Exchange Administrator program, you notice that your directory replication has failed. What three steps can you take to diagnose this problem?

_____

_____

_____

48. You add a server to your site and notice after a day and a half that the server has not been added to your site's Directory Service. You check the other server and notice that it has not added your site to its Directory Service. What could be the problem?

_____

_____

_____

Troubleshooting Exchange Resource Problems

49. Which NT tool do you use to increase the amount of pagefile space on your Exchange server?

_____

_____

50. True or False. If your hard disk is busy more than 90 percent of the time and if public folders seem to be the problem, delete the public folders causing the problem.

51. True or False. You notice that your server is page faulting heavily and your disks are busy 90 percent of the time. Your only solution is to add more physical memory to your server.

52. True or False. You notice that your gateway is constantly busy and that the queues for this gateway are growing. Your only solution is to add more physical memory to your server.

53. You suspect that your network is down between your MTAs. How can you verify this?

_____

54. Your MTA periodically goes down for no apparent reason. Which tools can you use to alert you of a downed MTA?

_____

55. Your users are reporting a problem sending messages to a host named Trigger. You know that a node named Triger exists on the network. What do you check?

_____

56. Your Internet Mail Service is rejecting messages and displaying the error message "Destination host is unreachable." You have pinged successfully to the other host using the host name and IP address. What could be the problem?

_____

_____

Troubleshooting Advanced Security

57. Which tool can you use to track error events with the KM Server?

_____

58. True or False. The KM Server will log only events of critical or error status.

59. Your users complain that they can't verify signatures on digitally signed messages from another site. You know the site has just been set up with a new administrator, who isn't very experienced with the KM Server. What could be the problem?

_____

_____

60. One of your users needs to send an encrypted message to another site, but the Encrypt button in the Create Message box is dimmed. What could be the problem?

_____

_____

_____

SAMPLE TEST

5-1 Marc is installing Exchange Server 5.5 at a large enterprise that has multiple sites. He receives the following error message during installation: "Unable to connect to server DWEZIL." The network appears to be up and running. What else could be the problem?

    A. Marc is installing on an early version of Exchange that does not support multiple sites.

    B. Marc is installing on a Windows NT Workstation 3.51.

    C. Marc does have administrative permissions on the server at the other site.

    D. Marc does have administrative permissions, but the Site Service account is on a Windows NT member server.

5-2 Theo is the Exchange administrator at a very large company. He has turned on Diagnostics Logging to assist in troubleshooting his server. He notices that his hard drive is quickly running out of space. What is the problem?

    A. Theo has chosen the maximum logging level for all components.

    B. Theo is experiencing disk thrashing.

    C. Theo has a RAID array that is experiencing errors.

    D. There is no problem with the server. Theo needs to buy more disk space.

5-3 Shannon is the site administrator for the Exchange servers at her local office. She reports to the Exchange manager that she has never seen the servers at the other sites appear in the Exchange Administrator program. She has run the link monitor, and the connections are present and mail is moving between the sites. What else can she do?

    A. Check her disk space.

    B. Restore her servers and run the ISINTEG utility.

    C. Check if the Directory Replication Connector has been set up correctly.

    D. Run full Windows NT diagnostics.

5-4   Selena has noticed that her users have been having problems with mail between sites. Messages are being returned to the senders because of size restrictions. She has checked the Connector property pages, and there are no size restrictions. Where else could she check for size restrictions?

    A. Each user's mailbox properties

    B. The distribution lists mailbox properties

    C. The custom recipients mailbox properties

    D. The Internet Mail Service property pages

5-5   Esee has noticed that directory replication between sites has failed. What should he do first?

    A. Check the Windows NT application log.

    B. Run the consistency checker on all sites.

    C. Check the Windows NT System log.

    D. Run the update now from the Server property pages.

5-6   Marc has not been able to send messages through the Internet Mail Service. It seems that the MTA is returning the message. What should he do?

    A. Check the Internet Mail Service address space, and enter `*.com` so that all SMTP mail is passed.

    B. Check the Internet Mail Service address space, and enter `*.com.smtp` so that all SMTP mail is passed.

    C. Check the Internet Mail Service address space, and enter an asterisk (`*`) so that all SMTP mail is passed.

    D. Check the Internet Mail Service address space, and enter `*.com` so that all `*.com` SMTP mail is passed.

SAMPLE TEST

5-7 A message from one of Chris's users is being returned when he attempts to send mail to someone on the Internet. All Exchange mail is received, and he can receive Internet mail. What is the first question to answer?

    A. Is the user configured to receive Internet mail?

    B. Is the user configured to send and receive Internet mail?

    C. Is the mailbox configured to send and receive Internet mail?

    D. Is the mailbox configured with the correct permissions?

5-8 Danny has added a new user to his Exchange server. The new user can log on to the server, and the server is available. But he can't connect to the Exchange server. What is the problem?

    A. Permissions are not set for the mailbox.

    B. Permissions are not set on the Windows NT account.

    C. Permissions are not set on the Exchange client.

    D. Permissions are not set on the Exchange server.

5-9 When troubleshooting a problem on the information store, Kathlyn notices that the replication status reads local modified. What does this mean?

    A. The current server's replica has not been modified, and the other copies in the site have been.

    B. The current server's replica has been modified, and the modification has not been propagated throughout the site.

    C. The current server's replica is in sync with all other replicas of this folder.

    D. The current server's replica is corrupt.

S A M P L E   T E S T

5-10   Alex is having a problem with errors when starting the information store, and users can't connect to the Exchange Server. Which utility can he use to help troubleshoot this problem?

   A. ISINTEG

   B. MTACHECK

   C. ISINTEG in Patch mode

   D. ISINTEG in Repair mode with save

5-11   Shannon is having a problem on her system. Her directory information is not the same on servers at different sites. She checks the Directory Replication Connector to ensure that the schedule is set to the default. What should she check next?

   A. The Windows NT application log for events that indicate a problem with the Directory Service

   B. The Windows NT Security log for events that indicate a problem with the Directory Service

   C. The Windows NT System log for events that indicate a problem with the system

   D. The Windows NT Exchange log for events that indicate a problem with the Directory Service

5-12   Danny is an Exchange Server supervisor, and his assistants notice that one of the hard drives is busy 90 percent of the time. His assistant has monitored Exchange to determine that the drive in question hosts user mailboxes. What is a good fix?

   A. Move the private information store to another server

   B. Move the mailboxes with the most activity to the server where the majority of the recipients reside to cut down the amount of network traffic

   C. Move the public information store to another server

   D. Move Exchange logs to another server

5-13   Kathy has received calls from users who are complaining that their mail is not being sent or received. After reviewing the situation, Kathy determines that the MTA queues are not moving. Which utility can she use to troubleshoot the problem?

    A. MTACHECK

    B. MTAChecker

    C. MTA Check and server integrity checker

    D. ISINTEG

5-14   Shannon has noticed that her messages are not being delivered remotely. During troubleshooting, she finds that her MTA queue is growing. The bandwidth is sufficient. What should she do to see if the destination server is available?

    A. Run ISINTEG

    B. Run Performance Monitor on the local server

    C. Run server monitor on the remote server

    D. Run server monitor and the Performance Monitor

5-15   Theo's user has called and reported an invalid address for a well-known user, John Smith. He could use the address before, but not now. The error message is "Recipient not found." What might be the problem?

    A. The GAL is corrupt.

    B. There are duplicate John Smiths.

    C. There are duplicate GALs.

    D. There are duplicate backups of GALs.

5-16 While troubleshooting a "host unreachable" error on her system, Elaine notices that there is no such host in the domain. What should she do next?

    A. Check the TCP/IP server, and make sure that the /etc/hosts file is in binary format.

    B. Check the TCP/IP server, and make sure that the /etc/hosts.equiv file is in binary format.

    C. Check the TCP/IP server, and make sure that the /etc/hosts.lpd is available for users.

    D. Check the TCP/IP server for an assignment to a DNS host server.

5-17 Which of the following components supports Diagnostics Logging?

    A. MTA

    B. Microsoft Mail Connector

    C. Internet Mail Service

    D. All the above

5-18 For which site objects can Message Tracking be enabled?

    A. MTA, information store, and Microsoft Mail connector

    B. MTA, Exchange Administrator program, information store

    C. MTA, information store, ISINTEG

    D. Information store, Internet Mail Service, and MTACHECK

5-19 John is using a TCP/IP connection to an ISP to run network connectivity using the Internet as a backbone. Which connector should he configure?

    A. Dynamic RAS Connector

    B. Internet Mail Service

    C. Site Connector

    D. X.400 Connector

5-20 When installing Exchange, which Windows NT account should you always use?

    A. Administrator

    B. Site Service

    C. Windows NT user

    D. Any account

5-21 You need to run the ISINTEG on the private information store, and you want to pass the results to a file called `privatelog.txt`. What is the correct command?

    A. `ISINTEG -pub -l publiclog.txt`

    B. `ISINTEG  -pri`

    C. `ISINTEG -pri  -l privatelog.txt`

    D. `ISINTEG -info_store`

UNIT

6

Final Review

You've studied this book and worked through all the study questions and the sample test questions. Now you're ready to do a final review. Get a pen or a pencil, give yourself 90 minutes, and be ready to start on the first of 56 questions.

1   Kathlyn is the Exchange administrator at a midsized company. While installing Exchange Server 5.5, she responded to the questions about NT accounts with all the default answers. Which account will be the default Site Service account?

    A. The NTAdmin Windows NT User account

    B. The Administrator Windows NT User account

    C. The ExService Windows NT User account

    D. The Exchange Site Service account

2   Ben is a new administrator of a midsized Exchange Server enterprise in a midsized company. He is in the last step of installing Exchange Server 5.5, which he has been told is optional. What is the last step?

    A. Running the Performance Monitor

    B. Running the Performance Server

    C. Running the Performance Optimizer

    D. Running the Start Services batch file

3   Dionicio is the Exchange administrator at a very large company that has multiple sites and servers. He wants some of his assistants to be KM administrators. Once he adds the individuals as administrators, what is their default password?

    A. Def_Pass

    B. Def_Sys_Pass

    C. password

    D. password_default

4   Alan's users are complaining that their messages are sometimes taking as long as 30 minutes to reach other sites and sometimes they don't get there at all. What can he do to get Exchange to warn him about this problem?

    A. Create an NT Performance Monitor

    B. Create a link monitor, set the Enter Warning state to a lower value from the 30-minute default, and set the notification alert

    C. Create a server monitor, set the warning state to a lower value than the 30-minute default, and set the notification alert.

    D. Create an NT Exchange alert

5   Marie is installing Exchange Server 5.5 on her server. She receives an "Error copying files" message. What is the cause?

    A. Other applications are running and currently locking the Registry or writing to the same files.

    B. There is no problem. Marie should simply reinstall.

    C. Marie's hardware is inadequate.

    D. Marie must stop the Task Manager.

6   Renee wants to create another Organization object in the Exchange Administrator program. Can she do this?

    A. No, she must create the Organization object in another instance of the Exchange Administrator program.

    B. Yes, she must create the Organization object in another instance of the Exchange Administrator program.

    C. Yes, she can use the -mul_orgs option when running the Exchange Administrator program.

    D. No, there can be only one instance of an Organization object. She can create virtual organizations using Address Book views.

7   Kristin, an administrator in a large organization, wants to allow assistants to manage sites and administrators. Which permissions and objects must she modify?

     A. She must assign permissions on the Organization object.

     B. She must assign permissions on the Server object.

     C. She must assign permissions on the Site and Site Configuration objects.

     D. She must assign permissions on the recipients.

8   Sally and Nicky are administrators for a large Exchange installation. Their company uses mixed versions of Exchange and Outlook 8.03 clients. In addition, users come in through IMAPv4 and POP3 Internet Mail clients. Sally has issued X.509 V1 certificates, but her S/MIME Internet users cannot choose S/MIME security. Why?

     A. They must install a Unix-compatible MIME security server.

     B. They must enable X.509 V3 certificates as well as V1.

     C. They must reinstall the X.509 certificates on the server.

     D. They must reinstall the X.509 certificates on the KM server.

9   Angie is a new Exchange administrator who is concerned about her site-server status. She wants to use a server monitor to monitor the status of the Exchange services and the links between each server. Can this be done?

     A. Yes, use the server monitor, add all the servers from each site, and specify the services she wants to monitor on each server.

     B. No, the server monitor will monitor only servers that are using TCP/IP.

     C. Yes, use the link monitor to check the services and the server monitor to check the communication links.

     D. Yes, use the server monitor to check the services and the link monitor to check the communication links.

10 Alex suspects that the Directory database has some inconsistencies. Some objects appear to be updated, and others do not. Which utility can he run to fix this?

 A. Directory Services Consistency Checker

 B. Directory Services Update Now

 C. ISINTEG

 D. MTACHECK

11 What do public folders contain?

 A. Messages that are shared among more than one user

 B. Databases that are shared among more than one organization

 C. Mailboxes that are shared among users

 D. All the above

12 Which utilities can you use to create an NT account with an Exchange mailbox?

 A. User Manager for Domains

 B. User Manager for Exchange

 C. Exchange Administrator program

 D. Exchange Administrator program for NT users

13 Bernadette wants to move a group of users to a different recipient container. She has placed all mailbox data in a personal folder on the users' hard disk. She has also exported all user information into an export file. She wants to import them into a new container. On the Directory Import Container form, which property must she modify?

 A. Template

 B. Recipient Container

 C. NT Account

 D. Export Container

14   Dawson wants to monitor his servers and links constantly, but he doesn't want to be the only one notified. He also wants other administrators to receive notification of a warning or an alert. How would he configure the monitor for more than one notification?

   A. Set the Monitor Notification properties to process more than one alert or e-mail message to various individuals.

   B. Set the Monitor Program properties to process more than one alert or e-mail message to various users.

   C. Set the Link Monitor Server Status property to process more than one alert or e-mail message to various users.

   D. Set the Windows NT Performance Monitor to alert his system administrator.

15   Daniel has installed Exchange on a old server with only the IPX/SPX protocol installed. After installation, his Internet Mail Service will not start. What is the problem?

   A. Daniel must start the service from the Control Panel.

   B. Daniel must restart the Exchange services.

   C. Daniel must install TCP/IP.

   D. Daniel must install TCP/IP and IIS 4.

16   The following are your Exchange Server objectives:

   ▪ Implement Exchange Server across four LAN segments connected by T1 lines

   ▪ Implement advanced security for Internet mail clients as well as Exchange clients

   ▪ Implement Directory Replication across sites

   ▪ Manage each site from a workstation in a general area

   Here is the proposed solution:

   Create four Exchange sites connected by an X.400 Connector for message transfers that can be scheduled. Each site will have a Windows NT workstation with the Exchange Administrator program installed for the administrator's central management, as well as servers to handle Exchange. One server in the corporate site will be the KM server. Each site will host the Internet Mail Service and Outlook Web Access on one of its servers. Each site will schedule Directory Replication every night at midnight.

Does this solution meet:

A. All objectives

B. Some of the objectives

C. None of the objectives

17   A site currently runs public information store replication every five hours. Shannon wants to run replication for a specific folder more often. Can she do this?

A. No, she must use the default public information store replication schedule.

B. No, she must use the site's public information store replication schedule.

C. Yes, she can modify the site's public information store replication schedule.

D. Yes, she can modify a folder's replication schedule, and it will override the schedule for the public information store.

18   Lupe has some users whose mailboxes are getting quite full. He also wants to purge some mailboxes of old and obsolete messages. In addition, he wants to take care of both these tasks while users are logged on. How can he do this?

A. He can write a script to purge the Mailbox files.

B. He can choose Private Information Store ➤ Delete Message.

C. He can select a group of users and then choose Tools ➤ Clean Mailbox.

D. It can't be done.

19   Which of the following components will Exchange Server 5.5 monitor?

   A. Directory

   B. Information store

   C. MTA

   D. Changes to the Exchange Administrator program

20   Harold has made numerous changes to his Internet Mail Service to optimize performance. But he notices that none of his changes have taken effect. What is the problem?

   A. He must restart his server.

   B. He must restart Exchange.

   C. He must restart the Internet Mail Service.

   D. He must restart Exchange across the site.

21   Larry is the Exchange administrator in the planning stage of a new Windows NT network. He has approximately 50,000 users who will be required to log in and use Exchange services as well as other network services. Which domain model should he use?

   A. Master

   B. Single

   C. Multiple-Master

   D. Multi-Master Resource

22   Which three types of addresses are created when you install Exchange Server 5.5 with the Internet Mail Service?

    A. MS Mail, SMTP, X.500

    B. MS Mail, X.400, cc:Mail

    C. MS Mail, SMTP, X.400

    D. Exchange, SMTP, X.400

23   Dana and Kelsey manage their Exchange server as a team, and they have decided to let certain users in each department manage users and distributions lists. In addition, they want to let these super users create and manage user accounts only. They do not want the users to modify any configuration objects. What can they do?

    A. Assign administrator permissions to the subordinates on the Organization object

    B. Assign administrator permissions to the users on the Site object

    C. Assign administrator permissions to the users on the Server object

    D. Assign administrator permissions to the users on the Site Configuration object

24   The objectives of Company ABC's disaster recovery plan require that all systems support automatic reboots in case of a power outage or a power surge. In addition, the manager of the IT department requires that all Exchange servers running monitors also automatically restart the services after the reboot.

The proposed solution is to create an account with administrator permissions on the site configuration and to configure the account's Start menu so that a shortcut to the Administrator program appears as:

```
C:\exchsrvr\bin\admin /m:monitor servername /m:linkmon servername
```

This solution meets:

    A. All objectives

    B. Some objectives

    C. None of the objectives

25   Kevin receives a call from several of his users complaining that they are not receiving any mail from Internet users. Kevin checks the service, and it is running. He attempts to connect to a host using ping, and that works successfully. His other TCP/IP commands also work. Kevin needs more information to troubleshoot. Which log file provides Kevin with detailed information on the Internet Mail Service?

A. TCP/IP Protocol

B. SMTP Protocol

C. TCP/IP Port 25 Protocol Event

D. Windows NT Performance Monitor

26   Bob and Kelsey manage an Exchange site. They are using TCP/IP as the network protocol over an extended LAN. Bob wants to use an X.400 Connector to schedule connections to other sites to cut down on network traffic. What must Kelsey create before he can create the X.400 Site Connector?

A. A TP4 MTA Transport Stack

B. A TCP/IP MTA Transport Stack

C. An X.400 MTA Transport Stack

D. A TP1/MTA Transport Stack

27   Logan has decided that with the expansion of his company he needs to add another server to his site. He configures an additional server for Exchange Server 5.5, with Internet Mail Service. He wants to make sure that the directory is correct and updated across the site. How can he do this?

A. From the Directory Replication property page, click the Update Now button

B. From the Directory Service General property page, click the Replicate Immediately button

C. From the Server's Directory Service General property page, click the Check Consistency button

D. Restart the Directory Service

┌─────── **FINAL   REVIEW** ───────┐

28   Devan wants to monitor communication links to foreign mail systems. She has configured the link monitor correctly, but users attempting to send mail messages to the link monitor recipients are receiving NDRs. What can she do to prevent this?

   A. Create a separate container and add the container to another organization

   B. Create a separate container, export the users from the first recipient container to the new one, and then hide the container by selecting the Hide from Address Book property

   C. Export the users from the old container to a new container

   D. Mark each mailbox with the Do Not Publish property in the Advanced Mailbox property page

29   What is the minimum hardware configuration required for installing Exchange Server 5.5 and all core components?

   A. Pentium 90 MHz processor, 24MB RAM, 250MB of free disk space

   B. Pentium 166 MHz processor, 48MB RAM, 1GB of free disk space (spread across several devices)

   C. Alpha Processor, 100MB RAM, 4GB of free disk space

   D. Pentium 33Mhz processor, 48MB RAM, 250MB of free disk space

30   You are migrating from cc:Mail 2.2 to Exchange Server 5.5. Your goal is to move users to Exchange while still using cc:Mail. After migrating users to Exchange mailboxes, you want to move them to the new Outlook client for Exchange Server 5.5. Can you do this?

   A. Yes, Exchange Server 5.5 supports cc:Mail V2.2.

   B. Yes, Exchange Server 5.5 supports all cc:Mail versions.

   C. No, Exchange Server 5.5 supports a minimum of cc:Mail postoffice 6.

   D. No, Exchange Server 5.5 supports a minimum of cc:Mail postoffice 5.

31 Prince Charles is having a problem with the Exchange Server 5.5 system at Buckingham Palace. His IS maintenance jobs run every 75 minutes, and the added overhead of users accessing their mailboxes is degrading performance. What can Prince Charles do to alleviate this problem?

    A. Modify the Site Configuration utility to run the IS maintenance jobs every 10 hours

    B. Modify the specific server's Public Information Store IS Maintenance tab and schedule the job to run once in the evening after users go home

    C. Modify the specific server's Private Information Store IS Maintenance tab and schedule the job to run once in the evening after users go home

    D. Modify the server's IS Maintenance tab and schedule the job to run once in the evening after users go home

32 John wants to know how many messages are queued for the Microsoft Mail Connector. Which component does he check?

    A. The Microsoft Mail Connector Interchange queues

    B. The MS Mail postoffice queues

    C. The Microsoft MTA Connector queues

    D. The MTA Queues property page

33 Joe suspects that the mailboxes on his servers have incorrect unread mail counts. Which utilities does Exchange Server 5.5 provide to diagnose and resolve mailbox counts?

    A. ISINTEG

    B. MTACHECK

    C. Message Tracking log

    D. All the above

34   Guy supports an Exchange server as well as Exchange clients, cc:Mail clients, and Microsoft Mail users. He has not completely finished his migration to Exchange. He wants to allow his Exchange users to view the addresses of cc:Mail and Microsoft Mail users, and vice-versa. How can he do this?

    A. Create a Directory Replication Connector

    B. Create a Directory Replication Connector after configuring a Site connector

    C. Create a Dirsync Server to synchronize the address lists with Exchange Server

    D. Create a Dirsync Server to synchronize the addresses with a Digital Equipment Corporation X.500 Directory Synchronizer

35   Your server has a disk that serves as the Public Information Store database disk. It has been recording a 90 percent busy rate. Upon monitoring, you find that the culprits for all the disk activity are several public folders. You decide to move the public folders to a server that has more resources available. Which tools can you use to rehome a public folder?

    A. The PFAdmin utility.

    B. The Exchange Administrator.

    C. PST files.

    D. None of the above. You cannot move public folders.

36   While monitoring her information store, Michaela notices that the average time for delivery counter and the active logon count are growing quite high. The information store disk is also creating an I/O bottleneck. What can she do to alleviate this problem?

    A. Add another site

    B. Add another virtual organization

    C. Add another server

    D. Add another MTA

37 Brandon wants to run NT backup automatically every night at 11 PM. He has a tape loader that will load tapes automatically. He also wants to back up the Registry. How can he back up the Exchange server database files and the Registry?

    A. Use NT Backup.

    B. Create a batch file with the `ntbackup` command to back up files and submit the batch file with the `at` command to run at 11 PM.

    C. Using the NT Backup GUI, create a script file and submit the script file to run at 11 PM every night.

    D. He must purchase a Colorado tape backup unit and software to schedule Exchange backups to run every night. This will also back up the Registry.

38 Raymond wants to manually synchronize the directories instead of waiting for them to synchronize in the next 15 minutes. What must Raymond do before synchronizing the directories?

    A. Pause Exchange using the Services applet in Control Panel.

    B. Use the `Net Pause MSExchangeDX` command at the command prompt.

    C. Stop and restart his server.

    D. Reinstall Exchange.

39 Which of the following items are core components of Exchange Server 5.5?

    A. Directory

    B. MTS

    C. Internet Mail Service

    D. Information Store

40 While reviewing his Exchange backup logs, Stan notices that some of his transactions logs are larger than 5MB. Is there a problem?

  A. No, all files are larger than 5MB.

  B. Yes, all files should be 10MB.

  C. Yes, all files should be 5MB.

  D. Yes, all files should be 2–5MB in size.

41 Cecil wants to install the Exchange MIB on her server. She has already installed the SNMP service and the TCP/IP MIB on her server. What must she do to install the Exchange MIB?

  A. Run the batch utility to install the MIB.

  B. Manually install the Exchange MIB.

  C. Remove the TCP/IP MIB and run the batch utility.

  D. She cannot. She must install the MIB on an NT workstation.

42 An Exchange administrator notices that the Exchange server's MTA appears to be down. After checking the service, he finds that the MTA is running but that the queues are quite long. What does this indicate?

  A. An incorrectly configured MTA

  B. A network problem

  C. A heavily used system

  D. All the above

43   Joe is an assistant to the Exchange administrator. The administrator calls in sick, and some changes must be made to the Site Configuration objects. Joe can create users and distribution lists, but has never before modified Configuration objects. While attempting to do so, he receives the error message "Access denied." What is the problem?

   A. Joe has not been given administrator permissions on the Configuration objects.

   B. Joe has not been given administrator permissions on the Organization object.

   C. Joe has not been given administrator permissions on the recipient containers.

   D. Joe has not been given NT administrator permissions.

44   John needs to give access to Exchange mailboxes to clients who travel and have access only to the Internet. His users would be using Internet Mail clients and Web browsers. What protocol support must he provide?

   A. POP3

   B. IMAPv4

   C. NNTP

   D. HTTP

45   Which Exchange Server 5.5 components support Message Tracking?

   A. MTA

   B. Information Store Site Configuration

   C. MS Mail Connector

46   Mandy wants to set up a dedicated public folder server in her site. Which property page must she configure to create a dedicated public folder server?

   A. Private Information Store General

   B. Public Information Store General

   C. Site Information Store General

   D. Server Information Store General

47   Which of the following are Exchange Server installation types?

   A. Typical

   B. Complete/Custom

   C. Laptop

   D. Portable

48   Joe wants to install the Exchange Administrator program on his NT workstation. Which installation option must he chose?

   A. Typical.

   B. Minimum.

   C. Complete/Custom.

   D. He cannot install Exchange Server on his NT workstation.

49   Angie has a problem with her information store database file. She suspects it is corrupt, and the ISINTEG utility doesn't fix it. Angie stops the Exchange services, chooses the Restore option from NT Backup, and is ready to restore the database file. Which option should she choose to restore the entire database file from the last full backup?

     A. Overwrite All Existing Data and Keep the Transaction Logs

     B. Keep Existing Data and Overwrite What's Missing

     C. Erase All Existing Data

     D. Overwrite All Database Files

50   Some of your users receive NDRs because they don't verify the address before sending the message. Which keystroke can you use to verify an address before sending a message?

     A. Tab+Enter

     B. Ctrl+K

     C. Ctrl+T

     D. Ctrl+Tab

51   Which Exchange component provides advanced security on Exchange Server 5.5?

     A. KM Server

     B. Microsoft Certificate Server

     C. MIME Certificate authorities on the Internet

     D. Advanced security on a user's mailbox

52   Mia wants to see where the Performance Optimizer has placed all the database files. Which property page can she view to see the database paths?

    A. Site Addressing General

    B. Information Store Database Paths

    C. Public Information Store General

    D. Server Database Paths

53   Gerald wants to support remote users by creating a list of addresses in a file that can be transferred to users. Which option can he use to create this file?

    A. From the Public Information Store General property page, choose Create Offline Address Book.

    B. From the DS Site Configuration Offline Address Book, click the Generate All button.

    C. From the DS Site Configuration Offline Address Book, choose Generate Address Book and enter the mailbox of the user who will be receiving the address book.

    D. You cannot create this file.

54   George's company wants him to limit the Internet addresses to which users can send mail. Which option can he configure to do this?

    A. Site Addressing

    B. Organizational Addressing

    C. IMS Address Space property page

    D. Microsoft Mail Address Space property page

55   What must be installed before you configure a Dynamic RAS Site Connector?

   A. Windows NT Server 4.0 RAS Service

   B. Windows NT Workstation 4.0 RAS Service

   C. Windows NT Server 3.51 RAS Service

   D. Windows NT Workstation 3.51 RAS Service

56   You have an existing MS Mail configuration, with a Dirsync Server configured as an MS Mail post-office. In order to allow Exchange Server 5.5 to exchange information with the MS Mail postoffice, the Exchange Server must be configured as:

   A. Dirsync Remote Requestor

   B. Dirsync Requestor

   C. Dirsync Server

   D. None of the above

APPENDIX

Study Question and
Sample Test Answers

Unit 1 Answers

Study Questions

Choosing an Implementation Strategy for Microsoft Exchange Server

1. Remote Procedure Calls

    Explanation: Remote Procedure Calls are based on client/server development.

2. Organization

3. Address space

    Explanation: For every MTA and/or connector, there must be address space entries that instruct the MTA how to get from one MTA to another.

4. TCP/IP Services for Windows NT 4

5. False

    Explanation: Exchange Server 5.5 requires that any site connection support RPCs (Remote Procedure Calls).

6. False

    Explanation: Exchange 5.5 code was developed to support Microsoft NT clusters.

7. False

    Explanation: During the planning stage of Exchange, you can choose how your sites are organized. You can choose to organize your sites by geographical, functional, or any other boundaries.

8. False

Explanation: Although it is much easier to manage if all servers share the same domain context, it is possible to build an Exchange site across multiple domains. In that case, you must configure every network connection with a username and password of the Site Service account for the remote domain.

9. Connectors

Developing the Exchange Server Configuration

10. Site Service.

Explanation: This account is used for Exchange services that communicate across core components, servers, or sites and also for maintenance.

11. 3

12. True

13. Location

14. True

15. Windows NT Services for Macintosh

16. Pentium 90 MHz

17. False

Explanation: The Site Service account is used for core component communication and maintenance on your Exchange server.

Upgrading to Exchange Server 5.5

18. Bridgehead servers

Explanation: The major change between Exchange Server 4 and Exchange Server 5.5 is to the directory. Update your bridgehead servers first, and then upgrade the servers in a site. If you have only one site in your Exchange organization, you can upgrade your servers in any order.

19. False

Explanation: You can upgrade from as far back as Exchange 4 only; Exchange 3 doesn't exist.

20. True

Explanation: Fault-tolerant upgrades are only available with upgrades from Exchange Server 5.

21. Back up

22. False

Explanation: Before upgrading you should back up the Exchange databases and not the NT directory.

Developing Long-Term Coexistence Strategies

23. Internet

Explanation: The Internet Mail Service provides connectivity with SMTP mail relay hosts and allows incoming SMTP mail to be delivered to Exchange users.

24. False

Explanation: The TCP/IP protocol is a network protocol and not an SMTP protocol. NNTP is used for newsgroups and not for SMTP.

25. True

26. True

Developing the Exchange Server Infrastructure

27. Containers

Leaf objects

28. System Attendant

    Information stores

    Directory database

    Message Transfer Agent

    Internet Mail Service

    Explanation: Of these core components, only the Internet Mail Service is optional.

29. System Attendant

30. Directory

31. Storage limits

32. True

33. Gateways

34. System Attendant

35. Directory database

36. Message Transfer Agent

37. Internet Mail Service

38. Public information stores

    Private information stores

39. E-mail addresses

40. False

    Explanation: Exchange 5.5 provides Outlook Web Access. Outlook Web Access gives your users the ability to read mail using a Web browser capable of using frames.

41. True

42. True

43. False

    Explanation: You can change the directory display name property on certain objects, but you cannot change the object name itself without reinstalling Exchange Server.

44. True

45. False

    Explanation: The private information store consists of mailboxes for users. Public information stores contain applications or data that needs to be shared by more than two people

46. True

    Explanation: Placing users who work together on the same server keeps the network traffic between servers at a minimum. Users who work together typically exchange more mail than users who do not work together. Because the mailboxes are on the same server, Exchange does not use the MTA to transfer user mail; instead, the mail message is placed in that recipient's mailbox and delivered directly when the recipient starts up an Exchange client.

47. False

    Explanation: Because Exchange Server 5.5 now supports differential address book downloads, users need to download only the changes since the last full download.

48. False

    Explanation: The System Attendant is an integral part of the Exchange core components and is not optional.

49. False

    Explanation: The Internet Mail Service supports bi-directional communication. This means you can accept mail and send mail through the same service.

50. True

    Explanation: Using the Internet Mail Service does in fact incur more processing overhead to convert messages from SMTP format to MDBEF format.

51. False

    Explanation: Exchange supports as many connectors as you need. Although there are some limitations on the types of connectors you can have on one server or in a site, the limits are fairly open.

52. 5

53. Private Information Store Storage Warnings

54. True

    Explanation: Exchange will use any of the listed network protocols, the only requirement being TCP/IP for the Internet Mail Service.

Developing Long-Term Administration Strategies

55. Admin

    Permissions Admin

    Service Account Admin

    View Only Admin

    User

    Send As

    Search

56. True

57. True

58. True

59. True

60. User Manager for Domains and the Exchange Administrator program

61. False

    Explanation: You can install the Exchange Administrator program only on Windows NT 4 platforms.

62. True

63. Hierarchy, data

Backup and Disaster Recovery Strategies

64. True

65. Storage media

66. Once

Planning Mailbox Document Recovery

67. False

    Explanation: As the Exchange administrator, you must determine the optimal retrieval time frame in which users can recover deleted messages.

68. Mailboxes, server information stores

Developing Security Strategies

69. Key Management

    Explanation: To use encryption, you must install the Key Management Server on one of the Exchange servers. Encrypted key pairs are generated for each mailbox that is enabled for security encryption and digital signatures.

70. True

Developing Server-Scripting Strategies

71. False

Explanation: Server-based scripting is available on every Exchange server.

72. True

Sample Test

1-1   A

1-2   C

1-3   A, B, C

1-4   A, C

1-5   B

1-6   A, B

1-7   A

1-8   A

1-9   B, C

1-10   A, B

1-11   D

1-12   B

1-13   A

1-14   A, B, C, D, E

1-15   D

1-16 A, B

1-17 D

1-18 A

1-19 A

1-20 A, B, C

1-21 A

1-22 B

1-23 C

1-24 B

Unit 2 Answers

Study Questions

Installing Exchange Server

1. False

   Explanation: To install Exchange Server, you must be logged on as the administrator.

2. False

3. Custom/Complete, Minimum, Typical

4. True

5. True

6. Join an Existing Site

7. Service

8. True

   Explanation: You must install from the Administrator account, but specify an account as your Site Service account.

9. Performance Optimizer

10. True

11. Site

Configuring Exchange Server

12. True

13. Delivery Restrictions

14. False

    Explanation: You can only enforce storage quotas from Exchange.

15. Custom

16. Pushed

17. Instance

18. True

19. Permissions

20. False

    Explanation: Anyone with Administrator access to a Recipient container can create, modify, and delete distribution lists.

21. Microsoft Mail, SMTP, X.400

22. True

23. Global address list, custom address list, and Offline Address Book

24. True

25. Container-level

Creating and Maintaining Exchange Server Connectors

26. True

27. Transport stack

28. True

29. True

30. Import, Export

31. True

32. Microsoft Mail

33. Connector Post Office

34. False

    Explanation: From the Site Configuration object, choose the connections container object. Select the Microsoft Mail Connector, and then choose File ➢ Properties.

35. True

Synchronizing Directory Information

36. Directory Synchronization (Dirsync)

37. True

38. False

39. True

40. True

41. Requestor

42. True

Replicating the Exchange Directory

43. True

44. Five (5) minutes

45. Directory Replication

46. A bridgehead server

Importing Data from Foreign Mail Systems

47. Directory Import and Export

48. True

49. Personal Address Book

Installing and Configuring Exchange Clients

50. True

51. 8

52. True

53. False

Explanation: Schedule 7.0+ is included as part of the client distribution.

54. Messaging Profile

55. True

Using the Message Transfer Agent

56. MTA

57. False

Explanation: The information store passes the message to the user's mailbox. In local delivery, the MTA is not used.

58. MTA

59. False

Explanation: The client simply posts the messages to the information store; the information store then determines if the message is local. If the message is not local, the information store passes the message to the MTA.

60. False

Explanation: A Site Connector is required to connect separate Exchange sites.

61.

Answer	Connector Type	Description
4	Site	1. Used for dial-up connections between sites. You must have an asynchronous connection between sites. You can schedule this connector.
1	Dynamic RAS Connector	2. Used for SMTP mail connectivity with an SMTP Mail Relay Host. Also used to connect two sites over an intranet or over the Internet.
2	Internet Mail Service	3. Used for connection to a CCITT mail system. Also used to connect two sites over an existing CCITT network.
3	X.400 Site Connector	4. Used for stable and high-bandwidth network connections. Used predominantly with a LAN.

62. True

63. True

64. False

Explanation: The Site Connector cannot be scheduled. Only the X.400 Connector and the Internet Mail Service can be scheduled.

65. False

Explanation: Only use the Dynamic RAS Connector to connect sites if there are no LAN connections.

66. True

67. A—Site Connector

B—X.400 Connector

C—Internet Mail Service

D—Dynamic RAS Connector

Understanding Internet Protocols and Properties

68. NNTP

69. False

Explanation: Exchange Server 5.5 supports only IMAP4.

70. Web browser

71. False

Explanation: POP3 only allows the downloading of unread mail to a user's Internet Mail client.

72. False

Explanation: If the server disables the Internet protocols, a user will not be able to enable the protocols.

Tracking Messages

73. False

Explanation: Message tracking consumes too much disk space and should only be turned on for troubleshooting purposes.

74.

Component	Circle Choice
MTA	Yes
Information Store	Yes
System Attendant	No
Directory Database	No
Internet Mail Service	Yes
Microsoft Mail Connector	Yes
Server Container	No
cc:Mail Connector	No
Site Configuration Container	No
Connections Object	No

75. Troubleshoot

Creating Public Folder Server Locations

76. True

77. Asterisk (*)

78. True

Configuring Security

79. Key Management

80. True

81. CA

82. True

83. DES

84. Bulk Enrollment

85. False

Explanation: An administrator can recover a forgotten password from the CA object Enrollment property page.

Sample Test

2-1 B

2-2 A, C

2-3 D

2-4 A, B, D

2-5 A, B

2-6 C

2-7   C

2-8   A, B

2-9   C

2-10   C

2-11   C

2-12   A, B, C

2-13   B

2-14   B, C, D

2-15   B

2-16   C

2-17   A, C, D

2-18   B

2-19   D

2-20   C

Unit 3 Anwers

Study Questions

Managing Site Security

1.   True

2.   True

3. False.

    Explanation: U.S. export laws allow only 40-bit encryption to be used outside the United States and Canada.

4. KM Server

5. False

    Explanation: To manage any of the CA and KM objects, you must be authorized as a security administrator. An Exchange administrator is not automatically assigned security administrator permissions.

6. Certificate Authority (CA)

7. Manage administrators, recover a user's security key, revoke a user's key, import or untrust another certification authority's certificate

8. You can e-mail the key to the user or hand the key to them personally.

9. False

    Explanation: The CA object allows bulk enrollment of users within different recipient containers.

10. Signing a message, sealing a message

11. X.509 v1, X.509 v3

Managing Users

12. False

    Explanation: You must be logged on as an Exchange administrator and delete the mailbox using the Exchange Administrator program or the User Manager for Domains add-in.

13. True

14. True

15. Directory Export and Import, the Exchange Resource Kit Mailbox Migration tool

16. Clean Mailbox

17. Age, Sensitivity, Read Items, Actions

18. False

    Explanation: Since the only recipient type that stores messages is a mailbox, you can only clean the mailbox of a user.

19. Clean Mailbox

Managing Distribution Lists

20. Assigning administrator permissions for the super user on the site; assigning ownership of the object to the super user

21. False

    Explanation: To improve performance across servers of unequal processing power, assign the most powerful server as the Distribution List Expansion server in the General tab of the Distribution List property pages.

Managing the Directory

22. Tombstone Lifetime; Garbage Collection Interval

23. A Directory database object that has been marked for deletion

24. Garbage Collection Interval

25. False

    Explanation: Multiple Address Books have only been supported since Exchange Server 5.

26. Remote users

27. True

28. Organizational global address list, the default recipient container, any recipient container, Address Book View containers

29. The Directory Consistency Checker

30. Update Now

31. 15

Manage Public Information Store Databases

32. Public Folder server

33. True

34. Private

35. The server to which the user is currently connected

36. Age limits

37. A replica in a public information store, all folders in a public information store, all replicas of a public folder in your organization

38. Delete item retention cleanup, delete expired public folder contents, synchronize the server's public information store with other servers, remove expired public folder conflicts

39. 15

40. Selected Time

41. False

    Explanation: Rehoming is the administrative task of load-balancing public folders across servers in your site. An Exchange administrator is the only user who can rehome public folders to another server's public information store.

42. PFAdmin utility, the PST file

43. From the BackOffice Resource Kit, Part Two (BORK)

44. False

    Explanation: You must use the Exchange Administrator program and have administrator permissions on the public folder.

Managing Private Information Store Databases

45. True

46. Storage Limits

47. Choose Item Recover ➤ Deleted Item Retention Time (days).

48. Issue Warning (K), Prohibit Send (K), Prohibit Send and Receive (K)

49. Prohibit Send and Receive (K)

50. Issue Warning (K)

51. No, only the administrator can change a user's storage limit.

52. 1—Mailbox Storage Limits; 2—Private Information Store Limits

53. C

Backing Up and Restoring

54. A 5MB file that holds Exchange transactions that will be written to a database

55. False

    Explanation: Circular logging uses one file to write transactions. As the file becomes full, Exchange writes over the part of the file that has committed transactions to the database.

56. True

57. Normal

58. You can restore to the last transaction committed.

59. True

60. False

    Explanation: Since the original transactions were written, Exchange wrote over the older transactions and can't re-create them. You must restore to the last full backup.

61. Full (Normal) makes complete copies of all the Exchange databases; Incremental copies file additions, deletions, and differences since the last Incremental or Full backup; Differential copies file additions, deletions, and differences since the last Full backup.

62. True

63. True

64. Run ISINTEG with the –patch option; run the Directory Knowledge Consistency Checker.

65. False

    Explanation: You can back up any Exchange Server database in your site.

66. Erase All Existing Data

67. False

Explanation: You must select Public and Private, even though you are only restoring the private information store.

68. `Dir.edb`

69. `<drive_letter>:\Exchsrvr`

70. `Pub.edb`

71. `<drive_letter>:\Kmsdata\kmsmdb.edb`

Managing Connectivity

72. A pause in the transmission, during which an acknowledgment is expected

73. False

Explanation: The window size is the number of checkpoints that can go unacknowledged before data transfer is stopped.

74. True

75. Connection Retry Values

76. Non-Delivery Report

77. Transfer Timeout

78. Whenever a change has been made or once a day

79. True

80. The current server

81. Routing Calculation

Sample Test

3-1   A

3-2   C

3-3   A, D

3-4   D

3-5   D

3-6   A

3-7   C

3-8   B

3-9   B, C, D

3-10   B

3-11   D

3-12   A, C

3-13   B

3-14   C

3-15   C

3-16   A, D

3-17   A, B

3-18   C

3-19   C, D

3-20   A, B

Unit 4 Answers

Study Questions

Configuring a Link Monitor and a Server Monitor

1. Server monitor, link monitor

2. True

3. False

   Explanation: The link monitor tests communication links, and the server monitor checks and maintains Windows NT Server services and Exchange Server services.

4. Exchange Server ping

5. False

   Explanation: Monitors are configured on a Server object. You must choose the server from which to build your monitor.

6. False

   Explanation: Monitors use log files to track events and to help troubleshoot problems with a specific monitor.

7. Normal, critical

8. Normal is 15 minutes. Critical is 5 minutes after a server goes into a warning.

9. False

   Explanation: The Bounce property for a link monitor sends Exchange Server ping messages for one round-trip between servers. The time it takes to return the ping message from the server is measured.

10. A server monitor

11. Clock Synchronization

12. True

13. Server Status

14. Warnings, alerts

15. True

16. Notification, Mail Message, Network Alert

17. False

    Explanation: You can assign as many notifications as you need on a monitor. You can also assign multiple types of notifications per monitor as needed.

18. False

    Explanation: The recipient of a mail message can be any valid e-mail address, although the recipient is usually the Exchange administrator.

19. Computers

20. Manual, automatic

21. Question Mark: Unknown
    Red Exclamation Point: Warning
    Green Up Arrow: OK, all checks are normal
    Red Down Arrow: Alert

22. True

Optimizing Exchange Server

23. Performance Optimizer

24. False

25. Directory, information store

26. 90 MHz Pentium

27. True

28. Sequential

29. True

30. Performance Monitor

31. True

32. Redirector, process, memory, logical disk, processor

33. Bytes Total/sec, Network Errors/sec

34. The % Disk Time NT counter of the Logical Disk object

35. The Elapsed Time NT counter of the Process object

36. The Page/sec NT Counter of the Memory object

37. True

Optimizing Foreign Connections and Site-to-Site Connections

38. False

Explanation: Using NDRs, you can test communication links to foreign mail systems and connectors.

39. Nonexistent

40. True

41. *Message or body returned from*

42. Messages Received NT counter in the MSExchangeMSMI object

43. False

Explanation: Exchange Server 5.5 includes support for the Internet Mail Service as well as support for SNMP.

44. Queued MTS-OUT counter in the MSExchangeIMC object

45. Connections Total counter in the MSExchangeIMC object

46. True

47. Inbound Messages Total, Outbound Messages Total

Monitoring and Optimizing the Messaging Environment

48. Secured, unsecured

49. False

Explanation: You cannot modify unsecured queues. You can only view the queues, and you can only view the contents immediately after a connection has been made to a connector and messages have been delivered into the queue.

50. Windows NT Performance Monitor

51. Remaining Replication Updates

52. Microsoft Mail Connector, Internet Mail Service

53. The Average Time for Delivery counter in the ExchangeIMC object

Monitoring Server Performance Using SNMP and MADMAN MIB

54. True

55. 1566

56. Maintenance and Directory Management

57. Manual, automatic

58. False

    Explanation: If you have already installed a MIB that did not ship with the Windows NT Server SNMP Service and Agent, you must install the Exchange MIB manually.

59. True

60. `Perf2mib.exe, Mibcc.exe`

61. False

    Explanation: Although you probably want to use an SNMP management application to view the MIB, you can also use the Windows NT Resource Kit tool, `snmputil`, to read from the MIB if you don't have SNMP management applications.

62. `1.4.311.1.1.3.1.1`

63. `software.systems., 38`

64. True

65. Total Loops Detected

66. Outbound Bytes Total

Sample Test

4-1   D

4-2   C

4-3   B

4-4   C

4-5   D

4-6   B

4-7   A

4-8   B, C, D

4-9   A, B

4-10   C

4-11   B

4-12   B

4-13   D

4-14   A

4-15   C

4-16   B, C, D

4-17   A

Unit 5 Answers

Study Questions

Troubleshooting the Exchange Server Installation and Upgrade

1. False

   Explanation: You should install from the Administrator account and specify an NT account for the Site Services account. If you use different accounts to install Exchange on other servers, you will not have permissions to add servers to the site.

2. True

3. The ESE97 key was not created in the Registry.

   Explanation: You must close all other running applications while installing Exchange. If one of those running applications is writing to the Registry at the same time you attempt to install Exchange, there will be a conflict, and the installation will fail.

4. Permissions: Install Exchange Server from the Administrator account. The account you are installing from does not have Exchange administrator permissions on the primary site.

   Network: The protocols between two servers are incompatible. Install a protocol between the two servers that supports RPCs.

5. There is not enough virtual memory configured for this server.

6. You must install the Exchange Administrator program on an NT workstation with the custom/complete installation type and choose only the Exchange Administrator program.

Troubleshooting Exchange Connectivity

7. Diagnostics Logging

Message Tracking

Windows NT Event Viewer application log

Message Queues

8. MTA

Directory

Information Store

Internet Mail Service

Microsoft Mail Connector

Microsoft Schedule+ Free/Busy Connector

Microsoft Exchange Connector for Lotus cc:Mail

9. None—Default

Minimum—Logs only high-level events

Medium—Logs high-level and medium-level events

High—Logs all events

10. Diagnostics Logging writes to the application log, and you use the Windows NT Event Viewer to view the log.

11. False

Explanation: You enable MTA Message Tracking by checking the Track Messages checkbox on the General property page of the host server's MTA property pages.

12. `<drive letter>`\exchsrvr\tracking.log\`yyyyddmm.log`

13. False

Explanation: You don't have to turn off the MTA; you can view the queues while the MTA is up and running. You must refresh the display periodically to view the changes made to the queues as messages are delivered and submitted. For a static view, you can turn off the MTA and view the queues.

14. Delete

15. False

Explanation: The Microsoft Mail Connector has a property page that displays the incoming and outgoing message queues.

16. Return or delete some of the oldest messages. If you can't do so, the outbound queue may be failing. Run the MTACHECK utility to fix this problem.

17. An instance with the same name previously existed and was incorrectly removed. Use a different name, or ignore the message.

You don't have permissions to create instances; ask the site administrator to grant you permissions.

18. True

19. True

20. False

Explanation: The Internet Mail Service can be used for transport across the Internet or used in an intranet for its routing and addressing features.

21. Site Connector

X.400 Connector

Dynamic RAS Connector

Internet Mail Service

22. Dynamic RAS Connector

23. You may not have configured Directory Replication, or Directory Replication has not been successful. Start and run a link monitor to check your connections. Then check the Directory Replication Connector at the remote site.

24. Using Message Tracking, follow the path of the Directory Replication messages to determine where the failure occurred.

25. Run a server monitor to check the connections between your server and the remote server. If the remote MTA is down, run the MTACHECK and restart the service.

26. You must configure a Directory Replication Connector. Directory Replication is not automatic across sites.

27. True

28. False

    Explanation: Although Microsoft recommends building a log of performance history on the Internet Mail Service for troubleshooting purposes, it is not required for Message Tracking.

29. True

30. Change the delivery restrictions on the Internet Mail Service on your local host.

31. From the Internet Mail Service's Internet Mail property page, in the Interoperability section uncheck the *Send Microsoft Exchange rich text formatting* checkbox.

Troubleshooting the Exchange Client

32. True

33. You must create a user account in the local domain for the user to establish trust relationships with the server.

34. Check the information store to verify that it is running. If it is not, run the ISINTEG to diagnose problems and then restart the Information Store.

Troubleshooting the Information Store

35. Diagnostics Logging

    Monitoring

    Message Tracking

    ISINTEG Utility

    Public Folder Status Information

36. The Exchange Administrator program's information store public folder resource status view

37. False

    Explanation: The information store views can be customized using the Tools menu in the Exchange Administrator program.

38. Client Version

39. Last Access Time

40. Total K

41. Number of Replicas

42. Deleted Items K

43. ISINTEG (Information Store Integrity Checker)

44. True

45. –pri

Troubleshooting the Directory Service

46. Diagnostics Logging

Monitoring

Message Tracking

Message Queues

47. Check the Windows NT application log for events that indicate a problem with the Directory Service.

Configure and start a server monitor session to verify that servers are transferring replication information normally.

Track replication messages between sites to identify the component that is causing the error.

48. Use the `ping` command or the `net use` command between servers to see if they communicate. If not, use your network management tools to locate the break.

Check the Windows NT Server Event Viewer application log to read the events associated with replication within a site.

Troubleshooting Exchange Resource Problems

49. The System applet in Control Panel

50. False

Explanation: Move the busiest public folders to a server that is not as busy as this server.

51. True

52. False

Explanation: Use the Windows NT Performance Monitor to check the rate of inbound and outbound messages and their sizes; add another gateway on another server to balance the load across the two servers or increase the schedule for this job.

53. From the command prompt, run the `ping` command or `net use` to confirm that the remote server is unavailable.

54. Server monitor with a Notification Alert

55. The address space for the correct spelling of the host name

56. Your DNS Server may be down or your TCP/IP network property does not reference a DNS server.

Troubleshooting Advanced Security

57. The Diagnostics Logging maximum log level

58. False

    Explanation: The KM Server will run all four levels of Diagnostics Logging.

59. Two KM servers have been installed in your organization. Remove one server and reinstall it as a slave to the master server in your local site.

60. Your user is not authorized to use advanced security. Enable security for the user from the Security tab of the Mailbox property page.

    Your user's security token has been revoked. Use the recover security key on the Mailbox Security property page for this user.

Sample Test

5-1	C
5-2	A
5-3	D
5-4	A

5-5	A
5-6	C
5-7	C
5-8	A
5-9	B
5-10	A
5-11	A
5-12	B
5-13	A
5-14	C
5-15	B
5-16	D
5-17	D
5-18	A
5-19	B
5-20	A
5-21	C

Unit 6 Answers

Final Review

6-1   B

6-2   C

6-3   C

6-4   C

6-5   A

6-6   D

6-7   C

6-8   B

6-9   D

6-10   A

6-11   A

6-12   A, C

6-13   B

6-14   A

6-15   C

6-16   A

6-17   D

6-18   C

6-19   A, B, C

6-20   C

6-21   C

6-22   D

6-23   B

6-24   B

Explanation: Although the command to start the monitors is correct, no autologon account is specified to log on automatically when the system reboots.

6-25   B

6-26   B

6-27   C

6-28   B

6-29   A

6-30   C

6-31   D

6-32   D

6-33   B

6-34   C

6-35   A

6-36   C

6-37   B

6-38   A, B

6-39   A, C, D

6-40   C

6-41   B

6-42   D

6-43   A

6-44   A, B, D

6-45   A, C

6-46   A

6-47   A, B

6-48   C

6-49   C

6-50   B

6-51   A

6-52   D

6-53   B

6-54   C

6-55   A

6-56   B

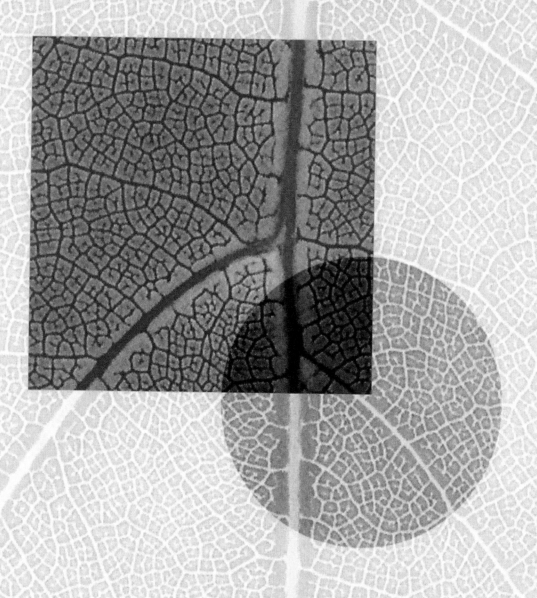

Glossary

ActiveX The set of Microsoft protocols that specifies how software components can communicate through the use of objects.

ADE See *Automatic Directory Exchange.*

Address Encapsulation Placing a sender's native Exchange address in the form of a valid SMTP address. The encapsulated address is placed in the FROM field of the message.

Address Space The set of remote addresses that can be reached through a particular connector. Each connector must have at least one entry in its address space.

Address Space Scoping A property that restricts a connector to transferring messages sent from a specified scope. The scope can be the organization, a site, or the server location within which the connector resides.

Age Limit A property that specifies how long a unit of data may remain in its container (for example, a public folder).

Anonymous Access Accessing a server without logging in with a Windows NT or other type of user account.

Application Programming Interface (API) A collection of programming commands (frequently called interfaces) that can invoke the functions of a program. Other programs can use a program's API to request services or to communicate with that program. For example, Windows 95 contains an API referred to as the win32 API. For an application to request a service from Windows 95, it must issue that request using a win32 API.

Architecture The description of the components of a product or system, what they are, what they do, and how they relate to one another.

Attribute A characteristic of an object. Attributes of a mailbox include display name, primary Windows NT account, and storage limits. The terms *attribute* and *property* are synonymous.

Authentication A process whereby an object, such as a user, is allowed to access or use another object, such as a server or a protocol. For example, you can configure the Microsoft Exchange Server POP3 protocol so that it allows access only to POP3 clients that use the Windows NT Challenge/Response authentication protocol.

Automatic Directory Exchange (ADE)   A program used to exchange global address lists across cc:Mail.

Back-End Program   A server application that provides services to front-end programs (client applications). Exchange Server is an example of a back-end program.

Backup Domain Controller (BDC)   A Windows NT server that maintains copies of the User Directory across a domain.

Bridgehead Server   A Microsoft Exchange server designated as a server to deliver data to another site.

Bulk Encryption Key   The random secret key generated by a client's security DLL used to seal messages.

Caching   Temporarily storing data in random access memory (RAM) where it can be accessed much faster than it could be from the disk.

CAL   See *Client Access License.*

CAST 40   A 40-bit encryption algorithm designed by Carlisle, Adams, and Tavares.

CAST 64   A 64-bit encryption algorithm designed by Carlisle, Adams, and Tavares.

cc:Mail   A Lotus mail system.

CCITT   See *Consultative Committee International for Telegraph and Telephone.*

Certification Authority (CA)   The central authority that distributes, publishes, and validates security keys. Exchange Server can be configured to perform this role. See also *Public Key* and *Private Key.*

Challenge/Response   A general term for a class of security mechanisms, including Microsoft-authentication methods that use Windows NT network security and an encrypted password.

Chat   A real-time, text-based, conversation performed over a computer network or networks.

Checkpoint File   The file (EDB.CHK) that contains the point in a transaction log which is the boundary between data that has been committed and data that has not yet been committed to an Exchange database.

Circular Logging   The process of writing new information in transaction log files over information that has already been committed. Instead of repeatedly creating new transaction logs, the Exchange database engine "circles back" and reuses log files that have been fully committed to the database. Circular logging keeps down the number of transaction logs on the disk. These logs cannot be used to re-create a database because the logs do not have a complete set of data. The logs contain only the most recent data not yet committed to a database. Circular logging is the default setting of the Exchange Directory and Information Store databases. Microsoft discourages the use of circular logging.

Cleartext   Unencrypted data. Synonymous with plaintext.

Client Access License (CAL)   The license, purchased from Microsoft, that legally permits a client to access an Exchange server.

Cluster Server   A Microsoft software product that enables multiple physical servers to be logically grouped for reasons of fault-tolerance.

Connector Cost   A numeric value assigned to a connector. The MTA uses connector cost as a criterion when it chooses from among multiple connectors that support the same address space.

Connectors   Software that manages the transport of data between Exchange sites (for example, the Site connector) or between Exchange and a foreign message system (for example, the X.400 connector, Microsoft Mail connector, and the Internet Mail Service). See also *Gateways*.

Consultative Committee International for Telegraph and Telephone (CCITT)   A international standards committee that defines electronic mail standards.

Container Object   An object in the Exchange hierarchy that contains and groups other objects. The organization object is a container object that contains the Folders, Global Address List, and Site objects.

Context Level   A level in the Exchange hierarchy that does not inherit permissions from other portions of the hierarchy. The three context levels are organization, site, and configuration. Administrative permissions must be assigned to users or groups individually at each of the three levels.

Cryptology   The study and implementation of hiding and revealing information.

Custom Recipient   An Exchange recipient object that represents a foreign message recipient. Custom recipients allow Exchange clients to address messages to foreign mail users.

Data Encryption Standard (DES)   A 64-bit encryption algorithm used by the U.S. Department of Defense.

Datagram   A packet that contains both data to be sent and information related to the transmission of the data, such as the network address of the packet's destination.

Decryption   Translating encrypted data back to plaintext.

DES   See *Data Encryption Standard*.

Desktop Information Manager   An application that can be used to manage many aspects of a user's activities, such as reading and sending e-mail, accessing calendar and scheduling information, and managing tasks.

Digital Signature   A personal and unique number included with a message that proves the sender's identity.

Directory Replication   The transferring of directory information to other servers in a site (intrasite) or to another site (intersite). Intrasite directory replication is automatic, but intersite directory replication must be configured through the Directory Replication connector.

Directory Replication Bridgehead Server   The Exchange server designated as the server that will send site directory information to another site. Only one server in a site can be assigned to replicate information with each remote site. There can be more than one directory replication bridgehead server in a site, but each must connect with a unique remote site. One server can, however, perform directory replication with multiple remote sites.

Directory Service   A network-wide descriptive directory that defines every Exchange object. The Directory Service is one of the five Exchange core components.

Directory Synchronization Protocol   The MS Mail protocol used to synchronize directory information between MS Mail postoffices. One server is designated as the dirsync server, and the other servers are designated as dirsync requestors. The dirsync server, maintains the master copy of a network's directory. The dirsync requestors send any new directory information to the dirsync server and request a copy of the master directory.

Dirsync Requestor   A type of MS Mail postoffice that sends its new directory information to the designated dirsync server and requests a copy of the master directory from the dirsync server. See also *Directory Synchronization Protocol, T1,* and *T3.*

Dirsync Server   A type of MS Mail postoffice that maintains the master copy of a network's MS Mail directory information. It also responds to requests by sending a copy of the master directory to dirsync requestors. See also *Directory Synchronization Protocol* and *T2.*

Distinguished Name (DN)   An X.500-style address that denotes an object's location in the Exchange directory hierarchy. An example DN is /o=widget/ou=chicago/cn=education/cn=jayw.

Domain Name Service (DNS)   A naming standard for hosts names on the Internet. Naming syntax is of host.subdomain.rootdomain.

Encryption   Scrambling data to make it unreadable. The intended recipient will decrypt the data into plaintext in order to read it.

Expanding a Distribution List   The process of determining the individual addresses contained within a distribution list. This process is performed by the MTA.

Export Utility   A Microsoft Exchange utility that enables the copying (that is, exporting) of the Exchange directory to a text file where it could be modified in a batch manner and then imported back into the directory. This utility is accessed through the Tools menu of Microsoft Exchange Administrator. See also *Import Utility.*

Extraction   The process of copying foreign message resources, such as mailboxes, messages, and so on, and putting them in a format that can be imported into Exchange. See also *Source Extractors.*

Filtering   The ability to display only messages that meet various criteria, such as sender, subject, date, priority, and others.

Folder-Based Application   An application built within a public folder by customizing properties of the folder, such as permissions, views, rules, and the folder forms library to store and present data to users.

Foreign System   A non-Exchange message system.

Frame   The unit of information sent by a Data Link protocol, such as Ethernet or Token Ring.

Free/Busy   Terminology used in the Microsoft Schedule+ application to denote an unscheduled period of time (that is, free) or a scheduled period of time (that is, busy).

Front-End Program   A client application, usually running on a user's workstation, that communicates with the back-end program, usually running on a server computer. Outlook is an example of a front-end program for Exchange Server, the back-end program. See also *Back-End Program*.

Fully Qualified Domain Name (FQDN)   The full DNS path of an Internet host. An example is `sales.dept4.widget.com`.

Function Call   An instruction in a program that calls (invokes) a function. For example, MAPIReadMail is a MAPI function call.

Garbage Collection Interval   Interval of time between the deletion of expired tombstones. See also *Tombstones*.

Gateway Access Component   The MS Mail software that permits a post-office to send foreign addressed messages to a gateway postoffice for delivery.

Gateway Address Routing Table (GWART)   The Routing table that contains all the address space entries for all the connectors in a site.

Gateway Postoffice   The MS Mail postoffice configured to receive messages to be delivered through a gateway.

Gateways   Third-party software that permits Exchange to interoperate with a foreign message system. See also *Connectors*.

Global Unique Identifier (GUI) An identifier for a specific Exchange information store.

Groupware Any application that allows *groups* of people to store and share information.

GUI See *Global Unique Identifier.*

GWART See *Gateway Address Routing Table.*

Hierarchy Any structure or organization that uses class, grade, or rank to arrange objects.

Home Server The Exchange server on which an object physically resides.

HTML See *HyperText Markup Language.*

HTTP See *HyperText Transfer Protocol.*

HyperText Markup Language (HTML) The script language used to create World Wide Web content. HTML can create hyperlinks between objects on the Web.

HyperText Transfer Protocol (HTTP) The Internet protocol used to transfer information on the World Wide Web.

Import Utility A Microsoft Exchange utility that enables the copying (that is, importing) of directory information into the Exchange directory. This utility is accessed through the Tools menu of Microsoft Exchange Administrator. See also *Export Utility.*

Importing The process of copying foreign message resources, such as mailboxes, messages, and so on, into Exchange.

IMS See *Internet Mail Service.*

Inbox The storage folder that receives new incoming messages.

Information Service A group of service providers for a specific product or environment. The information service for Exchange Server includes service providers for an address book, message store, and message transport.

Information Store   A database consisting of mail messages, data, and folders. One of the five Exchange core components.

Internet Locator Server (ILS)   A Microsoft server that monitors which users are online and available for collaboration, such as participating in a chat, a whiteboarding session, or even a videoconference.

Internet Mail Service (IMS)   A component that provides remote connection though an intranet or through the Internet. One of the five Exchange core components.

Internet Message Access Protocol 4 (IMAP4)   An Internet retrieval protocol that enables clients to access and manipulate messages in their mailbox on a remote server. IMAP4 provides additional functions over POP3, such as access to subfolders (not merely the Inbox folder) and selective downloading of messages.

Interoperability   The ability of different systems to work together (for example, the ability of two different messaging systems to exchange messages).

Interpersonal Messaging (IPM)   The X.400 standard for the format of an e-mail message.

Intersite   Transfer of information across site boundaries.

Intrasite   Transfer of information within one site.

Key   A randomly generated number used to implement advanced security, such as encryption or digital signatures. See also *Key Pair, Public Key,* and *Private Key.*

Key Pair   A key that is divided into two mathematically related halves. One half (the public key) is made public. The other half (the private key) is known only by one user.

Leaf Object   An object that does not contain any other objects. A mailbox object is an example of a leaf object.

Lightweight Directory Access Protocol (LDAP)   An Internet protocol used for client access to an X.500-based directory.

Local Delivery   The delivery of a message to a recipient object that resides on the same server as the sender.

Local Procedure Call (LPC)   An instruction that is executed on the same computer as the program executing the instruction. See also *Remote Procedure Call*.

Location Transparency   Being able to access resources without knowledge of their physical location.

Locations   A group of servers that will be searched first to display the contents of a public folder.

Lockbox   An encrypted secret key that is sent with a message.

MADMAN MIB   See *Maintenance and Directory Management MIB*.

Mail Exchanger (MX)   The designation of an SMTP mail server in a DNS database.

Mailbox   The generic term for a container that holds messages, such as incoming and outgoing messages.

Maintenance and Directory Management MIB (MADMAN MIB)   The Exchange MIB available for use with SNMP network console software.

Management Information Base (MIB)   A database used to set and retrieve values between a SNMP object and the console.

MDBEF   See *Microsoft Database Exchange Format*.

Member Server   A Windows NT server that participates in a Windows NT domain.

Message Transfer Agent (MTA)   A component responsible for transferring messages between Exchange servers and connectors. One of the five Exchange core components.

Messaging Application Programming Interface (MAPI)   An object-oriented programming interface for messaging services, developed by Microsoft.

Messaging Bridgehead Server   An Exchange server designated to deliver messages to another site.

MIB   See *Management Information Base.*

Microsoft Commercial Internet Server (MCIS)   A Microsoft suite of commercial-grade server applications marketed to Internet service providers, telecommunication carriers, cable network operators, and so on. Applications include MCIS Mail Server, Chat Server, and News Server, among others.

Microsoft Database Exchange Format (MDBEF)   The Exchange native e-mail format.

Microsoft Mail   A shared file system mail program.

Migration   Moving resources, such as mailboxes, messages, and so on, from one messaging system to another. See also *Extraction, Importing,* and *Migration Wizard.*

Migration Wizard   An Exchange program that extracts data from a foreign message system and imports it into Exchange.

Mismatch   The situation when an Exchange server determines through the Knowledge Consistency Checker (KCC) that it does not have all the Exchange servers in the site in its Replication List.

MTA   See *Message Transfer Agent.*

Multimaster Model   A model in which every server in a site has a copy of the site directory.

Multipurpose Internet Mail Extensions (MIME)   An Internet protocol that enables the encoding of binary content within mail messages. For example, MIME can be used to encode a graphics file or word-processing document as an attachment to a text-based mail message. The recipient of the message would also have to be using MIME to decode the attachment. MIME is newer than UUENCODE and in many systems has replaced it. See also *UUENCODE.*

MX   See *Mail Exchanger.*

Name Resolution   The DNS process of mapping a domain name to its IP address.

Network News Transfer Protocol (NNTP)   An Internet protocol used to transfer newsgroup information between newsgroup servers and clients (newsreaders) and between newsgroup servers.

Newsfeed   The newsgroup data that is sent from one newsgroup server to other newsgroup servers.

Newsgroup   A discussion group used by NNTP protocol.

NNTP   See *Network News Transfer Protocol.*

Objects   The representation, or abstraction, of an entity. For example, each Exchange server is represented as an object in the Exchange Administrator program. As an object, it contains properties, also called attributes, that can be configured. For example, an Exchange server object can have properties that give certain administrators permission to configure that server.

Offline Address Book (OAB)   A copy stored on a client's computer of part or all of the server-based global address list (GAL). An OAB allows a client to address messages while not connected to their server.

Offline Storage folder (OST)   Folders located on a client's computer that contain replicas of server-based folders. An OST allows a client to access and manipulate copies of server data while not connected to the server. When the client reconnects to the server, the OST resynchronizes with the master folders on the server.

One-Off Address   An e-mail address that does not exist in the Exchange GAL, but is specified as a message recipient by a user. One-off addresses are often used to send messages to Internet addresses that do not have corresponding custom recipients in the GAL.

Organization   The highest level object in the Microsoft Exchange hierarchy.

Originator/Recipient Address (O/R Address)   An X.400 address scheme that uses a hierarchical method to denote where on an X.400 network a recipient resides. An example is `c=us;a= ;p=widgetnet;o=widget;s=wilson;g=jay;`.

PDC   See *Primary Domain Controller*.

Personal Address Book (PAB)   An address book created by a user and stored on that user's computer or a server.

Personal Storage Folder (PST)   Folders that users create and use to store messages instead of storing them in their mailbox in the private information store. PSTs can be located on a user's computer or on a server.

Plaintext   Unencrypted data. Synonymous with cleartext.

Point-to-Point Protocol (PPP)   An Internet protocol used for direct communication between two nodes. Commonly used by Internet users and their Internet service provider on the serial line point-to-point connection over a modem.

Polling   A process that queries a server-based mailbox for new mail.

POP3   See *Post Office Protocol 3*.

Port Number   A numeric identifier assigned to an application. Transport protocols such as TCP use the port number to identify to which application to deliver a packet.

Post Office Protocol 3 (POP3)   An Internet protocol used for client retrieval of mail from a server-based mailbox.

Postoffice   An MS Mail server that stores messages.

Primary Domain Controller (PDC)   A Windows NT server that maintains the User Directory across a domain.

Private Folder   A server-based folder that is part of a user's mailbox. Private folders are stored on an Exchange server in the private information store. The Inbox and Outbox are examples of private folders.

Private Key   The half of a key pair that is known by only one user and is used to decrypt data and to digitally sign messages.

Professional Office System (PROFS)   An International Business Machine (IBM) host-based messaging application.

Property   A characteristic of an object. Properties of a mailbox include display name, primary Windows NT account, and storage limits. The terms *property* and *attribute* are synonymous.

Proxy Address   A foreign e-mail address of an Exchange recipient. The non-Exchange user uses the proxy address to address mail to the Exchange recipient. Proxy addresses for SMTP and X.400 are automatically generated for Exchange recipients at their creation. If the connectors for MS Mail and cc:Mail were installed, proxy addresses for those address types would also be automatically generated for Exchange recipients.

Public Folder   A folder used to store data for a group of users. Some of the features of a public folder are permissions, views, and rules.

Public Folder Affinity   A numeric value that assigns a cost to another site. When clients need to connect to public folders in another site, affinity numbers are used to choose the site.

Public Folder Replication   The transferring of public folder data to replicas of that folder on other servers.

Public Key   The half of a key pair that is published for anyone to read and is used when encrypting data and verifying digital signatures.

Pull   A procedure whereby a user finds and retrieves information, such as when browsing a public folder. Users accessing a public folder containing a company's employee handbook is a type of pull communication.

Pull Feed   A procedure whereby a newsgroup server requests newsfeed information from another newsgroup server. The opposite of a push feed.

Push   A procedure whereby information is sent (that is, pushed) to users. Users do not need to find and retrieve (that is, pull) the information. Exchange Server pushes incoming messages to MAPI-based Exchange clients.

Push Feed   A procedure whereby a newsgroup server sends information to another newsgroup server without requiring the receiving server to request it. The opposite of a pull feed.

RAS   See *Remote Access Services*.

Raw Mode   A specific operational mode of Microsoft Exchange Administrator that allows the viewing and manipulating of all the properties of Exchange objects. Can be initiated by running ADMIN /raw.

Recipient   An Exchange object that can receive a message. Recipients objects include mailboxes, distribution lists, public folders, and custom recipients.

Relay Host   An SMTP host designated to receive all outgoing SMTP mail. The relay host then forwards the mail to the relevant destination.

Remote Access Services (RAS)   A dial-up service provided on Windows NT platforms.

Remote Delivery   The delivery of a message to a recipient that does not reside on the same server as the sender.

Remote Procedure Call (RPC)   A set of protocols for issuing instructions that can be sent over a network for execution. A client computer makes a request to a server computer, and the results are sent to the client computer. The computer issuing the request and the computer performing the request are remotely separated over a network. Remote procedure calls are a key ingredient in distributed processing and client/server computing. See also *Local Procedure Call.*

Replica   A copy of a public folder located on an Exchange server.

Replication   The transferring of a copy of data to another location, such as another server or site. See also *Directory Replication* and *Public Folder Replication.*

Replication Latency   The delay period (the latency) that occurs after a change to the directory before the DS begins the directory replication process. Latency allows multiple directory changes to be sent during directory replication. The default replication latency period is 300 seconds.

Resolver Program   Client software that queries a DNS database to map a domain name to its IP address.

Resolving an Address   The process of determining where (on which physical server) an object with a particular address resides.

Rich Text Format (RTF)   A Microsoft format protocol that includes bolding, highlighting, italics, underlining, and many other format types.

Role   A group of permissions that define which activities a user or group can perform with regards to an object.

Scalable   The ability of a system to grow to handle greater traffic, volume, usage, and so on.

Schema   The set of rules defining a directory's hierarchy, objects, attributes, and so on.

Scripting Agent   The Microsoft Exchange Scripting Agent is a component that reads and executes a script attached to a public folder. It can carry out instructions by accessing databases, spreadsheets, gateways, and many other programs and services.

Sealing   The process of encrypting data.

Secret Key   A security key that can be used to encrypt data and that is only known by a sender and the recipients the sender informs.

Secure Sockets Layer (SSL)   An Internet protocol that provides secure and authenticated TCP/IP connections. A client and server establish a "handshake" whereby they agree on a level of security they will use, such as authentication requirements and encryption. SSL can be used to encrypt sensitive data for transmission.

Send Form   A stand-alone form that is sent from one user to another user.

Service Advertisement Protocol (SAP)   A Novell protocol that is used by servers to advertise their presence and services on a network.

Service Provider   A MAPI program that provides messaging-oriented services to a client. There are three main types of service providers: address book, message store, and message transport.

Shadow Postoffice   A postoffice without mailboxes. The Exchange MS Mail Connector Postoffice is referred to as a shadow postoffice because it does not contain user mailboxes and only temporarily stores incoming and outgoing MS Mail messages.

Signing   The process of placing a digital signature on a message.

Simple Authentication and Security Layer (SASL)   A protocol that provides authentication of SMTP client connections to an SMTP server.

Simple Mail Transfer Protocol (SMTP)   The Internet protocol used to transfer mail messages.

Simple Network Management Protocol (SNMP)   An Internet protocol used to manage heterogeneous computers, operating systems, and applications. Because of its wide acceptance and applicability, SNMP is well suited for enterprise-wide management.

Single-Instance Storage   Storing only one copy. A message that is sent to multiple recipients homed on the same server has only one copy (that is, instance) stored on that server. Each recipient is given a pointer to that copy of the message.

Single-Seat Administration   The ability to manage a number of sites, servers, and so on from a single application on a single computer.

Site   A logical grouping of Exchange servers that are connected by a full mesh (every server is directly connected to every other server) and communicate using high-bandwidth RPC. All servers in a site can authenticate one another either because they are homed in the same Windows NT domain or because of trust relationships configured between separate Windows NT domains.

Site Services Account   The Windows NT user account that Exchange Server components within a site use to communicate.

S/MIME   Secure MIME is an Internet protocol that enables mail messages to be digitally signed, encrypted, and decrypted.

Source Extractors   Software programs that can copy messaging resources, such as mailboxes and messages, from a foreign mail system and put the information in a format that can be imported into Exchange.

Standby Server   A server configured to be used in place of another server. If a server goes down because of a failure or is taken down for maintenance, a standby server can be brought online to provide continued service to users.

Store-and-Forward   A delivery method that does not require the sender and recipient to have simultaneous interaction. Instead, when a message is sent, it is transferred to the next appropriate location in the network, which temporarily stores it, makes a routing decision, and forwards the message to the next appropriate network location. This process occurs until the message is ultimately delivered to the intended recipient or until an error condition causes the message to be returned to the sender.

Subsystem   A software component that, when loaded, extends the operating system by providing additional services. The MAPI program, MAPI32.DLL, is an example of a subsystem. MAPI32.DLL loads on top of the Windows 95 or Windows NT operating system and provides messaging services.

System Attendant   A component responsible for maintenance and logging. One of the five Exchange core components.

Systems Network Architecture Distribution Services (SNADS)   An International Business Machines (IBM) store-and-forward protocol for the transmission of data. SNADS enables the sender and recipient to not have to be synchronized.

Target Server   An Exchange server in a remote site that is designated to receive messages from the local site.

TCP/IP RFC   Request for Comment that defines standards for TCP/IP.

Token   The packet of security information a certification authority sends to a client during advanced security setup. Information in the packet includes the client's public key and its expiration. A token is synonymous with a certificate.

Tombstone   Information created by the DS about a deleted directory object. The tombstone is replicated to other Exchange servers in a site to inform them of the deletion.

Tombstone Lifetime   The length of time a tombstone is kept before it is deleted.

Transaction Log   A file used to quickly write data. That data is later written to the relevant Exchange database file. It is quicker to write to a transaction log file because the writes are done sequentially (that is, one right after the other). Transaction log files can also be used to re-create data that has been lost in an Exchange database.

Trust Level A numeric value given an object that is used to determine if that object should be replicated to another location, such as a foreign directory.

T1 The interval used by dirsync requestors to send their postoffice address list to the designated dirsync server.

T2 The interval used by the dirsync server to compile a new global address list and to send that list to the dirsync requestors.

T3 The interval used by the dirsync requestors to rebuild their postoffice address list.

Uniform Resource Locator (URL) An addressing method used to identify Internet servers and documents.

Universal Inbox One inbox folder that receives incoming items from all outside sources and of all types, such as e-mail, voice mail, faxes, pages, and so on.

User Profile A collection of information for MAPI client configuration that specifies the services a user wants to use and how MAPI client applications are to look and behave.

UUENCODE Stands for UNIX-to-UNIX Encode, and is a protocol used to encode binary information within mail messages. UUENCODE is older than MIME. See also *Multipurpose Internet Mail Extensions.*

Web The World Wide Web.

Windows NT Services A Windows NT process created to perform specific functions.

World Wide Web (WWW) The collection of computers on the Internet using protocols such as HTML and HTTP.

WWW See *World Wide Web.*

X.400 An International Telecommunications Union (ITU) standard for message exchange.

X.500 An International Telecommunications Union (ITU) standard for directory services.

Index

Note to the Reader: Throughout this index, **boldface** page numbers indicate primary discussions of a topic or the definition of a term. *Italic* page numbers indicate illustrations.

MCSE CORE REQUIREMENT STUDY GUIDES FROM NETWORK PRESS

Sybex's Network Press presents updated and expanded second editions
of the definitive study guides for MCSE candidates.

ISBN: 0-7821-2220-5
704pp; 7¹/₂" x 9"; Hardcover
$49.99

ISBN: 0-7821-2223-X
784pp; 7¹/₂" x 9"; Hardcover
$49.99

ISBN: 0-7821-2222-1
832pp; 7¹/₂" x 9"; Hardcover
$49.99

ISBN: 0-7821-2221-3
704pp; 7¹/₂" x 9"; Hardcover
$49.99

ISBN: 0-7821-2256-6
800pp; 7¹/₂" x 9"; Hardcover
$49.99

A $50.00 SAVINGS!

MCSE Core Requirements
Box Set
ISBN: 0-7821-2245-0
4 hardcover books;
3,024pp total; $149.96

Microsoft® Certified
Professional
Approved Study Guide

STUDY GUIDES FOR THE MICROSOFT CERTIFIED SYSTEMS ENGINEER EXAMS

MCSE ELECTIVE STUDY GUIDES FROM NETWORK PRESS®

Sybex's Network Press expands the definitive study guide series for MCSE candidates.

ISBN: 0-7821-2224-8
688pp; 7¹/₂" x 9"; Hardcover
$49.99

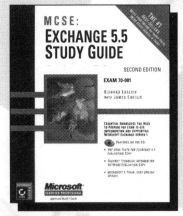

ISBN: 0-7821-2261-2
848pp; 7¹/₂" x 9"; Hardcover
$49.99

ISBN: 0-7821-2248-5
704pp; 7¹/₂" x 9"; Hardcover
$49.99

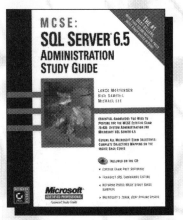

ISBN: 0-7821-2172-1
672pp; 7¹/₂" x 9"; Hardcover
$49.99

ISBN: 0-7821-2194-2
576pp; 7¹/₂" x 9"; Hardcover
$49.99

ISBN: 0-7821-1967-0
656pp; 7¹/₂" x 9"; Hardcover
$49.99

Microsoft® Certified
Professional
Approved Study Guide

STUDY GUIDES FOR THE MICROSOFT CERTIFIED SYSTEMS ENGINEER EXAMS